# In the shadow of her voice
## A Memoir of an Arab Woman
### Muna Alyusuf

You are my Fatema

Fatema for my beginnings
Fatema for my endings

You

Fatema for my silences
Fatema for my narratives
You are my Fatema

Within the shadow of stillness
I am possessed by a woman;
She tastes of silence and defeat.

I am possessed by a woman
who kisses the echo of my silence;

There I am
defeated by my trepidation
at the gate of truth

I behold a face that resembles my anguish; I hear a voice that resembles my muteness.
I sway between the edge of a dream and the taste of impossible. I sway between
the possibilities of my muteness and my rupture.

# In the shadow of her voice

## A memoir of an Arab woman

*Muna Alyusuf*

Fatema Sanctuary
PUBLISHING

Copyright © 2011 Muna Alyusuf

All rights reserved. No part of this publication may be reproduced or transmitted in any form or by any means, electronic or mechanical including photocopying, recording or any information storage or retrieval system, without prior permission in writing from the publisher.

The right of Muna Alyusuf to be identified as the author of this work has been asserted by her in accordance with the Copyright, Designs and Patents Act 1988

First published in the United Kingdom in 2011 by Fatema Sanctuary Publishing

ISBN 978-0-9569350-0-7

Produced by
The Choir Press, Gloucester

# Contents

| | |
|---|---:|
| Now and Beyond | *page* 1 |
| 1 Influences on Identity | 4 |
| 2 Closing and Opening | 34 |
| 3 Political Awakening | 49 |
| 4 Saudi Arabia Options | 83 |
| *Reflection/Monologue 1* | 97 |
| 5 Prison Memoirs | 99 |
| *Reflection/Monologue 2* | 133 |
| 6 Transition: From Prison to Prison | 136 |
| 7 Walking Away – Walking Back | 165 |
| *Memoir: Fatema, a Woman of Influence* | 192 |
| 8 Shattered Lives, Shattered Dreams | 193 |
| 9 A New Chapter | 211 |
| 10 Living in Transitions | 231 |
| 11 Transition – on to – Transition | 243 |
| 12 A Monologue: Shattered Silence/ Shattered Soul | 254 |
| *Memoir: Struck Mute by Persecution* | 271 |
| 13 Terror's Real Victory: The Surrender of Rationality | 273 |
| 14 Pilgrimage to Childhood | 289 |
| 15 Resumption of the Journey | 313 |
| 16 Two Thousand and Eight | 318 |
| Dedication: Fatema | 332 |

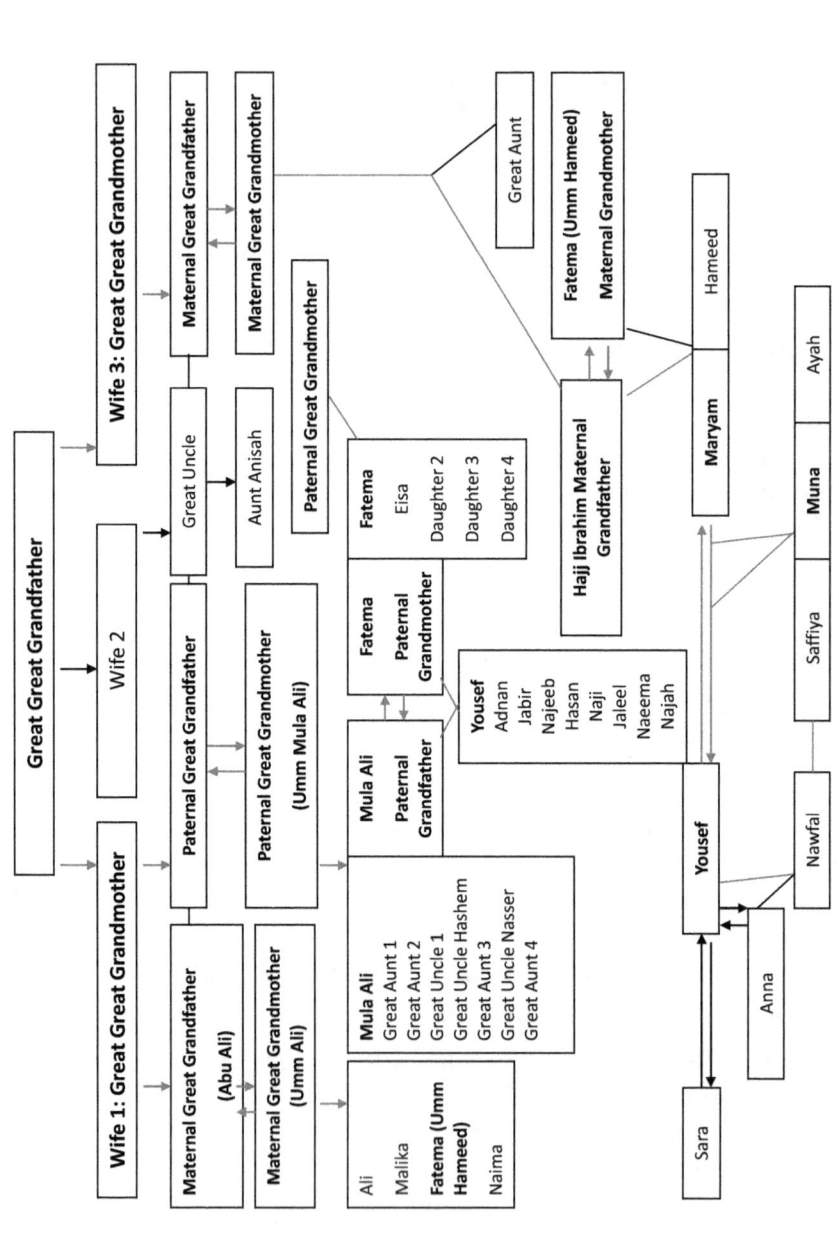

# Now and Beyond

As I approach the half-century mark in age, I reflect on my life as it has evolved over three continents. Now I am at peace.

Daily, I walk to my office via Hammersmith's Caffé Nero trailing in Rosa's warm Sicilian greetings – *'Buon giorno, Bella; Grazie; Ciao Bella'* – as if followed by distant supplications reminiscent of childhood. I smile as I recapture memories of my life's journey infused with the aroma and taste of Italian coffee. I wonder how those memories were created. I am not certain of what I can claim. The songs and the tunes have faded. The story lines are mixed and blurred. Clearly, however, I can hear my maternal grandmother's failing voice in humble supplication as she recited *suar* (*almuaowathat*) from the Quran to safeguard me from evil and to protect me from envy.

As I stir my coffee and contemplate my writing, I realise that I am stirring up my entire life. I know that for me the act of writing goes beyond taking risks. I not only freely, voluntarily bring to life the shadows and ghosts of my past, but I also contemplate the risks of persecution to myself and to my loved ones.

Distracted by the aroma and taste of my coffee, I compare it to cardamom-spiced Arabic coffee, my beverage of choice. I drift into contemplation of the beautiful, smiling woman with henna-coloured hair cloaked in a black *hashimi thobe* who intrudes in my thoughts. *Graciously, she extends her slender hand with the offer of a cup of Arabic coffee.*

I recall my paternal great grandmother's precise etiquette, the many times she returned the small coffee cup untouched until it contained the exact quantity required by her coffee-cup rule – less than half full – or it would be returned. Without uttering a single word of instruction, she would repetitively return the cup until we mastered the protocol.

On crossing the road to my office, I recall the many roads and borders that I have crossed during my life. The most exhilarating was that childhood crossing between my parents' relatively modern home and that of my maternal grandmother Fatema, Immy Um Hameed. Dreamily, I approached Fatema's ancient beautiful carved wooden gate, an entrance to a sanctuary she had created for three little girls, my sisters and me. I long for the simplicity and security of those days of endless journeys to and within her sanctuary.

As I watch school children descending from the London bus, a vivid memory of my sisters and me en route to school intrudes to supersede this moment. Daily, we three little girls exited for the bus, attired identically in long-sleeved, full-length blue school uniforms with white collar and pleated waist with ribbons tied to the back. The black shoes accumulated dust daily. Our dark brown hair tied in a ponytail completed the picture. *I turn now and see my mother standing before the mirror, her beautiful hands brushing our sleep-tangled hair, coaxing it into order.*

I grew up moving between homes and searching for a homeland. I studied, played, ate and slept in the same rooms where my parents grew up. They had played there as children and had started their lives there as a married couple. I close my eyes and savour the smell of the thatched mud and palm-frond homes that absorbed humidity. I recall the coolness that those walls radiated in the midst of summer's humid heat and the distinct smell of damp straw mats after washing to generate further coolness.

I feel blessed for having had access to both original extended family homes. Both maternal and paternal homes were of two levels and square shaped in design with an open courtyard. Each large, beautiful carved wooden gate featured a smaller gate. Exclusively, the large gate opened only for delivering goods and home supplies while the smaller gate remained open for resident and guest access. Conscious that my current walk parallels London's River Thames, I recall the family home with its *khuaida'a*, the small wooden gate that lead to the *shariaa*, the stream that ran along the back alley way.

During my childhood and into my teenage years, my maternal great uncle and his family occupied the original extended family home. The barn was in the courtyard where my great uncle – who traded in salt – kept his few donkeys and mules. My paternal grandparents' barn had a cow paddock and a chicken pen. Their house was recognised for its special status as the host to *elaziyah*, a place of commemoration, a place where tributes were paid to the memory of our Martyrs, the twelve Shia Imams. On those grounds, my ears were pierced. On those grounds, I observed my youngest aunt as she walked from her bed to the bathroom after being circumcised.

Today, I write for the two women who inadvertently conspired to give me the gift of voice, my mother Maryam and my maternal grandmother Fatema "Immy Um Hameed". I write these memoirs as a letter that will not be delivered nor read by either.

To Maryam, I am eternally grateful for her demand that I say thank you when it was not due, that I say sorry when no wrong was done and mostly for the love that no one but she could have given. I write for my mother and her mother, my maternal grandmother, Fatema. Both embodied kindness, fairness, generosity, forgiveness and transparency. They left no room for contempt. I am grateful to you, Maryam and Fatema, for making possible a childhood and a life full of love and joy beyond despair. I am grateful for the gift of my distinctive voice, your miraculous gift to me. Fifty years on, I walk sheltered in your supplications as your voices reverberate from the doors of heaven.

# 1

# Influences on Identity

Quite simply, on 5 June 1982, my life was disjointed. In that defining moment, my life was split into before and after. At the age of twenty-two years, two months, two weeks and five days, *I was sentenced without a trial to the solitude of political imprisonment for an indefinite period.*

Before and after the incarceration, a sorrowful beauty has defined my life. Later in life, I traced the sorrow, the pain in my journey of healing. Born in Safwa, under the care of a blind midwife, I entered the world after the sunset (*maghreb*) prayer on 17 March 1960. I was blessed with the only thing a child needs: an indomitable will to survive.

## Seeds for tomorrow

Safwa is one of the small coastal towns in the Eastern Province of the Kingdom of Saudi Arabia (KSA) on the Arabian Gulf. It is located between Qatif and Rahima-Ras-Tanura. The visible burning gas from refineries miles away marked its skyline. Palm tree farms fringed its borders and created a band of green around the residential areas and along the seashore. A distinctive aroma of humidity mixed with green grass and palm trees defined the village.

My parents are second cousins. My paternal grandfather Mula Ali and my maternal grandfather Hajj Ibrahim are first cousins. Mula Ali was the oldest of four boys and four girls; my great uncles Hashem and Nasser were the same ages as Mula Ali's oldest children. Hajj Ibrahim had one sister; both Hajj Ibrahim and his sister married their first cousins. Mula Ali married Fatema who bore him many children. Only nine of those children survived – seven boys and two girls: Yousef, Adnan, Jabir, Najeeb, Hasan, Naji, Jaleel, Naeema, and Najah. My father Yousef is the oldest. Hajj Ibrahim married his first cousin, also Fatema, who bore him five children. The only two survivors were my mother Maryam and my uncle Hameed.

At the beginning, my paternal and maternal grandparents lived in the extended family home. In time, my paternal great-grandfather who had a large family of his own had saved enough money and bought another house not too far away from the original extended family residence where he moved his own family. Initially my paternal grandparents were allocated two rooms in the new residence. Meanwhile, the extended family continued to share the palm tree farm. My paternal grandfather was trained to become a Mula, a reader, a literary man who studied religion locally and conducted some religious services, including marriages. However, my grandfather refused to divorce husbands and wives, maintaining his position to participate only in the process of unity of marriage, not the separation. It was my paternal grandfather Mula Ali who advised his cousin, my maternal grandfather Hajj Ibrahim, to seek work with Aramco (the Arab American Oil Company).

Prior to 1964, my memories are of the stories told to me by my mother and other family members. My first conscious memory was in the summer of 1964, and it was of my mother on what must have been a special day: the day my father returned from the US for the first time. I remember my mother with her modern, bobbed haircut. In a lovely white halter style, sleeveless, V-necked dress with a narrow waistband, she preened in her room, as if in preparation to wed. My maternal and paternal grandmothers, my aunt Anisah, my mother's first cousin whom I knew as my aunt, and a few other women who were helping her dress surrounded her. To me, my mother appeared ethereally beautiful. Although we were in the same room, my sisters and I watched from what seemed to be a distance.

Between 1964 and 1967, my memories are a fragmented ensemble of stories, songs, smells, words and adventures. My mother is a gifted storyteller and the listener is bound to fall in love with her stories about her marriage and my parents' early days together.

I knew my parents' story primarily from my mother's narrative and my father's letters posted to her from 1961 until 1976. To my mother, those letters are the only beautiful account of his love and relationship with her. My father's letters to my mother have given me the privilege of discovering my parents anew and nourishing my heart with love and compassion I didn't have the chance to witness. In addition, they introduced me to a man whom I have consciously known as my father only since I was age sixteen.

At twelve years of age, my father sought employment with Aramco and began on 6 May 1951 as an office boy. On 20 December 1955, my parents married and lived together for six years before my father left for Beirut and subsequently the US in pursuit of further education. When they married, my father was seventeen and my mother was thirteen. My mother, Maryam, says that my father had told my grandfather Mula Ali that if he were to marry, he would only marry Maryam. My father insists that it was not love, but an arranged marriage.

On their wedding night, according to custom, two women accompanied my mother: her first cousin Najibah, and her aunt Zahrah. In our community this was a common ritual to ease the transition from single to married life and to help orient wives and husbands. The following morning, and customary to the tradition of the time, my father gave my mother 80 silver riyal (coins) so that she would lift the veil and reveal her face. My father was not disappointed, as my mother was known for her beauty. According to my mother, he had known of her beauty before he chose her having briefly shared the extended family residence. When they first married, my parents had a room in the family home with my paternal grandparents, great grandmother, great uncles, aunts and uncles. Each couple had a room to share with their children.

Eight months after their marriage, my father travelled to Egypt and returned with trendy dresses and lingerie. Often my mother says, *"I was your father's queen."* My mother recalls that my father presented the dresses to my paternal grandmother first as customary in order that she could choose one for herself or as a gift for one of her numerous sisters-in-law. My father deeply loved and respected his mother, so he often indicated that he would appreciate and love my mother even more if she developed closer ties with my grandmother. At the beginning of her married life, my mother resisted his expressed wish. According to my mother, she was too young and preferred to go her own way. Despite all the similar guidance and advice from older aunts and cousins, my mother refused. Later, she confessed that at age thirteen she only wanted to play.

On 20 October 1958, exactly two months before my parents' third wedding anniversary, my sister Saffiya was born. Shortly before Saffiya's birth, my father joined Aramco's homeownership programme, obtained a housing loan and built a house for his young family in Safwa. My father bought the land for five thousand riyals as Aramco then did not give land as part of their homeownership loans. My father chose the blueprint from the few choices Aramco presented to him. In the summer of 1959, he moved his young family into their new home. Among her friends, my mother was the first to have a house of her own.

I grew up in this beautiful, three-bedroom house which was built on one level. It had one large living room, a dining room, two bathrooms, a big kitchen and a beautiful spacious veranda. The house was tiled throughout. Our kitchen was divided into two parts: the smaller functioned as a "dirty" kitchen, where heavy cooking such as frying food took place. The other part was devoted to preparation of lighter foods and snacks.

I recall that despite my mother's warning not to cook in her absence, we sisters could not resist playing chefs. It was in the smaller kitchen that my younger sister Ayah and I experimented to develop our childish cooking skills. It was in this small kitchen that I once accidentally burned Ayah's hair as we attempted to imitate our mother's sweet dishes. There too, Ayah once accidentally spilled hot oil on my foot.

In the style of the community, the house had two entrances. The first one entered from the main road and was used by family members and women. The second entrance for male friends and guests and tradesmen, was located on the alleyway behind our house and was accessible from the side road.

The entrance from the main road led directly into the garden, which half encircled our house on the right. The door into the house was of steel and green glass and led into the corridor. On the right were the children's rooms. To the left were the family bathroom and the back entrance to the kitchen. At the end of the corridor, an arched doorway divided the house. On the more formal side of the house, the family room, which doubled as a dining room, dominated the centre between my parents' master bedroom and the formal living room. Beyond were the entrances to the veranda and the main entrance to the kitchen.

The formal living room was designed in a crescent shape with its own en suite bathroom. The furniture was Western style with two elegant sofas and comfortable armchairs, along with coffee and side tables. Off the family room and to the right of the kitchen was the stairway door to the traditional walled roof. There we slept on hot summer nights.

I recall as young children when Ayah and I sat patiently next to the stairway door while Saffiya was locked under the stairway. She and our cousin Muneer were being punished for shredding one of uncle Jabir's notebooks. Ayah and I would sneak to her whatever food would pass through the slight opening between the wooden stairway door and the tiled floor. We respected no concept of a punishment that resulted in depriving us of our sister.

The back door opened onto the enclosed veranda which we used during the summer for sleeping. The family room, my parents' room and the formal living room overlooked and had access to the veranda. Retaining the tradition of two separate entrances, my parents maintained the traditional segregation of the sexes. In addition, my mother temporarily and transiently learned to embrace the new way of mixing with friends who didn't believe in gender segregation. My mother loved my father so much that she accepted his vision of modernity. However, she never became totally comfortable with his newly adapted customs, particularly the mixing of men and women.

Shortly after Saffiya's birth, and noticing the increasing influence of the traditional and conservative community on my mother, my father decided to quickly move his young family from Safwa to Rahima-Ras Tanura. There, they lived in my uncle Adnan's house, which was closer to my father's permanent workplace and removed from the influence of the small community. My father made this move in order that he and my mother could live according to his view of how young married couples should establish a home and family life. My father had a vision for his family life, his relationship with my mother and of intergenerational relationships. He established strict rules, including how my mother was to dress and use her spare time. My mother was expected to be at home when he returned from work. Thus, he focused on re-educating and re-training her. He encouraged her to read and write, building on what she had learned in the traditional school *lemaalem*, where young children learned to read, write and to memorise the Quran.

By then, my parents had forged their own friendships within their community; some of them were my parents' relatives and old friends, some were my father's old colleagues. They became part of a seven-family pod of friends who were also neighbours. My great uncle Hashem and aunt Anisah were part of this pod of friends. We grew up within this small community within our community, and we grew up to cherish the friendships we forged through our parents.

My parents, especially my mother, enjoyed the privileges of living independently from the extended family. Six months later, my father was transferred to Dhahran. Due to his transfer and the change of his schedule, my parents moved back to Safwa. My father was only home on the weekend (Thursday and Friday). Therefore on weeknights, my mother would take Saffiya to her parents' home where I was later born. We continued to live like this after my father departed to pursue his education. Despite his long absence, the rhythm and routine of our home continued, as if my father was still there.

Initially, my father left home for Beirut, Lebanon, to obtain his high school certificate. In June 1961, he left again to attend summer school at the International College of Beirut, situated opposite the American University of Beirut in Alhamra. In September 1961, he returned home for a couple of weeks before leaving again for Lebanon to complete his high school requirements. On his departure this time, my mother was pregnant with my younger sister Ayah.

In June 1962, he graduated and returned home briefly after Ayah's birth. Then in July of 1962 he departed on a fateful journey from which he never fully returned to our family. At that time, he took up a scholarship to the US. Initially, he went to Lewisburg, Pennsylvania and then to Yellow Springs, Ohio, for his bachelor's degree. My mother remembers that my father cried often, as he feared for their relationship during the approaching extended separation. According to my mother, he returned home exactly two years and four months later, a changed man.

Upon his return from the US in 1964, that changed, distracted husband–my father – travelled to Kuwait. When he returned, he took his mattress from the master bedroom to the formal living room and slept there. Filled with anguish, my mother searched for an explanation. She found it inside my father's leather wallet: a picture of an American woman. When my mother confronted my father, he denied having any relationship with the woman, telling her, *"She is only a friend."* My mother recalls that she and my father fought until it was time for him to return to the US. Upon his departure, my father told my mother that she would receive one of two documents: either an airline ticket to the US or a divorce petition.

After returning to Ohio around May 1965, the tone of my father's letters changed significantly. Departing from the terms of endearment of earlier years, he addressed her formally as Dear Maryam Ibrahim, or dear sister. There was no more passion in his letters. Through them I can trace the end of their relationship. In May 1966, my father used the word "divorce" for the first time in a letter to my mother. My father had fallen in love with another woman, the woman who was in the photo my mother found two years earlier in his wallet. Later, Anna became our stepmother and the mother of the only brother we have, our brother Nawfal who was born at the end of 1971.

My mother recalls her painful journey through my father's betrayal and the challenge of the ensuing separation. Rather than informing my mother of his plans directly, my father sent letters to my uncle Adnan and another to his maternal uncle Eisa. In those letters, he informed them of his irrevocable decision to move on with his new life, a future in the US with Anna. He told them that he planned to divorce my mother and to marry his American girlfriend.

During that time, it was the routine on weekends that my uncle Adnan resided in our house. Unexpectedly uncle Adnan told my mother that she was going to the US to join my father. Further, he indicated that he was buying her an airline ticket. My mother was stunned. Suddenly, she was asked to go to the US, not directly by my father, but by his brother. As my father had told her that she would receive an airline ticket or a divorce petition, she doubted that it was his wish for her to join him. It was clear to her that she could not leave three little girls – ages eight, six and four – without a parent.

As my mother waited for a sign from my father, she questioned uncle Adnan. She was not convinced by his answers. Due to her vigilance, my mother found a letter cut into pieces in the trash bin. She collected and pieced the bits together. Alone, my mother read the four-page, double-sided letter that shaped her future as a separated and single mother of three children.

My mother had no say whatsoever in her future. My father did not address the letter to her or discuss the matter with her as he had promised. In this matter of supreme importance to my mother, he behaved in a manner contrary to his liberal progressive character. Deliberately or involuntarily, he followed the traditional male-dominated practice of dismissing the voice of women. He had forgotten, or chose to ignore, that it was her future that was on the line; he had forgotten that she was the one who had the right to know his decision first.

First, my mother took the letter to my aunt Anisah, her cousin, best friend and confidante. My mother asked my aunt to accompany her to my paternal grandparents' home to inform her in-laws.

My mother recalls the five-minute walk to their home as lasting a lifetime. There, she handed my father's shredded letter to my grandfather. Thus, he learned that his oldest son was planning to divorce his wife. For a second time, my paternal grandfather was deeply saddened for her. As a child, the town doctor had mistakenly diagnosed my mother with a terminal illness. Now she confronted divorce at the age of twenty-three, with three small children – all girls.

My grandfather took the only action he thought might work. He campaigned to stop my father's planned marriage by lobbying my father's friends. According to my mother, they all opposed my father's planned divorce and remarriage. Boldly, my grandfather went a step further to persuade my father's supervisor to stop the marriage. My grandfather's lobbying and friends and family boycott did not deter my determined father. He was deeply in love with a modern, liberal and Western-educated woman.

In 1966, my father returned. When he told my mother that she was forbidden to him as a wife, she knew that he had divorced her. A few years later, my mother learned that a forged divorce decree had been issued in her absence and without her consent. This meant that the divorce was unlawful. Although in writing, the divorce decree was never acknowledged or registered officially in Saudi Arabia. As polygamy is illegal in the US, possession of a divorce document was the only way my father could legally marry his American wife. In the true sense and legitimate practice of Islam, a non-consensual divorce is illegal, as both marriage and divorce require consent and public notices of intent. Thus, legally, my parents never divorced; however, they separated never to be rejoined as husband and wife. My father remained in the US until 1976 – with the exception of almost two years between 1967 and 1969, when he and Anna, his new wife, lived in Safwa and Dhahran.

While my father was happily remarrying, my mother became ill. Perhaps the community of women around her entertained the idea that he was bewitched and that my mother was cursed. Fatalistically, they might have concluded that my father had remarried and that was that. The house where my mother was crowned as a young bride is the house where her heart and life were shattered. The windows of our house were shut and the curtains were closed, as even the faintest ray of light hurt her eyes. As a child, it seemed to me that my mother was bedridden for an eternity. During that period, my maternal grandmother, Um Hameed, stayed with us and took charge of the household.

In the initial recovery stages, my mother crawled. She wore leather sandals that combined the smell of Vicks mentholatum and leather. *"It felt as if I were being burnt alive"*, my mother would say. She was shocked and paralysed, unable to walk properly. I remember how sick my mother was. Her face was pale, her eyes no longer sparkled and there were no more colourful elegant dresses. The stylish haircut disappeared. Many familiar and unfamiliar women and men came and went checking on her and sometimes on us. Some remained at the door, while others entered. As a child, I learned to recognise eyes without hope. Ayah, still a toddler, started to call my mother "crippled". Thereafter, and in many senses of the word, "crippled" defined my mother's life.

I do not know how long it took my mother to regain her sense of her own existence and of ours. To me, it seemed an eternity, while my mother recalls that it took months.

In the end, my mother had no choice except to regain her strength and get on with life despite my father's departure. She was a beautiful young woman with three little girls. She had no say and no choice except to accept life as it was. If she wanted to care for us, she had to stand on her feet again and prove to her family and community that she was worthy and capable of bringing up three girls. She could have remarried, but if she did she would have lost custody of us. In that case, we would have been handed into the care of my paternal grandparents. Remarriage was not an option for my mother because of us, her three little girls, and because she was still deeply in love with my father and remained that way.

Although my mother struggled with my father's absence and the unreliable, insufficient monthly financial allowance, we had a beautiful childhood. She filled it with her love, wit, singing, laughter and heavenly cooking. She loved life in spite of her situation. She loved to sing and laugh.

When Saffiya started school, every morning Ayah and I would follow her to school which was set up in an old rented house in one of the oldest residential areas of town a mile away from our home. We waited with the guard until her school day was over despite the school warning my mother against us waiting there. We eventually stopped following Saffiya to school.

A few years later, we left our gate to board the bus to our school, which had been relocated to a newly built Aramco facility in the newly developed part of town that came to be known as the labourers' town. This is a big plot of land where Aramco developed its homeownership programme to include land ownership plus loans to build homes. Aramco was building and maintaining schools around the Eastern Province as a show of support to the community.

My mother gave us a daily allowance, some of which we saved for later, and some we spent on the purchase of sweets. The old woman with the sweet kiosk moved from her corner near the old school to a new location near the new school bus stop. In the winter, she sold roasted sesame and molasses balls, as well as cooked garbanzo and black-eyed beans, which were served with vinegar and Tabasco sauce. Generally, we shared what we bought except when we were not on good terms with one another.

Daily we returned from school to hear our mother singing as she cooked. She was strict and disciplined us carefully. She never spoiled any of us when healthy or sick. Through experience, we learned to read her eyes and body language. In public, she used a silent sign language by which we could determine what we were allowed and not allowed to do. She allowed our home to be used as our playground where our cousins, relatives, friends and neighbours were all welcome. Our house was also open and accessible for my uncles and their friends on weekends.

Whenever there were enough of us and we were at our home, or at the home of Um Hameed or of my aunt Anisah, we children always played games of *sadah ma sadah* (tag and chase), *itghobiyah* (hide and seek), and *almakhatah* (hopscotch). Sometimes at night we would play *hrooq alfai* (burning shadows). Our home always seemed open and adequately large to accommodate countless adults and children. It was a reflection of my mother's generosity and kind heart. She seemed to always have something to offer her guests. My mother, a genuine fatalist, accepted life and made the best of it. She had a natural gift for touching peoples' hearts and sharing their joys and their sorrows.

Because we were young and none of my uncles was present, we lived in our house during the day but slept at my maternal grandparents' house. Immy Um Hameed would also sleep with us when my grandfather was working the night shift. Even after they separated, my mother kept the order of the house as if my father was there. We had chores and curfews. My mother did not mind us playing but expected to return to a home as clean as she had left it. When we three were older, my mother felt adequately safe for us to sleep at home.

The presence of a constant male role model in our house was fragmented. My uncles came and went according to their timetables. Despite being in charge of our house, my mother always seemed willing to abandon that role as soon as one of my uncles was present.

My maternal uncle Hameed, my mother's only sibling, had his rotation of living with and taking care of us. Uncle Hameed and my mother shared a similar sense of humour, a talent for story telling, and a trace of naivety that characterised their attitude toward life and people. Like the many other adults in our life, he was responsible for looking after my sisters and me and also in charge of entertaining our cousins, and our friends who joined us. Despite Uncle Hameed's conservative and strict religious orientation, he would take us to Hajj Ibrahim's farm without any pre-conditions regarding the performance of our religious duties or demands about our dress. He would allow us to stay with him and his friends as they listened to their favourite radio programmes. He would share whatever sweets he had such as *halwa* (a cornflour, starch-based sweet) and *rahash* (a sesame paste sweet). He included us in his chores around our home and that of my maternal grandparents. He organised outings to the beach outside the boundaries of our small town. He always managed to sort out an automobile ride for us whenever an opportunity presented itself through his friends. Without dictating or demanding, uncle Hameed remained a constant support to my mother.

When my paternal great uncle Nasser and my uncle Adnan were present, the rhythm of the house and our diet would change. Our breakfast and dinner would include foods that were not available otherwise. We enjoyed the wholesome aroma and taste of peanut butter, marmalade, strawberry jam, Kraft cheese, fresh sliced bread, doughnuts, cinnamon rolls, V8 and orange juices that were a novelty to us. When my uncles cooked for their friends, the dinner menu extended beyond our typical cheddar cheese sandwiches, cold rice and yoghurt or the simple tomato and egg dishes to proper complete meals of rice, fish or meat, salads and fruits.

My sisters and I relished those times. It was as if we were on a short holiday. As soon as my uncles left, our life would return to its normal rhythm. It was within the security of that normal rhythm among my sisters and nurtured by my mother and her mother that I grew to become who I am today.

It was during this period that fortuitously, my uncle Adnan stepped in my mother's way and stopped our circumcision. He blocked her plan. Vaguely, I remember them arguing when he warned my mother against having us circumcised. He told her: "Their father disapproves of such practices." I can only assume that my mother had great respect for the opinions of my uncle and my father. Perhaps she doubted the tradition, although in our community it was deemed necessary for the purification of women. Miraculously, my sisters and I were saved, although circumcision was considered *taharah* (purification) and was deemed good for girls. I have a vague memory of my youngest aunt Najah's post-circumcision. I thought how lucky she was to receive the ceremonial care and attention. I was too young to comprehend the meaning of circumcision. In the end, my clitoris was saved.

Much later in life I became aware of socially mandated violence toward women. I recognised that as a child I was envious of the ceremonial process that served as justification of the practice to the sexually impaired woman, not resentful of or outraged by it. In later years, I continued to question how as a child and a young woman I had accepted such gross impairment for the sake of the social code of purification.

Clearly, political activism was not an all-encompassing holistic route to full awareness of our socially conditioned oppression. While my journey to sovereignty, to claiming my own voice, had seemed comprehensive, I realised in time that women's issues were always secondary to everything else.

However, change was imminent. The first adult education programme for married women was launched amongst my parents' close circle of friends. This small circle was composed of men who were all relatively progressive thinkers. This was reflected in their views of life, of their wives' roles and of child rearing. In our house, the programme operated as two classes for a few hours in the afternoon. Eager to learn how to read and write, women filled up the classrooms. The same teachers who taught the children in the public school during the morning taught the mothers in the afternoon.

In the middle of her fifth-grade studies, my mother discontinued her pursuit of further education. I am not sure of her reasons. Perhaps she did so in defiance of my father, as it was he who had wished her to continue. Or perhaps she lost interest on realising that she had lost him to another woman.

Eventually, the women stopped coming and the school closed down. The beautiful voices of women echoing within the walls of our home stopped, imparting a sense of emptiness into my heart.

Nevertheless, my mother was amongst the first women in Safwa to sponsor practitioners from the Aramco community health centre to deliver lectures to women. I remember the persuasive posters on immunization, polio and the food pyramid that were mounted on the walls of the classrooms in our home and in the family room. My mother used her family and friends to publicise the sessions. As there were no telephones, she must have relied on my uncles to organise such seminars.

### The seasons

During the summer, our time was divided between home where we played with our relatives and friends or at the home of our grandparents, Um Hameed and Abwiye Hajj Ibrahim. Throughout those long, glorious sun-filled days, we went to Abwiye Hajj Ibrahim's date palm farm. We started going with him when the date fruit was at the *khalal* stage before becoming fully ripened. Hajj Ibraim would allow us to eat the *khalal* and Um Hameed would sometimes make *khalal* necklaces for us. We would spend hours playing and picking *lauz* – fruit particular to the Arabian Gulf – and figs while Hajj Ibrahim harvested fresh dates.

After the farm visit, we would return home to Um Hameed. Each would carry her harvest of *lauz* and figs, eating a few on the way home. Sometimes, we would wait until we got to her house to consume what we had harvested. On some days, Um Hameed would serve us sugar-sprinkled sliced tomatoes or sliced melons to nourish and cool us.

We would gather around Um Hameed and watch her treating the straw. Then she would braid it into strands and then sew them together. From this, she made beautiful straw mats for sitting, some for food containers and various sizes of baskets in which to store dates. Very practically, Um Hameed made hanging straw baskets to keep cooked food out of the reach of cats, flies and insects.

Um Hameed would signal the end of the summer season with the production of *salooq* from a special variety of red dates. In this process, she boiled the dates before storing them for later use as snacks. At the end of the summer date season, Abwiye Hajj Ibrahim would bring down the ripe dates to dry them on the straw mats laid on the rooftop of their house. Taking turns, Um Hameed and Hajj

Ibrahim would turn the dates so they dried thoroughly. Then they would store them in the straw baskets for consumption throughout the year. Hajj Ibrahim ate dates with his meals and often as a snack with fresh melted butter, buttermilk or yoghurt.

My maternal great-grandparents, Abu Ali and Um Ali, lived with Immy Um Hameed and Abwiye Hajj Ibrahim. During the winter, we spent the afternoons in Um Hameed's house with great-grandfather Abu Ali who had been a rope maker. He had one goat whose name was *Farhah*. Abu Ali only drank goat milk and despite our reluctance to try, he always offered it to us. Traditionally, my maternal great-grandfather was the first to be served lunch. Um Hameed would place the small coffee cup filled with melted butter in the middle of his plate of rice. The main dish – *bzar*, which is fish, lamb or other item – was placed on the side. Before eating the rice, he would spread the melted butter over it with his fingers. My sisters and I learned to love buttered rice as our great-grandfather had. From him and my maternal grandfather, we picked up various eating habits such as dipping our fresh or dried dates in cooked butter to begin our meals. With Um Hameed, we were allowed to do things that my mother would never allow or approve.

Abu Ali built fires in his *manqalah* (portable fire place) of either natural coal or wood. We would gather around him while he told stories: some fairy tales, some stories of the old days. Often he would roast chestnuts for us. Sometimes he allowed us to roast them.

This beloved maternal great-grandfather would save his fruits, nuts and sweets to share with us three sisters and cousin Wafyah. We received a share of everything that his nephews and nieces gave to him. As we did not go to Um Hameed's house every day, the fruit might be either over ripened or partially rotten. He still gave it to us and we gratefully accepted and ate what our little stomachs could manage.

In the fall, we would impatiently wait for Abwiye Hajj Ibrahim to harvest the sesame seeds. Hajj Ibrahim would bring the sesame seed branches with their loaded pods and place them for drying on the rooftop straw mats that Um Hameed had arranged. When ready for harvesting, Hajj Ibrahim would take us to the rooftop to watch as he shook the pods and the sesame seeds fell onto the mats. Then, we would help Hajj Ibrahim gather the seeds and roast them. Into our eager extended hands, he would place the freshly roasted warm sesame seeds. From our hands, the seeds went directly into our watering mouths, justifying the wait for them.

During the winter when Hajj Ibrahim did not work the late night shift, he would wake before the call for the *fajr* (dawn) prayer. Always he went to pray in the *Dirah* (old town) mosque near the old extended family home where he grew up. On his return from the mosque, Hajj Ibrahim would stop at the bakery to buy fresh Arabic flat bread and then stop by the grocer for Kraft cheddar cheese and watermelon jam. Sometimes he would purchase *halwa* (a cornflour, starch-based sweet) or *rahash* (a sesame paste sweet). Once I heard him ask Um Hameed to recite *almuawathat*, the specific Quran verses that protect people from evil and envy. On that day, he explained to Um Hameed that men at the bakery and the grocery were envying his granddaughters. Hajj Ibrahim was worried and wanted to take precautions to protect us from evil and envy.

Spring was always a festive season as it ended two months of sorrow: *Muharram* and *Safar,* the first and the second months of the Hijira calendar. The two months mark the death memorials of the Prophet Muhammed (peace be upon him) and the majority of the Shia Imams. *Ashura,* the tenth day of the month of *Muharram,* commemorates the memory of the martyrdom of Imam Al Hussain bin Ali bin Abi Taleb and his family and followers in Karbela. Throughout *Muharram* and *Safar* women gathered in *aziyah*. An *aziyah* is a place of remembrance where women pay tribute to our Imams by reciting the stories of martyrdom and grief. The hall and grounds are also used to celebrate the births of prophets, messengers and Imams.

During our childhood, we were not in the habit of attending the *aziyah*. My mother did not encourage us to accompany her. We went only when we needed her or when she asked us to meet her there. My sisters and I were happy to stay at home to act or play. During the months of *Muharram* and *Safar*, women wore only black dresses. Many children also dressed in black, especially if they were going to *aziyah*. In general, mothers avoided dressing children in bright colours or new clothes. Like the adults, we respected the commemoration of martyrdom and refrained from chewing gum, eating pumpkin seeds and watching television. Later during our teens, we stopped following these guidelines during *Muharram* and *Safar*. In our youth, we learned about the sacrifice of Imam Hussain who willingly engaged in a battle to restore justice. Not until I was well into adulthood did I learn the full story of the struggle of Imam Hussain and members of his household to reinstate the moderate, just way of Islam and that of our Prophet (pbuh). As an adult, I learned of the political and religious contexts of such battles. Imam Hussain did not sacrifice himself and his family in vain, he did so to preserve the essence of Islam, that of justice and moderation. Long before the death of Imam Hussain, the Shia school had positioned itself as a leading radical school of thought in Islam.

Within our family, as in many other Shia families, every new thing, every happy event had to wait for spring. As young as my sisters and I were, we had learned to wait patiently to celebrate. New dresses and new shoes were saved for the spring. Maryam would send us to Um Hameed who would adorn our hands and feet with henna. She would apply the cool dark green paste into the palms of our hands and wrap them in soft cotton cloth to avoid staining our beds. The scent of *rriyhan* and white *razqi* (Arabic basil and jasmine) anointed people and homes. After the two months of symbolic mourning, women changed into colourful dresses with gold necklaces, earrings, bracelets and rings, adorned by the henna on their hands and feet. Many weddings and other celebrations took place during this festive season.

Of course, we would celebrate Prophet Muhammed's (pbuh) birth. Women in the same *aziyah* would exchange the books of mourning to read and chant in celebration of the Prophet's birth. *Nethour* – offerings of food made to Allah to symbolise gratefulness for answered prayers – were prepared almost every day during spring. The offerings would be of rice, meat or traditional desserts cooked on the grounds of the *aziyah*. Alternatively, they might be of traditional *tanoor* bread filled with *halwa* or *rahash* sweets. The *Nethour* would be consumed on the grounds or divided into servings for distribution among the attendees to share with their families.

Prophet Muhammed's (pbuh) birth wasn't the only one we celebrated. The births of other prophets and messengers such as Jesus and Moses were celebrated in the same manner. The birth of the Virgin Mary – Maryam bint Omran – was also celebrated.

In addition to the spring festivities, our small community celebrated the two *Eid* occasions just as in every other Muslim community. *Eid il Fitr* marks the end of Ramadhan and celebrates the end of the fasting month and *Eid il Idha* marks the conclusion of the *Hajj* (the annual pilgrimage to Mecca) rituals. For the *Eid* celebrations, Um Hameed adorned our hands and feet with henna. Hajj Ibrahim was responsible for hanging our special rope swing made by our maternal great grandfather Abu Ali. He would secure it between two tall date palm trees in front of their house.

Both *Eid* celebrations extended for three days. On the first day of Eid after breakfast, we would pay respect and praise to my mother's parents, Um Hameed and Hajj Ibrahim, and receive their blessings. Then, my mother would take us to pay respect and praise to my paternal grandparents Mula Ali and Immy Um Yousef, wishing them a blissful *Eid*. From there, we proceeded to visit our great aunts and uncles repeating the same rituals. For the remainder of the three *Eid* days, we savoured them at the home of Um Hameed, alternating between the swing, games and the treats collected through our visits to other family members.

During these *Eid* occasions, the first day would begin with the communal *Eid* prayers, followed by the slaughter of a lamb or a goat, another offering of thanks. Children gathered in the courtyard to watch as two of the adult male family members restrained the *thabiha* (the animal to be slaughtered). While reciting the name of Allah, one held the animal down and the other with a large sharp knife quickly slit the windpipe, throat and arteries of the neck to minimise the animal's suffering. We watched until all the blood was drained. Then the men would cut off the head, skin the carcass and cut it for cooking. Not everyone could afford a lamb or a goat. Alternatively, some people slaughtered a chicken, a rooster or a duck.

My favourite time during the *Eid* festivities was at dawn, just between sleep and awakening, when I listened to the faint voices of women quietly conversing with my mother. Still in bed, I would savour the aroma of the traditional sweet dishes made for such occasions. The mornings of *Eid* would be filled with the fragrance of spiced milk as it boiled with cardamom and saffron, cooked flour and *suyaa* (vermicelli). *Suyaa* is cooked with sugar and oil and is spiced with cardamom and saffron. Some cooks add eggs to make it healthier. My mother would make one of the traditional dishes: *fatitah, khabisah* or *asidah,* all of which have the same basic ingredients of cooked flour, sugar and oil. Some varied the dishes with eggs and added cardamom, saffron and rose water. *Khabisah* and *asidah* are served in a smooth-paste texture. *Fatitah* is served as it crystallises into varied size crumbles.

That was *Eid*. In my memories, it always began with the beautiful voice of a woman, that of my grandmother, Um Hameed. That would be followed by the voices of one of my great aunts or one of the neighbours talking to my mother, wishing her and us a blissful *Eid*. *Eid* was in the aroma-filled air of my mother's cooking as we anticipated the swing. *Eid* was filled with women's voices, children's laughter, swings, food and my mother's heavenly cooking in her simple kitchen. In the midst of festivity, my mother would sing a sad song questioning the disposition of the *Eid*'s annual return. Would the *Eid* bring blessings or memories of grief?

At the end of the *Hajj* and the summer season, gifts arrived. My mother returned home from neighbourhood visits bearing gifts from friends. Women visited us to deliver gifts they had gathered as they travelled to Mecca, Medina, Iraq, Iran and Syria. The gifts would be wrapped in a *mishmar* (a colourful cotton body wrap), a *hashimi thobe* (traditional robe made of black lace fabric) or in *heram salat* (the white prayer garment). The gift would include pieces of beautiful cloth for each of us and one for her. Depending on where the travellers had been, the gift might have hazel nuts, *melibis* (sugar-coated almonds), or a mixture of sugar coated and salted chickpeas, peanuts and zahdi (dried dates that were a specialty of Medina). If the traveller was in Mecca and/or Medina, a few rosaries and prayer mats might be included. My mother would roast the peanuts before we removed the shells for eating. We shared everything, enjoyed everything and were grateful for the kindness of people.

My mother felt indebted, as she did not have the means to travel and bring back gifts. In the absence of a husband, her resources were limited. Despite the limitation that kept her from travelling, my mother had a reputation for being generous as she shared whatever she had with guests and neighbours. Most importantly, she opened her heart, her home and extended genuine kindness and hospitality.

During the fall, winter and spring, Allah bestowed rain, a blessing to us and the desert. In our young lives, we forever chased rain and rainbows. Sadly, our attempts to catch the rainbows failed, as the rainbows receded ever further as we walked toward them. In those carefree days, we were set free to walk and run in the rain as if being purified and blessed by Allah. Mud covered our bare feet and legs and our young slender bodies were drenched. Happily, our mother provided us with pots and buckets in which to collect rainwater. Carrying them on our heads, we balanced with acrobatic skill. At times, we placed the empty containers on the rooftop for collection later. Voraciously, we drank as much as we wanted, allowing it to purify our bodies and souls. We welcomed the rainwater soaking as a counterweight to the dryness of our desert land. Letting our hair down, we circled freely in a water dance, in celebration of all that earth might reciprocate in return for the skies' gift. Although my mother was strict, she intuited the divine connection between a child and Mother Nature. The sounds, the tastes and the aromas of childhood were embodied in the seasons.

## My father returns

At the end of 1967, my father returned to Saudi Arabia with his new wife Anna. Briefly, he returned to Aramco before he resigned to join the University of Petroleum and Minerals in the Eastern Province. He rented a house in another part of town. Due to the distance, we children had to be accompanied by an adult on our walk there.

Anna, my first stepmother, must have arrived with various assumptions. Perhaps she imagined that her husband's children would welcome her with open arms. Indeed, she was welcomed with open arms by many family members, which caused my mother much pain. Much later, my father said that I had rejected Anna both emotionally and socially, as I distanced myself totally from her.

Anna learned Arabic, wore the abbaya (veil) and learned the Quran. After accepting Islam, she went to *Hajj*. My mother recalls that Anna went to *Hajj* along with my paternal grandparents, a parent in law's privilege that was bestowed on my mother much later in life.

My mother – who had long dreamed of going to *Hajj* – was unable to fulfil her duty until many years later when my maternal grandfather

Hajj Ibrahim provided the financial support. At the time of Anna's pilgrimage, my mother did not complain, but her body language revealed her sorrow. As the first wife and one born into Islam, she was not afforded the opportunity to go to *Hajj* while my father made that possible for his second wife who was a convert to Islam.

My mother had done nothing to deserve such an indignity. Whenever she felt let down or that life was unfair, she sang, recited poetry or repeated proverbs to restore her spirits. She had an inspiring way of overcoming the unfairness of life. My mother's spirit was a spirit free from contempt; she believed that people loved her and no one could do anything to help her. With the help of her strong faith and Eliya Abu Madhi's poetry that she recited, she put misery behind her. Madhi's poetry speaks against complaints, against depression. It is poetry that uplifted the spirit and made us realise how privileged and fortunate we were to have so much that we could enjoy.

Anna would gather we three sisters, my mother and my aunt Anisah with her four children – Muneer, Yonis, Wafyah and Yaseen – to teach us the English alphabet, numbers and a few songs. During the eighteen months when they lived near us, my father continued inviting his friends to our house and had my mother cook for them. I did not understand why she continued to obey him. Perhaps it was out of love or perhaps under the false hope that he would return to her some day.

Before 1968, my sisters and I had known only hand-made dolls. My mother taught us and helped us make our own dolls. We would collect the sticks and she would provide us with the leftover fabrics. She would embroider the face giving our dolls beautiful eyes, noses and lips. My mother had a way of buoying our spirits without making us feel deprived in any sense.

In 1968, during Anna's mother's visit to Saudi Arabia, we were presented with manufactured dolls from the US. With their blonde hair and blue eyes, the dolls did not bear any resemblance to our appearance. They were as alien to us as the people who brought them. However, we accepted them and shared them with our close relatives and friends until the dolls fell apart.

*I buried the year 1968 in the depths of my soul. It was a year of one painful memory: a memory of a window and a child with suppressed memories that wouldn't be unlocked until twenty years later in 1988.*

Suddenly, television appeared in our lives. I do not remember exactly when or how it arrived in our house; it must have been 1969. The small silver box, in black and white, broadcast English programmes over an Aramco channel. While the official Saudi national television channel was only launched in 1965, for a long time it was the Aramco channel that we watched.

As there were few children's programmes, we watched the news, Charlie Chaplin, Laurel and Hardy and *I Love Lucy*. The favourites were movies such as *Batman*, *Superman*, *The Mask of Zorro*, and John Wayne's cowboy movies. We did not know English, nor did we need the language. Influenced by those programmes, we were convinced that cowboys were the good guys and Native Americans, the "Indians", were the bad guys.

We were obedient and yet creatively destructive children. We were creative in that we put every piece of furniture to good use. The suitcases became sleighs for sliding down the stairs. Chairs, coffee tables, side tables and stools were used to create small caves, forts and tents. We children turned furniture and home accessories into theatrical objects and were oblivious to the destruction we created.

Our house was a big theatre. We did not need dolls. With the aid of our four cousins – Muneer, Yonis, Wafyah and Yaseen – we started acting out what we watched on TV. Initially, we used our house as the theatre and movie set, later moving into our cousins' house. Our best productions took place during the afternoons and especially during school holidays.

We seven children were the original crew. Muneer, my cousin, was the informal leader of the group and Ayah, my younger sister, was his assistant. Sometimes when our relatives and friends were present, we would invite them to join us. Through these short acting productions, we dictated which of our relatives and friends were part of our exclusive circle.

When the boys were busy with their outdoors activities, my sisters, cousin Wafyah and I would act out novels such as *Little Women*. My mother's room became the dressing room and her wardrobe became ours. It was rich with stylish imported dresses, high-heeled shoes and cosmetics. My mother's dresses were tailor-made for her in Al Khobar or purchased in Dhahran, Cairo or Beirut. According to my mother, my father selected and purchased them for her. My mother remembers, "There was nothing out of bounds, you used and ruined everything I had." It was my mother's trendy dresses that made us look like Little Women. We all had a favourite, mine being my mother's dark olive-green satin, sleeveless dress with flattering V neckline and narrow waistband. When it was my turn to wear it, I felt grown up and beautiful. The grounds of our home nourished the seeds of friendship that bound my sisters and I to Wafyah whom we claimed as our sister.

We would recite and act the dialogues without understanding the plot or its context. *Little Women* with the March girls – Jo, Meg, Beth and Amy–remained a favourite, an exciting part of our summer holiday. I have no recollection of how we allocated or chose roles. I do not recall how we portrayed Meg's vanity, Jo's hot temper, Beth's shyness and Amy's selfishness. We were familiar with America as the name of a country somewhere in the world. We could not locate Massachusetts on the map, nor did we understand the meaning of the American Civil War.

To a lesser extent, we played women's characters from Leo Tolstoy's *War and Peace*. Russian society during the Napoleonic era was as alien to us as Massachusetts. Nevertheless, the roles of Natasha and Sonya Rostova, Maria Bollkonskaya and Elena Kuragina were part of our days as well.

Among our sisters and cousins, we maintained agreements to save our allowances to purchase treats after playing. When money was not available, we made sugar sandwiches for our afternoon snacks. If we were disciplined in saving our allowances, we would treat ourselves to locally made popsicles, sold by a Yemeni man who came around the neighbourhood. Sometimes in our impatience, we would go and knock on his door to get what we wanted. Later when ice cream, soft drinks and chocolate became available, we switched to the newest available treat and the popsicle man disappeared. Using Coca Cola and Miranda drinks, my sister Saffiya started making mini-popsicle cubes at home and then sold them to us. One favourite winter memory is of using the kerosene heater or the stove to melt wrapped chocolate pieces before we sisters ate them.

In August 1968, we moved with my mother into my aunt Anisah's house temporarily. My aunt was finally convinced to accompany my uncle Hashem to the US during his last year of university. My mother cared for seven children, the three of us and my aunt's three boys and one girl. Aunt Anisah's mother also moved in with us to help my mother. During that time, I learned to share the love of the only parent I had with other children whom I forever regarded as my siblings.

During that period, my mother initiated us into the observances of our Islamic duties. It was time for us to start fasting during Ramadhan. We began with brief training periods to prepare us to fast throughout the long days. I remember Immy Um Hameed saving leftovers and giving us permission to eat a little to sustain us.

The following year, the leftovers disappeared and we fasted from sunrise to sunset, for the full month of Ramadhan. From then, we paid attention to the *msaher* (a drummer) who goes around the neighbourhoods and calls people by name to wake up for sahoor, the last meal before sunrise. Sometimes, the *msaher* also called the children by name to encourage them to wake for *sahoor*, before fasting throughout the day.

Ramadhan's days and nights are defined by the spirituality of prayers, supplications and absolute submission to Allah through refraining from all obscene and irreligious displays. It is a month that is intended for worship and devotion to Allah. Refraining from food and water from sunrise to sunset was easy when compared to the requirement to be calm, kind, forgiving and patient while so deprived. Sharing and giving are the essence of Ramadhan. Before sunset, we children were summoned to the kitchen to assist with the dispatch of food to neighbours, family members and friends. In those days, there were specific dishes to share. The most common was *harrisah*, a dish made of whole wheat and veal. Other popular dishes were starch-based sweets such as *sagoo* and *insha* (corn starch). Each child was dispatched to deliver food; each returned with food, according to the tradition of reciprocation.

For us in the Muslim Shia community, Ramadhan is marked two weeks before its official commencement with a humble celebration that we call *Nasfah*. It is celebrated on the fifteenth of Shaban, the eighth month of the Hijira (lunar calendar). The *Nasfah* marks the middle of the month preceding Ramadhan (the ninth month) when the countdown begins. It is also a celebration of the birth of the twelfth and last Imam, Al-Mahdi.

My mother would make fabric tote bags with long handles for us. These we hung around our necks and shoulders while going door-to-door singing songs of blessing in return for sweets. This tradition begins in the afternoon finishing with the call for prayer at sunset. It is then repeated in the middle of Ramadhan when we took our tote bags and again went from door-to-door singing to mark the fifteenth of Ramadhan, the birth of Imam Hassan Ibn Ali. The countdown then began to the celebration of *Eid el Fitr* at the conclusion of Ramadhan.

During our school holidays, my mother sent us for lessons to Um Abbas, an elderly woman and the mother of a neighbour. She taught us how to pray. Afterwards, my mother would observe us praying at home to ensure that we did it correctly. We made mistakes, laughed and played games until Um Abbas gave up on us. Later, Um Abbas, our prayer teacher, was admitted into an old people's home, the first mother in our small community so stigmatised. Our small community never forgot and never forgave the children of Um Abbas, none of whom was willing to look after her at home. It was and still is a blight on their reputation, an undignified act for both Um Abbas and her children.

Thereafter, we continued to pray with my mother at home. In the evening, I would stand next to her to perform the *maghreb* (sunset) and *Isha* (night) prayers. I triumphed when after concluding the prayer I could recite the names of the twelve Shia Imams. It is a Muslim Shia routine to end prayers by re-affirming our commitment to Allah. We begin with "Allah is my God, Muhammed is my Prophet" and then we list the Imams in descending order beginning with Ali bin Abi Taleb. At night, when getting ready for bed, I practised the descending order of our Shia Imams so as to avoid mistakes as I concluded my prayer. In our house, my mother encouraged us to pray without punishing us if we did not.

In our house only, my uncles could tease us when we prayed. As my paternal grandparents were strictly religious, it was impossible for them to have teased my aunts when they prayed. Uncle Hasan would make tempting offers around prayer time. He would say, "Those who pray won't go to the picnic with me." Sometimes we would hide the fact that we prayed so that we could go to the picnic.

There were no picnic baskets, no sandwiches, no drinks or treats. Our picnics consisted of walks to the beach or the desert sand dunes. Typically, we started just after lunch and walked toward the sand dunes on the outskirts of Safwa. Sometimes we would sit in the shade – when we could find it – while my uncle hunted: a rabbit, a *dhub* (a large desert dwelling-lizard) or *jarad* (grasshoppers), any and all of which were roasted and eaten. At other times, we would return directly home.

On these picnics, we walked in our flip-flops. Proper shoes were only for school and out-of-town adventures. Often, we would go barefoot, which I enjoyed with the soft burning touch of desert sand. Generally, I continued praying, although I abstained when unable to resist the picnic invitation. When I was caught out, I missed some of the picnics.

We comfortably moved between different religious expectations and commitments. At home we lived with two contradictory examples: that of my mother and her family's religious simplicity and her commitment to teaching us how to practice Islam without force or punishment; and that of my uncles' indifferent attitude toward religion.

Beyond the boundaries of our home, we were exposed to the paternal side of the family who meticulously adhered to religious rituals and traditions. At my maternal grandparents' home, we were gently reminded to pray, but were left to finish our childish play. The contrast to my paternal grandparents' home was stark. There, religious duties and obligations were tightly observed and reinforced; children were reminded and ordered to pray. Wherever we were, we adapted to these different ways of discipline.

The number of adults who disciplined us, guided us and dictated to us what to do and how to behave varied from house to house. For me, as long as Um Hameed and my mother Maryam were present, life was fine. A woman with limited financial resources, Maryam's heart is as big as the world; she loved everyone and accommodated everyone. We happily adjusted, listened and obeyed. But we managed also to do what we wanted to do.

My sisters and I were permitted to go out with relative freedom compared to other relatives and friends. We were free to go to Immy Um Hameed's house to play with our cousins. Also, we could visit the grandchildren of my great aunt Khaltie Malika, Um Hameed's sister who lived next door to Um Hameed.

The way of life for Khaltie Malika's family was quite different from ours. At that house, the girls were not allowed to leave their home except with their mothers. They were rarely allowed to go with us to the farm. They were also not allowed to attend the formal public school but instead they experienced *lemaalem,* the traditional home schooling like many other Safwa families. Much later, my cousins, who were our ages, enrolled in adult education. They worked hard and caught up with their formal education.

Some girls who attended public schools also attended *lemaalem* for a few hours a week to learn how to correctly read and recite the Quran. My female cousins also helped their teachers with the chores and looked after her children if needed. As they grew older, the girls were taught to cook, clean, wash clothes and take care of children. For some home teachers, this was what they requested in lieu of teaching fees.

At the time, I never questioned being one of the girls who were attending public school to be educated, to be able to read and write, nor did I feel privileged. My ability to read and write did not alienate me from my female cousins. At the end of the day we were all the same, just girls. We all matured into womanhood and into our own realistic and unrealistic dreams.

### My body

Between 1968 and 1969, we began swimming in the *shariyah,* the water canals that branched out from the few natural springs around town. In Safwa, there were three natural water springs: *el-ain el wastiyah* (the middle spring), *ain el janwbiya* (the south spring) and *ain daroosh*, which was nearest the home of my paternal grandparents. There were also three major water canals that ran through the springs and nourished the numerous farmlands.

I learned to name the water canals in their descending order as I walked from our west-side home to my paternal grandparents' house, located on the east side of town. First, I crossed the water canal known as *Shariyah Qmaih*, which basically divided the east from the west side of town. To the west of *Shariyah Qmaih* was the new town, which was called *Kharij* (outside). In *Kharij*, there were no water springs or canals. The second canal, *Shariyah le-traiji*, was immediately behind my paternal grandparents' house. As I walked further toward *Dirah*, the old town, I would reach *Shariyah el Oasaiyee*, the third canal. They were all within walking distance of our house and that of Um Hameed.

Those residents, like my paternal grandparents, with houses bordering the water canals were fortunate. These families had access from their back doors to the canal where they erected a temporary *hdhar*, a wall of palm tree branches. This secluded their own *mithar* (toilet) and provided private waterways where women could bathe. As we walked along the canals, we often crossed open toilet areas, as not every family was able to secure and seclude a private space. Our fortunate families had their private baths and toilets built into their homes. To go to other parts of town, visit other family members or to reach H*ammam abu Niss* (the Half-Riyal Bath), we had to cross the open toilet lands where we were unable to avoid the human excrement.

Primarily, my sisters and I went to *el Oasaiyee* to bathe. We would deprive ourselves of sweets and treats in order to save our daily allowances for bathing in the *hammam*. When we had saved half a riyal each, we treated ourselves to *Hammam abu Niss* for a fun bathing experience. The family whose house was located almost in the middle of the *Shariyat el Oasaiyee* operated the Half-Riyal Bath. We would proudly hand in our half-riyals and enter through the house to the changing room leading to the bath.

There we would leave our clean clothes with our *abbayas* [veils] on a cement deck along with our brushes and slippers. We would then walk into the bath where on one side there was a wide cement floor leading to steps into the water. The waters were always steaming hot during the winter and lukewarm in the summer. I enjoyed the experience of going to the *hammam* with my sisters Saffiya, Ayah and my cousin Wafyah. Our feminine bond was grounded in the sharing of such simple experiences. I knew that women paid attention and noticed my breasts developing and the changing colour of my nipples. There were only glances, no words. I started noticing that women were sometimes reluctant to bathe in the *hammam*, but did not understand why they chose not to bathe at certain times of the month. The *hammam* was a comfortable and familiar place.

During this same period while my father and Anna were still living in Saudi Arabia, they also took us with them to the swimming pool at the Aramco senior staff compound in Ras Tanura. When Aramco was established, it built various compounds with the senior staff camp designated for American nationals. I am not sure if my father had achieved senior status then. I assume that he and Anna had friends who lived there. It was during these visits that we were introduced to swimming pools where people swam in swimsuits. Two different worlds collided in my childish mind as I moved between the feminine bonding experience within that natural warm bath enclosure and that of the chlorinated water of an open swimming pool for foreigners.

Foreigners, mostly Americans, seemed comfortable in their skimpily clad bodies. Women, men and children walked around the pool in their swimsuits and swam together as if it was the most natural thing to do. Those women around the swimming pool behaved differently from the women at the *hammam*. I preferred the women at the *hammam*.

My sisters and I investigated and analysed how different these women were from the women in the *hammam*. In the changing room, we would lie flat on the floor as close as possible to the shower cubicle and try to see what these foreign women looked like naked. We could not imagine what women of the *hammam* would think if they saw women, men and children all swimming together. Probably, they would have blushed with embarrassment, and said: "*Asteghfer Allah*". Be penitent to Allah!

Until that time, I had never seen a naked woman before. This was especially true of my mother, as she would not even allow us to stay in the same room when she changed clothes. Thus, in the *hammam* I saw some women bathe topless. Others wore cotton undergarments that revealed everything beneath when wet. The *hammam* was a window into a secluded world that only existed in public baths, *ain* or *shariyah*, and only for women.

Within that fascinating world of women, I trained my ears to listen to the coded language in which women referred to their sexuality, joked about their sex lives and their husbands' sexual habits. Water served as a potion, a lubricant, to awaken and free women's voices. Disciplined and stern women relaxed and talked easily of censored topics while we listened. They trusted that we were just children, naive and carefree. I listened as women teased and joked, sometimes with loving care and sometimes with sorrow.

In the *hammam* and the *shariyah,* women almost always came together with their daughters, sisters, relatives and friends. Women bathed and helped other women bathe. They gave each other a good scrub, washed and brushed each other's hair. The *hammam* was the only place where women and girls partially or fully exposed their bodies without being made to feel shame. It was during these short-lived experiences that I began to have an idea about how my body would develop and how much body hair I might have when I grew older. In the *hammam*, older women often stripped naked, ordered us to scrub their backs and to bring their towel and slippers closer to the steps. I thought that one day I would be able to order children about in the *hammam*.

Little then did I realise how fast my small world was changing. Abruptly, the water springs, the canals and the *hammam* dried out. For ever, I lost the right and the opportunity to strip naked and order younger women around when bathing. I lost the right of access to the *hammam* rituals; rituals that belong to women within the *hammam* experience. I lost the access to women's uninhibited voices. Involuntarily, I lost the right to a natural relationship with my body at a critical stage of my development. The sensual and harmonious relationship that had been nurtured through the feminine world of the *hammam* was shattered with its closing. From that time forward, my body existed only in shadow. Divided, my body and I existed in isolation from each another. I acknowledged its existence only when it required hygienic care. Otherwise, it was a thing apart with which I was uncomfortable.

# 2

# Closing and Opening

Although my father and Anna left Saudi Arabia in 1969, I have no recollection of their departure. In my memory register, there is no record of hugs or farewell wishes. The experience has always been a blank page, with no attached documents and no emotions.

I do have one distinctive memory from 1969. It was the considerable commotion created in our small community by Apollo 11 and Neil Armstrong's moon landing. I remember the misgiving and fear that this was the sign of the world coming to an end. In that small community, it was simply not possible for a man to land on the moon, even if it had been shown on TV.

I have a clear memory of my sister Ayah's response to my paternal great-grandmother's disapproval of her nail polish. "Grandma," Ayah said, "a man has landed on the moon and you are disapproving of my nail polish!" I also remember the reaction of my paternal grandparents' neighbour, a taxi driver, who relentlessly argued with his customers. He sought to convince them that a man could not have landed on the moon, as the earth was flat and it did not revolve. His triumphant proof was that since building his house, the gate had never changed direction and it had always faced west. Soon the moon landing was forgotten.

My life veered away from the focus on man's new frontier. It was a quiet life with slow yet profound waves of change approaching. Life resumed its normal patterns with the moon regaining its romantically poetic status, unsoiled by the landing. My cousins, my sisters and I continued our acting rehearsals. Luckily, we were never tempted to enact the landing on the moon.

At the end of 1969, or the beginning of 1970, aunt Anisah and uncle Hashem returned from the US. My mother, my sisters and I continued to sleep at their house. My uncle returned with a modern stereo set. Thus at my aunt's house, we learned to dance to the 70s' songs such as "Come on, baby, let's do the Twist" and "Sugar, Sugar ah Honey", despite our total lack of understanding of the rock and roll culture. That too passed and the Twist fad faded.

On 28 September 1970, our carefree days were disturbed by the news of Jamal Abdel Nasser's death. At aunt Anisah's house, we watched his funeral procession on TV. The house went silent. The whole town went silent. Perhaps, the entire world went silent, except for the weeping that filled the Arab world. I remember the crying all around me. There was a pronounced stillness and sadness, as if a dream close to realisation had been aborted.

With Nasser's death, a generation, a whole nation, lost hope as its dream of unity was shattered. With his death, it lost the only man who had the qualities to be endorsed as a legitimate spiritual Arab leader. I was only ten, and yet I was overwhelmed by an impenetrable sense of loss. I felt abandoned. There were no more songs for Arab unity; there were no more songs for the Arab world. Jamal died. Jamal died. There were no more rousing inspiring speeches. Men no longer gathered in silence to listen to Nasser, to listen to the voice of Arab dignity, to the voice of determination and possibility. Tears surged, as if suddenly I had become an orphan.

I recalled a day after the 1967 Six-Day War when Um Hameed interrupted us to point out demonstrations in the streets. She said: "I would join the men if I were allowed." Women were not allowed to participate, but as female children we could. I remember marching at just seven years old alongside one of my uncles and his friends. The men protested against Israel and the US in the aftermath of that war between Israel, Egypt, Jordan and Syria. The men demonstrated and called for the destruction of Israel. They reiterated their support for Egypt as an Arab country. They demonstrated against Israel's atrocities and its new occupation of Palestinian homelands: of Sinai in Egypt and the Golan Heights in Syria. Men carried Jamal Abdel Nasser's pictures and chanted. I have no recollection of when I stopped marching and returned home to Um Hameed's.

Despite the setback of the 1967 war, this was the first concerted celebration of Arab Nationalism and the freeing of our nations from colonisation. We listened, learned and sang songs such as "The land speaks Arabic" and "My beloved homeland, the Arab homeland". Egypt had been attacked because President Nasser confronted the West, because he dared to dream of a united Arab world. The majority of Arab nations identified with Nasser's dream. Although it was Egypt in the front line, we sang in honour of other liberation movements such as the Algerian war for independence. We sang for a woman, Jamila Buhraid, the Algerian freedom fighter, a symbol of independence from colonialism. Primarily however, we sang for Arab unity and for Palestine.

Brought up in a home that embraced Arab Nationalism, I was inspired by Nasser's speeches and his enthusiasm for a united Arab future. A framed photograph of Nasser hung in our living room. This was the case in most of the homes around us. Between 1967 and 1969, political arrests were at their height in the Eastern Province as in other parts of Saudi Arabia.

I have a vivid nighttime memory of my mother and aunt Anisah collecting mounds of books and Nasser's photos for burning behind the kitchen in our house. Still, I recall the anguish and the tears the day Nasser died, as if dreams and hopes were only possible with him as leader. We cried for a future that was lost before it was fully conceived. Nasser was a leader with noble intentions but with common human flaws. Today, he remains, in every sense of the word, the spiritual leader of Arab Nationalism.

## A childhood surrendered

Quite unexpectedly, I woke one day to another death. Unprepared, I surrendered my childhood. I reached puberty and became a young woman. Of all the possible places, it happened in the bathroom. I had just finished bathing when I noticed a streak of red water rushing down the tiled floor. I had a moment of panic and suppressed a scream. I was hoping for an injury. I was only eleven years old. Silently, I protested, "I am still just a child." My protest was met with an empty internal echo. There was nothing, no pain and no signs, only that red streak. At age eleven, I somehow understood, but I hoped that my mother would find some other cause. I was not ready. I felt as if had been caught off guard. I felt cheated of my childhood.

My knowledge of menstruation was limited to the mysterious reusable cloth pads I saw drying on the clothesline. Momentarily, I went blank on sight of the blood. I reached for and tucked tissues between my thighs and waited for my mother. With that jolting shift out of childhood, I experienced an unwelcome burden as womanhood descended upon me. With that jolt, I entered unfamiliar territory; I became a woman.

My rite of passage out of childhood was a silent moment. I lost my childhood and stepped over the threshold alone. On joining me, my mother's only comforting act was to teach me how to use the pads. Overnight, I had to learn a new way to walk, to sit, to talk and to behave. My body betrayed me. Rapidly, it began to change.

I denied the change and believed that I could deny it as long as no one noticed. Without immediate compensation, I lost my innocence. My activities were more restricted and more closely watched. New boundaries of right and wrong, of what was allowed and what was prohibited were added to the already existing list of licit and illicit activities. I had to reconsider all that I had taken for granted as a child. My friendships with male cousins were becoming more limited.

Although she had received some formal education, my mother had never thought of preparing us for changes in our bodies. She had never discussed with us what to watch for, what to expect, how to notice changes in our bodies and what to do when our menstrual cycle started. Thus, she taught me in the way that she was taught: she gave me one lesson. Very businesslike, she showed me how to fold the cloth pad, how to secure it, how often to change it and how to wash it. She advised that I should expect this intrusion once a month. Vividly, I remember her instruction to "Keep it to yourself. This is not something you speak of."

Before me, of course, my sister Saffiya had her period. She had never spoken about it. Although we never discussed it, Ayah and I knew that Saffiya's cycle had started. That was *not* a topic for discussion. Later, Ayah was lucky in keeping the onset of her cycle to herself. No one knew that she had entered womanhood, as disposable sanitary pads had entered our lives by that time.

I struggled. My body had changed beyond my control. There was no way it would go unnoticed. With sisters, it was impossible to disguise my condition. I had become plump and my sisters started calling me chubby and fatty. Even my beautiful, waist-length, wavy hair could not conceal my body or compensate for the weight gain. I consoled myself with the hope of losing weight. Although I would eventually lose weight, that was in the future.

While I could ignore my body, I could not ignore being called fat and chubby and I could not ignore the glances. Compared to my sisters, I was fat. I was unable to conceal my weight and my monthly menstrual period. As I became violently ill, I had no control over the monthly misery. I would stay in bed for the first two days because of the cramps, the back pain, the vomiting and diarrhoea.

My body had betrayed me. When I walked, I sensed that my body weight *sounded* heavy. I walked awkwardly during my period, as I feared that the pad would become unsecured. I left traces of blood on my bed sheets, my underwear and worse my school uniform. I had a peculiar smell and I hated that odour of dried blood. I felt that people around me noticed my odour. In those near-paranoid periods, I began to limit myself and sought solitude during those days.

My relationship with my menstrual cycle was limited to daily hygienic care each month. Beyond that, there was no connection. There was no recognition of hormonal changes and their impact on my body and my mood changes. I did not know what hormones were and I am certain that my mother shared my ignorance. There was no celebration of the lunar cycle as it mysteriously influenced my femininity. Although in so many ways a female, I did not necessarily want to be feminine at that stage.

I struggled emotionally and socially. I felt displaced. I was neither a child nor a woman; rather, I was suspended between two stages of life, exiled from one, not fully qualified for the next. I was no longer permitted my childhood but I did not have full access to womanhood. While I was allowed to participate in certain children's activities, simultaneously I was asked to assume more chores in preparation for womanhood. The boundaries and new responsibilities constricted, pinched, leaving me with the feeling of entrapment.

With womanhood approaching, I was initiated into veiling but not yet as a compulsory custom. Rebelliously, I wore the veil improperly. I did not cover my face, as my family did not mandate this. I did not hold the veil tightly around me to conceal my body and my clothing. In the security of our house, I was not required to veil or to wear the *mishmar* to cover myself even in the presence of men who were not recognised guardians.

I felt trapped at the gate of womanhood. In that period, I stayed home more than I went out. For security, I involved myself with my mother and her relatives or friends. This is when I learned to love the kitchen.

The kitchen was where life happened and the world revolved around. It was also where I learned to smoke. Although Western-style cigarettes were frowned upon for women, they traditionally smoked *Qadoo*, the *shishah* (water pipe) without penalty. While they smoked, they shared their tears, laughter, sorrow, complaints and gossip. Women arrived to visit with my mother while she cooked. Some would join her in the kitchen and some would sit against the wall facing the kitchen door. One of my new grown-up chores was to prepare the *Qadoo,* which eventually led me to smoke.

Every new day brought more chores, more expectations and more boundaries. My world began to revolve around running errands and chores. My world centred on what I was and was not allowed to do, on how to walk, talk and laugh. Gradually, I began to relish these new expectations.

It was during this period that I became curious about my paternal grandparents' life. I expressed interest in spending time at their house with my two aunts, Naeema and Najah. My paternal grandparents lived in a truly extended family house. They shared it with the families of my great uncle's two wives, my paternal great-grandmother and the family of a fatherless distant cousin. Together, they all lived in an old styled two-storey Arabic home with a spacious two-section courtyard: one covered and one open. At the main entrance was a beautiful large traditional carved wooden door that enclosed a smaller gate.

Life was different in the home of my paternal grandparents. There were more rules and respect was equated with fear. At their house and in their presence, children did not talk much and only spoke when addressed. Religious practices were strict and applied to children as well. My aunts and my paternal grandmother prayed together; therefore, during my visits I would pray with them.

My older aunt Naeema, following in the footsteps of her mother, had a talent for dressmaking. During the early stages of my paternal grandmother's married life, she had earned her living from sewing dresses and undergarments for women. She charged one riyal per piece, a very modest price indeed.

My aunt Naeema knew how to use grandmother's sewing machine, a black Singer that was placed atop a small wooden trunk. The trunk had small drawers where she kept the thread, bobbins and needles. Endlessly, I would sit and watch my aunt holding the handle as the wheel turned the needle to do the work. She had a few dress sketches, patterns and designs and a genuine talent for the work.

At that time, my aunts had already travelled with my paternal grandparents to Iraq and neighbouring countries. They had exotic stories about other people in different lands. I found it fascinating to listen to them. My aunts seemed sophisticated and well travelled. They also had dolls and souvenirs that they brought from other lands.

In the absence of my father, the family relationship had remained formal. Therefore, my mother and the three of us would visit my paternal grandparents typically on formal occasions. These generally included when they returned from travel, during the two *Eid* celebrations and on occasions when one of them was sick.

I recall the occasions when my mother, my sisters and I sat in my paternal grandmother's room or the tiny living room. Always, we formed a row in age-descending order. We would only speak when we were addressed. My paternal grandmother's room was always tidy and clean. She had a metal sleigh bed under which was storage space. Included in her under-bed storage were treats, which she would offer to us before departure. She kept her hairbrush and clips, her Brylcreem and Vaseline hair tonic on an embroidered white cloth on the top of a small stand next to her bed.

In her room, my grandmother always kept a small porcelain pot filled with rose water. Before her afternoon outings, she would pour the rose water over her hands and wash her face. Afterwards she dried her rose-watered hands on her veil or dress. Many years later, she would leave the rose water pot in the family room and invite us to duplicate her ritual as we took leave in the afternoon. My paternal grandmother, her clothes and her room were always pleasantly redolent of perfume, Arabic fragrant oil, incense and rose water. My paternal grandmother had rituals that she followed strictly. Before putting her freshly laundered clothing away, she would perfume each piece then fold it neatly and place it on the shelves of her cupboard. The image of her performing this ritual by her bedside is indelibly imprinted in my memory.

There was no doubt that entry to her room was permitted only during formal occasions or by invitation. Such an invitation to my paternal grandmother's room signalled her endorsement of our trustworthiness. Her room was decorated with silk flowers, Quranic verses in exquisite calligraphy and a painting of Imam Hussain. In addition, there was a painting of a man rowing a boat across a beautiful lake. My aunts warned us (my sisters and I) that according to my paternal grandmother, the man in the painting (whose name was San Sanao) would come to life to abduct misbehaving children.

My paternal grandparents' house had a different rhythm compared to the home of my maternal grandparents. My paternal grandparents lived in a communal, extended family style, i.e., they cooked and ate together. The women of the house – the daughters and sisters-in-law – divided and shared the household chores. Without question, my paternal great-grandmother was the true matriarch of the house.

Lunch was always served to two separate groups: males and females. When food was limited, men always got the largest portion of the main dish. Rice was always plentiful and women and children received more rice than meat or fish. Little boys would normally eat with the men; however, if they misbehaved they would be sent back to eat with the women.

My paternal grandmother Fatema had her own special status; she was the oldest son's wife and also a mother of seven boys and two girls. She was a beautiful, influential, well-respected woman who was admired for her wisdom. She had a stern face but radiated a well-modulated compassion. My paternal grandmother was firm and took her life seriously. She took good care of my grandfather and of her children.

As my paternal grandmother and my mother gave birth at almost the same time, my grandmother was busy looking after her own young children. Thus when we were young, we did not often have the opportunity to be looked after by her. That task was left for Um Hameed, my maternal grandmother.

Only once, my mother left me in the care of my paternal grandmother. On that occasion, my parents went on holiday leaving both Saffiya and me in the care of our grandmothers. At that time, I was around three months old. With only an eighteen-month age difference between us, Um Hameed did not feel that she could look after both of us day and night. The agreement was that my paternal grandmother would look after me during the day with both of us sleeping in the home of Um Hameed. However, my paternal grandmother could not look after me as she had promised. Instead, she left me to be cared for by the wife of one of my great uncles. In the end, my maternal grandmother, Um Hameed, took me back after I became very sick and malnourished.

On becoming aware of our world, my sisters and I developed a healthy understanding of the significant differences between our paternal and maternal grandparents. While we enjoyed their company and embraced the kindness and love our parental grandparents bestowed upon us, the relationship was defined by respect and formality. We enjoyed my paternal grandmother and shared her love for ice cream and popsicles. She taught us how to make homemade buttermilk popsicles, which we relished. Nevertheless, we longed for a special relationship with our paternal grandmother similar to that we had with our maternal grandmother. After all, we were the daughters of her eldest son and her first granddaughters.

My four paternal great aunts were a part of this extended family household. They had inherited part of the house according to the Islamic law of inheritance. Two of my great aunts were *Mulayat* (readers) for the commemoration of the martyrdom of the Shia Imams. Mulayat are recognized and renowned for their beautiful voices when reciting the history of martyrdom. They used the spacious courtyard every day to hold *elaziyah* during the commemoration.

## Closing and Opening 43

At about the time of my puberty, I started sitting through these commemorations. For most of the time when visiting, I would stay upstairs in my grandparents' quarter. Most of the extended family women gathered there for *elaziyah.* On this spiritual social journey, women gathered, wept and remembered the Shia Imams who were either assassinated or died in battles.

While the other family members took their afternoon siesta and before the women gathered, I would sit and watch my paternal great uncle's wife Alawiyah enter the *aziyah* from the side door connecting their home to the main family home. Quietly, she would sprinkle water over the courtyard to cool the ground. Then, she would roll out the straw mats and rugs under the shaded area. I loved observing how beautiful and serene she always looked. Two or three other women would arrive to help her bring out the *Qadoo* (water pipes) from the kitchen where they were routinely stored. Then they would wash them and change the water. One or two women were designated with the responsibility to tear the tobacco leaves and set them aside to await the women's arrival. Then they would soak the tobacco leaves in water and start a fire of coals. Other women were assigned with brewing Arabic black coffee (*qahwa sawda*) for the *aziyah*. There was no cardamom and no saffron, just black bitter Arabic coffee, as bitter as the anguish of *Ahl el Bait.* Gradually, other women, mostly family members and relatives would gather.

The distant humming voices of women would launch these daily ritual gatherings. Between late noon and early afternoon the hum of women laughing, complaining, quarrelling and even crying signalled the beginning of their daily ritual. Remotely, I could sense the mood of the beginning. When the reading began, the mood of the women changed as they listened to the epic of *Ahl el Bait*'s martyrdom. The women, overcome by grief, cried as if it was the last time they would ever hear the epic. They knew of course that they would be here the next day doing the same thing. I questioned if women's tears didn't relate to their lives as much as they related to the compassion and empathy they felt toward *Ahl el Bait*.

In memory, my steps race back to the aziyah and to the unending tears and voices of women. Those memories are infused, defined by the seasonal drinks and aromas of *elaziyah*, an offering of *Ahl el*

*Bait*. While *elaziyah* indicated mourning and anguish for *Ahl el Bait*, the memories are inextricably associated as a child and a grown up with seasonal tastes. For the spring and summer in the *aziyah*, they served the refreshing sugar-loaded lime juice and Vimto. During the fall and winter, hot, freshly brewed ginger roots, cinnamon sticks and dry lime teas were offered at the end of the congregation. In the *aziyah*, it seemed that women stopped only to start weeping again immediately.

I marvelled at the curious ways that women deal with their own lives as they shifted moods after listening to the reading. I marvelled at their tender compassion. Within that circle of compassion, I matured in the company of women, listening to them while I rested against one of the first-floor panels of my paternal grandparents' house. I watched as women clad in their black abbayas made the best out of their lives, the best that they could.

I loved visiting their home for my paternal grandfather had a small library. It contained numerous religious and non-religious books, novels and old magazines. Mula Ali's well-maintained library was always closed but never locked. Often, I would go there quietly, select a book and sit reading on the Persian carpet, resting my back against one of the many hard cushions lined against the walls of the small room. My paternal grandfather did not mind as long as I did not take or damage any of his books. He had a collection of books on the Prophet's wives, their knowledge and contributions to Islam. I was fascinated by the wives' courage in challenging, questioning and demanding their rights from the Prophet himself (pbuh). From those books, I formed a beautiful image of the their voices but as those voices were excluded from our public school curriculum, we were not encouraged to emulate them.

It was at my paternal grandparents' house that I first experienced stark gender differences. As men had more rights, they were able to make demands. My uncles had the right to discipline my aunts. There was a stark divide in the relationships indicating that males had higher status than females.

It was also at my paternal grandparents' house that I witnessed women and children eating men's leftovers. As a well-respected Mula, my paternal grandfather had many friends who came to visit him from neighbouring towns or far away places. It was customary that when the man of the house had guests, all of the cooked food was served to his guests. The only exception to this rule was when there were women guests accompanying their husbands. Then only enough food to serve the male and accompanying females was prepared and served. The women of the house cooked and served lunch leaving nothing in the pots and pans. Mula Ali would not appreciate his wife if–without his permission – she reserved food before his guests were served. Of course, my paternal grandmother never reserved any food without his permission and never asked for it even when she could have. The men would eat to their satisfaction and return the largely empty serving dishes to feed the awaiting hungry women and children. No one complained. It was simply the custom of the house.

Over time, I became aware of the subordinate status of women and the hardships they endured in my community. Silently, I pledged to challenge the status quo of women as represented by my mother. Abandoned with the responsibility for bringing up three girls, my mother was stigmatised in our community as she had no sons and thus was deemed unfortunate. We lived with the pitying glances and words of *maskena* (poor thing), if only Allah had given her a son. In our community, we lived with proverbs and rhymes about girls such as "The father of boys has gold chairs. The father of girls has wooden chairs." One of the rhymes is a dialogue between a mother of boys and a mother of girls as follows:

> You, the misfortunate mother of girls:
> In the middle of the road, your consignment is abandoned.

The mother of girls replies:

> When the daughters of the misfortunate become women,
> They wed the boys of the fortunate
> They, then bring their mother dignity and fortune.

Another was the pessimistic rhyme about girls as it speaks of boys as:

> They are the veins of steel
> Securing luck

Even if divorced, their mother's return home is guaranteed
They are the face of their timid mother
And they revoke her misfortune.

I wanted to put an end to the recitation of such rhymes and the quoting of such proverbs. I wanted to stop being made to feel as if my sisters and I were the curse of our mother's life. I questioned the proverbs and rhymes as they deviated from Islamic teachings and practices. The commonly quoted proverbs and rhymes reflecting gender inequalities did not concur with what I learned about the beliefs and faith in Allah's Will and Creation.

My mother did not allow us to internalise or believe those cruel rhymes. She would say, "*Intoo be el-dinya* [To me you are the world], do not listen to what they say." My mother alternated between strength and weakness. When she displayed weakness, I would pledge to myself never to be weak, never to become subservient to anyone or anything, including my heart and desires. Much later, my mother divulged that during her final two pregnancies, she believed that she carried a son; on both occasions, she was gifted with daughters.

Throughout puberty I continued to be extremely quiet and obedient, especially with my mother. I had always listened and did what she had asked of me. I was a follower. I followed my sisters' plans and executed them as if they were my own.

I had always been aware of my role as a middle child. When my sisters had a fight, I tried to remain neutral when and if I could. Many times I would be pulled into their conflict by one of them, usually Ayah, the youngest. I had always given in to her, be it in choosing food, games, even gifts that were brought to us. I did so to save my mother from one of Ayah's tantrums. It was my way to keep balance. I would let Ayah choose first, as I would happily give up my first choice if it were her preference. I was happy with whatever was left and I had learned to enjoy whatever I had.

My mother never laid a hand on me. No one laid hands on me except my sisters who punished me for not being punished. I accepted this code of justice, as my sisters could not possibly go after my mother. I was the only available target. My sisters mostly went after my long hair, my crown and my curse, which they snatched and pulled.

## Closing and Opening 47

I do not exactly recall when between 1971 and 1972 the shift in my interests occurred. I had begun losing interest in my own childhood and in my sisters. I had begun to lose interest in our childish games and of being called names. I know that this was the only time in my entire life that I was tired of my sisters. I began to slowly withdraw into a world of solitude where I found comfort in books and complete silence. My sisters had no interest in my new-found world. I did not mind their lack of interest, as in this realm I was a leader. I indulged myself. They still found new unpleasant names for me.

I continued with my chores. At this time, they included bringing gas cylinders home. I would roll them through the streets until I reached home. I also learned how to replace the empty ones. I got my hands into everything from changing light bulbs to fixing television and radio sets. With my total lack of knowledge of electric and electronics work, I claimed that I could fix things. Sometimes it was successful and things would be fixed temporarily. What made it work was my stubborn persistence. Eventually, I became tenacious when it came to fixing things and finding solutions. I noticed the dismissive glances that said, "You are but a girl. This is a temporary phase that will pass." I was determined to learn and to be able to do everything considered "boys' work". Thus, eventually I developed a reputation and a new identity as a "tomboy". My defiance manifested into aggression that was limited to throwing stones and empty glass bottles at boys who dared to call me that name.

I have always been interested in books, particularly literature and history. My father had left a small collection of books, including a copy of Nizar Qabbani's poetry, al Manfalouti, and Taha Hussein. I shied away from reading Qabbani's sensually provocative poetry. I would open the hard cover of *Qalat li al-samra* [The Brunette Told Me], (1944) and *Tufulat nahd* [Infancy of a Breast], (1948) to immediately close them and put them aside. I was a committed reader of *Al Arabi* (equivalent to *National Geographic*) and Alnahdha, two of the leading publications of Kuwait. I read current and outdated issues with the same interest.

I was eleven years old when I read Victor Hugo's *Les Misérables*. I still remember reading the novel in three days, along with completing my school homework. I remember that I didn't sleep much until I finished the book. The most fascinating book I read during that time was *One Thousand and One Nights*. A girl I befriended in my fifth-grade class introduced me to it. During one of my after-school visits to her house, she shared it with me. I was mesmerized. I started reading, skipping the stories of Aladdin and the magic lamp, Sinbad and Ali Baba and the forty thieves. I had found the magic of *One Thousand and One Nights* beyond the scope of those legends. The enchanted stories and the implicit language of both the licit and illicit love stories fascinated me. The fantasies of passion, love and desire between witches, djinns and humans, the homosexual and bisexual relationships–all of which was prohibited to an eleven-year-old – made it the more fascinating to read. I wasn't allowed to take the book home. My classmate gently reminded me to keep what I read to myself.

*One Thousand and One Nights* was the doorway into learning about my sensuality and sexuality. During those afternoons, I wondered if the book was bewitched, i.e., did it have the power to transmit never before experienced sensations through my body? Unable to understand the sensations and too shy to ask my classmate, I nevertheless feverishly pursued reading despite the near overwhelming sensations.

# 3

# Political Awakening

I moved beyond *One Thousand and One Nights*, and started reading Ghassan Kanafani's collection of short stories. With my limited understanding of the Palestinians' plight, I confess that I did not fully understand what I read. Nevertheless, my interest had shifted.

In 1974, my uncle Adnan and his American wife Louise returned home after he graduated with a Master's degree from the USA to work in Al-Khobar. My great uncle Nasser also returned to rejoin Aramco after graduating from University. However, it was with the return of my uncle Najeeb and his ulterior political motives that I gained access to numerous and varied books. I read Maxim Gorky's *Mother*, Boris Pasternak's *Doctor Zhivago*, Naguib Mahfouz's Cairo novels, and I continued reading Ghassan Kanafani's books.

My rebellion against strongly held community rituals and religiously associated codes began around this time. My paternal grandparents, my paternal great-grandmother, her granddaughter and my aunts temporarily lived with us while their house was under renovation. Before that time, we had never dared to turn on the television during the months of *Ashura* and *Safar* or during the commemoration of Imam Ali's death in the month of Ramadhan.

After the elders left the house to attend the commemoration of *Ahl el Bait*, my sisters, cousins and my aunts would turn on the TV thereby violating the Shia community code during the remembrance of Imam Ali's death. That year, the most acclaimed Syrian social comedy television shows were aired during the month of Ramadhan: *Sah el Noum* (Wake Up) starred Duraid Laham and Nihad Qalie, known widely in the Arab world as Gowar and Husni al

Burazan. We did not comprehend the political undercurrents of the show at the time. We simply enjoyed the comedy and for Gowar and Husni we disobeyed and challenged the rules. We certainly did not appreciate then that the show was a masterpiece of Syrian and Arabic TV, a virtual cornerstone of modernity.

Carefully, we locked the doors in order to switch the TV off before my grandmothers and my mother returned home. One evening, the three women returned earlier than usual. They were so furious to find all their children and grandchildren glued to the set that they almost broke the door to the house. My paternal grandmother held a hammer against the set and would have broken it if it was not for the few of us who wrested it from her hand. She threatened to break the set if we did not repent. We continued to secretly watch TV during the months of mourning.

Years later, during the 1980s my paternal grandfather Mula Ali broke the *Ashura* prohibition; he would return home after he finished his commemorative reading and follow the news of the Iraq–Iran War. Mula Ali's mother, my paternal great-grandmother, muffled her words of disapproval of him watching the news.

None of the women of the house, including his mother, had the courage to challenge him. Still, we were not allowed to watch television during those mourning periods, unless we were watching the news with him. Much later the prohibitions for *Ashura* and *Safar* were relaxed in our family.

I was thirteen when the disappointment of the October 1973 war sparked my interest in and fascination with politics. Until then my struggle and frustration with the status of women had only led me to read about women in early Islam. I was fourteen when I was exposed to the wider Palestinian resistance literature. *Al Hadaf* was one of the first political magazines to which I was introduced. It was founded by Ghassan Kanafani as the voice of the "Popular Front for the Liberation of Palestine". Like many before and after me, my political initiation was through Arab Nationalism and the Palestinian cause.

When I was fourteen, the Arab Nationalist Movement, which was based on Constantin Zureiq's thinking, was a safe political entry point for women living in a conservative and traditional Muslim community. The Arab Nationalist ideology was revolutionary, placing secular Arab unity over that of religion. It gave us hope and allowed us to dream of unity, strength and progress. It proposed to revolutionise Arab consciousness leading us all to democracy through the adoption of a socialist secular ideology. Given our ultra-conservative upbringing, it was easier to gravitate toward the Arab Nationalists than to Marxism, which later became the overarching ideology for our political agenda. If the Arab Nationalist Movement's local representative had proposed Marxism at first, I believe that I would have rejected it, as Marxism was then associated with atheism.

I was introduced to Charles Darwin's theory of evolution and natural selection. For some time, I ricocheted between belief in the creation of Allah and the creation story of nature. Intellectually, I began to have doubts about Allah and religion. I wrestled with questions of ritual: to pray or not, to fast or not.

By age sixteen, I was initiated partially into the political movement with its now declared Marxist ideology. While on the rooftop of Um Hameed's house, I would remain awake until dawn when I could no longer see shooting stars. As children, we had been told that shooting stars are intended to burn non-believers: *"On you will be sent (O ye evil ones twain!) a flame of fire (to burn) and a smoke (to choke): no defence will ye have"* (The Holy Quran, *Surah ar-Rahman*, 35).

Gradually, I stopped fasting and praying along with some other relatives and friends. Among the young political recruits I knew, none had the courage to admit to a change in these practices or to stand up for our new beliefs. We all lied to our families. For a long time, I pretended to pray and fast but I was not seriously adhering to any of my former Islamic rituals. One day during Ramadhan, my younger sister Ayah discovered me having lunch with friends from my new world. I sensed the threat of exposure. This was the first time that I experienced blackmail and how it feels to try to buy someone else's silence. It was one thing to devote myself to the cause of Arab Nationalism and quite another to become an atheist.

Was I ever completely doubtful about Allah? I know now that I was never certain. However, my spiritual journey was not destined to follow the conventional route. I was not convinced that Allah wanted the believer to worship out of fear. I believed that there must be something more powerful than fear. I refused to believe that the fear of punishment led to the love of Allah. There must have been more to being a believer, much more than a minority Muslim Shia community could explain to me at that time. Islam was simpler and more just than is commonly believed today. What I independently read and understood in the Quran was not what I learned at home and at school.

My allegiance to women was now transferred to men. At the time, only they could provide access to the realm of political activism. To forge alliances with men was and I believe is still the only way for women the world over to participate politically.

In 1975, King Faisal died and his successor, King Khaled, bestowed clemency on all political prisoners of Saudi Arabia. This modest clemency coincided with the possibility of travel abroad. That summer I left Safwa, my hometown, for the first time in the company of my two sisters, my two aunts, Naeema and Najah and two uncles Najeeb and Jaleel. It was a first vacation abroad for my sisters and me. We went to Kuwait, Iraq, Syria and Lebanon.

During that trip, I sensed that there was something more to the books and the magazines I was reading than just believing in Arab Nationalism. In Kuwait, Iraq, Syria and Lebanon, various other Arab nationals visited us. Numerous books and magazines were given to us to be smuggled back home.

We were used as a cover-up, a political shield to disguise more organised, more dangerous activities engaged in by the men. Then, we did not mind, as this seemed a fair exchange. We got to travel; uncle Najeeb did politics.

Behind the scenes, the flame of political conflict flickered to life and was escalating in Lebanon between Palestinians and Lebanese. On leaving Lebanon, I hoped to return the next summer. Lebanon was then approaching twenty-five years of civil war. In fact, it was twenty-nine years before I returned to Beirut. I returned home to Safwa longing for my mother, for everything that was familiar. Memories of the summer holiday faded rapidly.

Love enveloped me as if it had been waiting for my return. On a late afternoon at the end of summer 1975, I saw him – a shadow-like being – walking across the road from our house. I realised that the boy was wearing a wig; I noted that the high collar of his *thobe* looked different. I was attracted by his eyes, his hazelnut coloured eyes. My heart moved. From behind the main gate, I peered out again; my heart quivered. I fell in love.

## Love and politics collide

In my journey toward love, I drifted toward my maternal grandmother, Immy Um Hameed. In that extraordinary period, her house was my homeland. Sheltered in her sanctuary, I wandered innocently into the forbidden domain: love, a strict cultural taboo.

At age fifteen, I fell in love with Suhail, whose allegiance was to another political party. I loved Suhail and I was terrifyingly aware of being exposed. Until then I had behaved properly, i.e., done what I was told to do. My mother was a strong woman when it came to bringing up girls. She had to be strict in a community where she and we were under constant surveillance.

I was in love, but terrified. I relaxed when I received the blessing and the protection of Batool, Suhail's mother. She blessed our love; I trusted that Suhail would not hurt me, while under the care of his mother, nor in her absence. Suhail was to be in my heart and my life forever. Although we were not relatives or neighbours, a bond was forged. Our bond contradicted the norms of social relations.

My first kiss, my first caress, my first sweaty palm, my sensuality was awakened in Suhail's sanctuary of love and devotion. Unexpectedly, he came into my life without permission or an invitation. It seemed that I stumbled on him on my way to school and gravitated toward that which was forbidden.

The second time I met Suhail was by coincidence; I was visiting some of his relatives who happened also to be his neighbours. I was in love and I had to find a way to meet him; thus, I befriended Suhail's cousin, Haniyah, who lived next door to his family. I drifted partially away from cousin Wafyah; she alone among my family and friends knew of my love for Suhail. I retained some study routines with Wafyah but limited them to a few times a week instead of every day. Some time was required to establish a new study routine with Haniyah. I told my mother that Haniyah needed after-school tutoring in science and English.

At Haniyah's house, we – Suhail and I – met and studied in the same room. For some time, we conversed through glances before we verbally revealed our feelings. Eventually, we had the courage to hold hands, thereby breaking social boundaries. At the time, Suhail was in the habit of leaving open the top buttons of his *thobe* permitting his confident exhibition of his prized gold necklace, not a customary practice at that time. Indeed, society frowned upon such display. In my eyes, he seemed so sheltered, so fragile and so spoiled.

Between 1975 and 1979, Suhail and I remained deeply in love, although of profoundly different views. Between 1979 and 1982, we were out of love frequently. In a community where love is taboo, I felt extremely lucky to love and be loved not only by Suhail, but also loved, welcomed and protected by Suhail's mother, Batool. She was as much a mother to me as to her son. I had a special bond with her. I sustained my routine visits to her house even when Suhail and I were no longer on good terms. We both loved Suhail. She recognized that my love of her son was profound; therefore, she loved me beyond my relationship with him.

In the end, our relationship was exposed. Our secret became public knowledge and it became more difficult to meet him. From that time forward, my visits to Um Hameed's house remained the only place from where I could go to Suhail's house.

Loving Suhail was my first real act of defiance. I chose an outsider. We belonged to different political ideologies. I followed the revolutionary communist line; Suhail chose the New Left ideology. In addition, I chose Suhail without my guardian's pre-approval. We were in a community where love was taboo; while it might exist, it could not be acknowledged. Ours was a love that was savoured together only briefly. Nevertheless, it was a love that endured through distance, time and the many lives we both lived.

Suhail and I agreed that if stories were songs ours would be "*Aaz el Naas*" (The Dearly Loved People) by Abdel Haleem Hafez. Our names are engraved in its lyrics. Our love and desire for each other was boundless, but had no chance of survival. While Suhail dreamed of our future as lovers, as husband and wife, I lived in the reality of eternal parting. Twice we bonded and twice we parted. During the brief time that we shared, what Suhail and I never realised or understood was that our love and friendship transcended both of us. The love and friendship remained despite our mutual decision to separate and to pursue independent lives.

As a young woman, I knew that there were boundaries and that men dictated them. To my uncles, I was a woman incapable of knowing my own mind and of knowing what was good or what was bad for me. Of course, the men of my family knew these things with perfect certainty. Thus, they rejected Suhail, as he was not good for me.

I was trapped between wanting to be in love with Suhail and wanting to be in politics. I was threatened with exposure and coerced into breaking with him. In the most exquisite of ironies, my uncle, Najeeb, who was leading us toward change and freedom, leading us to where women have a voice and a choice, gave me no choice. He was the uncle who had introduced me to politics. He was one of the leaders of the party into which I was indoctrinated. It was he who introduced me to Marxist political ideology.

Vividly, I remember that fateful day as the entire family gathered for lunch. Uncle Najeeb first hinted that he knew about my relationship with Suhail. I recognised the coded language as he conversed with my uncle Jaleel. They both hinted at the possibility of exposing my love relationship to the family, to my paternal grandparents and to my mother.

I was certain that everyone noticed my anxiety. My beating heart pounded my chest. I lost my appetite. My words, my voice were trapped somewhere between my heart and my vocal cords. I can still taste the anxiety that preceded fear; I can still taste betrayal and coercion. I had never before experienced such vulnerability. At age sixteen, I did not have the strength to confront my uncles. I did not have the power to fight for a future with Suhail. I did however continue to love him and to move into and out of his love confusing both of us.

Subsequently, I read Nawal el Saadawi's book, *Women and Sex* (Cairo, 1969). My world and my sixteen-year-old head reeled, as I read and re-read el Saadawi. Shrewdly, male political and cell leaders endorsed el Saadawi's books and thereby co-opted and undercut her message. We were to discuss everything we read with our male cell leaders. Although we were encouraged to express our opinions, men determined the "appropriate" analysis and the "correct" applications of what we read.

El Saadawi clarifies how women's sexuality is linked to the social, economic and political contexts in which she lives in the following passage: "The ignorance of woman's mental and psychological abilities is more critical and common than the ignorance of her sexuality. Socio-historical conditions cooperated to reduce woman's humanity to merely an object -a body".

El Saadawi redefines the concept of honour from that of an intact hymen – the definition of honour in our Arab cultural reality – to a definition that applies to both sexes. I wondered about my own hymen; how could protecting this unseen mucous membrane and keeping it intact secure my honour, my reputation? It was indeed a mystery.

El Saadawi explains that if personal honour is measured by chastity as a moral value then it should be applied to both sexes not only women. "*When a value is forced upon one of the sexes, or one of the social classes, the value ascertains its immorality. It is then no longer a value, but is a law by which the dominant group in the existing social structure dictates its own values in order to control the other groups.*" It would take me years to challenge the boundaries of the gender status quo.

El Saadawi observed that young girls in Arab society encounter many obstacles while maturing and exploring their sexuality. They are limited by the lack of accurate information and proper education with regard to their sexuality. Instead of being prepared for the onset of menstruation, many young girls are left in the dark, unprepared for the event. Such neglect is born of ignorance. I could relate my own experience to that described by el Saadawi.

Subsequently, I proceeded to read el Saadawi's analysis of the origin of women's inferior status as set forth in Engels' work *The Origin of the Family, Private Property and the State*. In her analysis, el Saadawi provides an understanding of the actual basis that underlies women's oppression. For me, it was a revelation to read:

> Woman encounters different forms of oppression and limitation imposed by laws, norms and rules. Because of such oppressive conditions, woman has learned how to repress her sexual needs along with social and political ambitions. What happens in the case of woman is that when she fears the others' power, she denies her real needs and

ambitions and replaces them with those of others. Woman struggles for her rights, but she is usually overpowered by man. Woman is then forced to escape into passivity, and her action transforms into reaction.

What was my frame of reference for internalising el Saadawi's arguments? I did so within a context that was dictated totally by men. I did not question or doubt the interest or the propriety of men to limit my sovereignty. At that time, I failed to recognise that no man or woman could empower me by giving me books or support. I had to fight for myself. I failed to recognise that I had to be my own master. I had to trust my intuition that I was capable of understanding what I read and my belief that I have the right to choose without others dictating to me. I had yet to honour my independent analytical and critical thinking ability.

On reflection, the self-serving caveats of my political leaders vis-à-vis sexuality and sexual freedom were fascinatingly contradictory. Subtly, we were enjoined to redirect our energy to higher political aspirations, rather than "wasting" time contemplating sexuality. On further reflection, my willingness to exchange the words of Allah for those of the male messengers of Arab Nationalism and Marxism is astonishing. Only much later, I realised that in our patriarchal society the words of men will always outweigh the words of women. Years later, I understood that the voices of women are but an echo of those of men.

Thus, my first course in sex education was el Saadawi's *Women and Sex*. For the first time, I read about and understood women's anatomy, sexuality and sexual organs. Finally, I understood the sensations I experienced when I read *One Thousand and One Nights*.

I proceeded then to learn about the different types of circumcision. In our community, the circumcision of the clitoris was common. I learned about the functions of the clitoris, the hymen, the uterus, the ovaries and female hormones. My education was not limited to the physical aspects alone; it included the social and psychological. I came to understand the meaning of virginity.

Of most importance to me were el Saadawi's revelations about scientific and medical facts versus traditionally conventional community beliefs and practices. I understood that el Saadawi was not promoting sexual liberation. She was promoting a constructive understanding of sexuality both physical and psychological. Her aim was to educate and to equip women with the scientific and rational knowledge necessary to challenge the boundaries of culturally imposed conventional beliefs and practices, thereby redefining the gender status quo. El Saadawi concluded:

> Besides being courageous, persistent and powerful, women need knowledge and awareness to strengthen their unity. Women should recognise that any attempt to change society should be directed toward social conditions, and dominant misleading knowledge in society. Women should realise that their success in liberating themselves depends on their actual participation in transforming the society to a socialist one which will grant equality regardless of colour, sex or social class. I believed in the possibility of transforming society.

I believed that one day I would participate in changing the status quo, perhaps in changing the world around me.

At age sixteen, I was naive in politics and inexperienced in male/female political dynamics. By then, I had studied Engels' *The Origin of Family, Private Property and the State*, the book referenced in el Saadawi's *Women and Sex*. However, I failed to make the connection between what I was learning and how our groups and discussions were constructed. Long afterwards, I came to understand that the Party's analysis directed us to a pre-conceived end with little or no consideration of the present circumstances. Then, I simply accepted the group dynamics without question. Thus, I developed blind spots, which grew bigger until 1982 when I began to question everything.

I had devoured el Saadawi's books, which served as my portal to Marxist literature and the communist philosophy. Later, el Saadawi's other books – *Woman is the Origin* (Cairo 1971) and *Men and Sex* (Cairo 1973) – became available. I continued reading her novels and short stories. The Party leaders permitted me to read her books (and indeed all books) with the implied understanding that they would be discussed. This was to ensure that I could be redirected if I did not grasp the Party's correct analysis.

In the group sessions, I would listen and observe. I was cautioned not to take too seriously el Saadawi's research hypothesis and arguments about female sexuality and sexual freedom; their intent was merely to raise awareness. I was to recognise the Party's correct position and redirect my sexual energy usefully to a higher political aspiration rather than spending too much time contemplating sexuality. I continued reading el Saadawi as I became fascinated with the women's liberation movement. At the end of the book, she introduced her idea of equality: to be equal regardless of gender, colour or class. The Quran reinforces the same concept; we are all equal before Allah.

El Saadawi had extended an invitation to the reader to think analytically and independently. She advised the reader to question even scientific research if it did not make rational sense. In her view, the questioning of authority must go beyond the narrow questioning of the bona fides of the ultimate decision maker to the questioning of all authorities that control and manipulate the mind.

I was challenged to question and to examine things differently. I began to comprehend equality in general terms and specifically in terms of gender equality, freedom and honour. Inevitably, this led me to endorse women's liberation as a political issue.

At the time, I did not take these ideas further. El Saadawi had an authentic voice that resonated within me. Through reading her books, I became interested in the Arab women's movement although at that time this was not a priority. For the present, I was totally focused on my induction into the Arab Socialist Action Party's Philosophy and Agenda League in order that eventually I would be deemed trustworthy and thereby eligible for membership.

Sometime in 1976 when I was sixteen, my father, constantly present in his absence, returned home to Saudi Arabia to live and work in Riyadh. We saw him only during his short family visits to the Eastern Province. In my life, my father was displaced, fitting neither in my past nor my present. I felt nothing for him and my indifference translated into aloofness toward him. Certainly, he had the virtue of being patient and composed. I maintained my unspoken decision to distance myself from him. Given that he had come and gone as he wished, I had no interest in rearranging my life to accommodate him. He was my father and that was that.

On one occasion, there was a reunion between the five of us: my father, my mother and we three daughters. We sat in the formal living room of my mother's home. My memory is fixated on the ruptured mood of that reunion. While the broken family had re-assembled, there was nothing to salvage and nothing to savour. On that occasion, my father was there only temporarily as he was based in Riyadh far away from our hometown and us.

During the summer of 1976, Saffiya graduated from high school. She left for the US to pursue higher education. Initially, my father arranged for her to live with his, by then, ex-wife Anna, and my step-brother, Nawfal, who was about five years old. Thus, my father sent Saffiya to live with the very woman who had lured our father away twelve years earlier. I was surprised by my mother's meek, submissive acceptance. Apparently, she accepted that he still had the right to decide what was best for us even though she was the one who brought us up after he abandoned the family.

Soon after Saffiya departed, my mother, Ayah and I were moved out of our home, the house that my father had built for his young family in 1959. We were never to return there. I left the house that sheltered my childhood and my adolescent dreams and fears. Within its walls, I lived out my love stories, wrote my love letters and read beautiful poetry and novels. Most importantly, in the confines of its walls, my womanhood was shaped.

Yet we did not look back or say farewell. We did not ask its permission to leave. We did not thank it for sheltering us and keeping us safe. We did not pay tribute to the only home we had ever owned and where we had experienced the best years of our lives.

By the time we moved out of our home to live with my paternal grandparents, the furniture and the usage of each room had drastically changed. Various family members had lived in it, some for short and some for longer periods of time. In the end, my mother returned to her first marital home, the one that she left at age fifteen. She returned to the same house where she began life as a young bride.

I did then and still today find comfort in closing my eyes to walk the corridor of our home. It lives yet in my memories and dreams. I loved the tiled floors. I mopped them and counted every tile, always admiring the dark olive green, grey and silvery colouring which gave our house extra warmth.

Like us, our home was abandoned. It was emptied of its soul that was composed of our voices, our steps, our songs and laughter. Gradually, it deteriorated. Later that year, I realised that my mother, Ayah and I had unwillingly consented to surrender our right to the only home we had ever known. In order for four of my uncles to complete their newly built houses, my paternal grandfather sold our home to cover the financial shortfall of their government loans. My "no" had no value among those men. Not only was our home sold, it was demolished and replaced by a new apartment block. Since then, at every opportunity when I am in Safwa, I make the pilgrimage to the site of our former home. I pay tribute to my childhood memories. I see my sisters, our cousins and friends playing tag and chase or hide and seek around the house.

I was soon distracted from the painful move as I became absorbed in reading Russian literature. Between the ages of sixteen and nineteen, I read Lenin, Marx and Engels and much else. I endeavoured to understand and reflect on what they wrote, the ideas they articulated and how they would become manifest within my life.

Soon, I was reading Karl Marx's *German Ideology*, *Communist Manifesto* and *Capital: Critique of Political Economy*; Fredrick Engels' *The Origin of Family: Private Property and the State*; and Lenin's *Utopian and Scientific Socialism* and *Between the Two Revolutions: Articles and Speeches of 1917*. I read Mao Zedong, Kim Il-sung, Pablo Neruda's poetry, Che Guevara, Ho Chi Minh, and many other books, magazines, and articles. I was eager to join the Party but I was not yet deemed ready.

I persevered in my study, grasping to understand and adapt the complex ideas expressed in my reading, as exemplified by the following:

> Morality, religion, metaphysics, all the rest of ideology and their corresponding forms of consciousness, thus no longer retain the semblance of independence. They have no history, no development; but men, developing their material production and their material intercourse, alter, along with this their real existence, their thinking and the products of their thinking. (Marx, *German Ideology* (1845)).

Although difficult, the study of Marx enabled me to put el Saadawi's books into a solid research framework. Nonetheless, Marx's books challenged the way I was taught to think and to analyse the world, its morality and religious ideologies. My understanding of faith had shifted from religion as a statement of truth to religion as an ideology that was created by social consciousness rather than by the divine. The shift took me to the crossroads of doubt. In retrospect, I am not sure today if I was mentally ready for that transformation. All I know is that I was hungry for something that made sense; something that made what I knew and observed in the world around me comprehensible.

> The ideas of the ruling class are in every epoch the ruling ideas, i.e. the class which is the ruling material force of society, is at the same time its ruling intellectual force. The class that has the means of material production at its disposal has control at the same time over the means of mental production, so that thereby, generally speaking, the ideas of those who lack the means of mental production are subject to it. The ruling ideas are nothing more than the ideal expression of the dominant material relationships, the dominant material relationships grasped as ideas. (Marx, *German Ideology* (1845)).

> The materialist conception of history starts from the proposition that the production of the means to support human life and, next to production, the exchange of things produced, is the basis of all social structure; that in every society that has appeared in history, the manner in which wealth is distributed and society divided into classes or orders is dependent upon what is produced, how it is produced, and how the products are exchanged. From this point of view, the final causes of all social changes and political revolutions are to be sought, not in men's brains, not in men's better insights into eternal truth and justice, but in changes in the modes of production and exchange. (Engels, *Socialism: Utopian and Scientific Socialism* (1880)).

> It is, therefore, from the history of nature and human society that the laws of dialectics are abstracted. For they are nothing but the most general laws of these two aspects of historical development, as well as of thought itself. And indeed they can be reduced in the main to three: The law of the transformation of quantity into quality and vice versa; 2. The law of the interpenetration of opposites; and 3. The law

of the negation of the negation. (Engels, *Dialectics of Nature* (1883)).

Marx and Engels' historical analysis of the division of power and the development of the ruling class made rational sense in terms of the evolution of humanity; also, to a certain extent it explained the roots of current world events. However, their analysis did not reflect the way I lived in this remote, anonymous and unrecognised small village. That study did offer me a vision of a revolutionary idea, of freeing Palestine and Arab worlds from the grasp of colonialism. I continued reading Marx and Engels and the many other Marxist and leftist revolutionary writers fully conscious that to be labelled or identified as a Marxist was to be labelled and identified as an agnostic.

> We develop new principles for the world out of the world's own principles. We do not say to the world: Cease your struggles, they are foolish; we will give you the true slogan of struggle. We merely show the world what it is really fighting for, and consciousness is something that it has to acquire, even if it does not want to. (Marx, *Letter from the Deutsch-Französische Jahrbücher to Ruge* (1843)).

I had to read everything more than once in order to grasp the meaning. I sought to find parallels and relevance in my own circumstances. It took me years to construct my own understanding of the Marx and Engels quotes above and much more. I was not clear about my own knowledge, consciousness and awareness. I did not have the slightest idea as to how the self is constructed and how we develop socially. At the time, I was only age sixteen. Only at age thirty did I become fully conscious of my own awareness. After I studied sociology and then the sociology of knowledge years later my world expanded. I was then able to reconstruct and further develop my own knowledge and awareness.

I was able in debating – like other people around me – to casually quote the master theoreticians including Lenin's *"Without revolutionary theory there can be no revolutionary movement"*; *"A lie told often enough becomes the truth"*; and *"Can a nation be free if it oppresses other nations? It cannot"*. Of course I facilely interjected the thoughts of Mao Zedong: *"If you want to know the theory and methods of revolution, you must take part in revolution. All genuine knowledge originates in direct experience"*; and *"There is in fact no such thing as art for art's sake, art that stands above classes, art that is detached from or independent of politics. Proletarian literature and art are part of the whole proletarian revolutionary cause"*.

The successful party applicant could quote Ho Chi Minh's *"We have a secret weapon ... it is called nationalism"*; *"It was patriotism, not communism, that inspired me"*; and *"Nothing is more precious than independence and liberty"*. Finally of course, we introduced Kim Il Sung: *"It is wrong to try to avoid the struggle against imperialism under the pretext that independence and revolution are important, but that peace is still more precious";* and *"The oppressed people can liberate themselves only through struggle. This is a simple and clear truth confirmed by history".*

My view of political events, my view of reality was filtered through these postulates and philosophical arguments. They were far removed from the reality of my life. They were contradictory to what I was learning at school. I wanted to be a revolutionary. I entertained images of me fully clad in my veil leading people in national demonstrations. I did not doubt the possibility of it happening one day. That image was *not* congruent with the reality of my life. Revolutions need to have the right components, the right historical formula in order for the masses to lead revolutionary change. At that tender age, I did not realise or understand that reality.

### Political rejection: Disillusionment

I believed I was ready for Party membership, as I was one of the most committed readers. I put my love on hold; actually I totally gave it up. For the sake of politics, I was willing to surrender love.

To my dismay, I was not successful. I was only eligible to join as a supporter, not as a full member, although I was willing to do all that was asked of me. I convinced myself that the young women and men who were selected must have met the criteria. Of course, the criteria or standards for membership selection were never explained to us. I remained a supporter until 1981.

To a certain extent, my new friendships were monitored and largely pre-approved and my existing friendships were altered.

There were houses and families that I was not to visit; there were others that I could visit but only for limited periods because those people were not aligned with the Party. Those not so aligned were judged unworthy of investment. There were friendships that were presumed insignificant and unworthy. And there were my numerous dear friends, including Suhail, whose allegiances were to entirely different political views and agenda or to none at all. I was persuaded, or coerced, to control certain relationships. While I loved my friends dearly, I nevertheless sought the Party's approval of my readiness and worthiness for membership.

At the time, I justified my conformist behaviour on the basis of a greater, noble cause. I never questioned what justified the cause. Therefore, I accepted and functioned within the newly imposed limitations on where to go and who to befriend. Family norms were replaced by Party norms. I behaved in accordance with the Party's disciplinary policy and began to resist and reject my mother's code. It seemed insignificant and irrational compared to that of the Party.

Nonetheless, and for the love of my best friends from whom I was banned, I broke boundaries and promises. I lied to the Party's cell leaders and members not only about the time I spent with my friends, but also about how much joy I had being in my friends' company. I did not foresee that these special ties to my friends had created and would always be a sore spot where the Party's leaders are concerned. It would be much later that I became conscious of how marginalised I was. Marginalised by my love of humanity!

My allegiance to women was pushed to the bottom of my priority list. I did not pay attention to the glaring contradiction in gender inequality, despite struggling to voice my opinion. I forgot el Saadawi's advice that in order for women to effectively change their status, they must first become an organised social group. Only with organised group power can women significantly alter laws and reconstruct their social institutions. Unfortunately, the likelihood of women organising and exerting power within that tribal patriarchy was and is still limited.

At that stage of my life, I only focused on government oppression and the larger society. I ignored the more immediate gender oppression, the one that is harder to detect and more difficult to revolt against even within a progressive liberal movement. I doubted my intuition. I doubted my ability to be critical at such a young age. It did not seem reasonable that with my limited exposure to the world I could be more knowledgeable than the Party leaders.

Within the Party, I was labelled as being "too serious" and unable to take a joke. Each time I protested sexist or other inappropriate behaviours, I was dismissed as not being able to recognise that a joke was intended. I struggled with "jokes" about waiting for men to finish their meetings; about acting as a cover for the political activities of men; about preparing meals and serving tea and coffee when meetings extended to the early hours of the morning; about being told that a man's explanation was needed in order to understand the point of a book or an article; and about woman's lack of understanding of her own self.

My commitment to the Party's philosophy, to liberating people and to liberating women deepened. And yet, my feminine voice failed me. I was so clear about my commitment to women; however, for the sake of advancing in politics, I had unconsciously traded off my voice. I started to dismiss and downplay my awareness and disapproval of the gender-based allocation of chores and tasks and the absence of women members from the leadership committee.

The dream of the Arab Socialist Action Party and therefore Arab Nationalism was advanced relentlessly and mechanically. For me, that dream, that ideal, bore the seeds of destruction within its original structure. It mirrored Marx and Engels' argument that the social evolution and the eradication of a historical social era or a regime carry within it the seeds of its own destruction. This was the case with the fatally flawed Arab Socialist Action Party, a party in which I was not selected for admission until I was twenty-one.

I rationalised that the period of indoctrination was not the time to question or challenge. Thus, I was largely silent. By then, I had lost the edge I had at age thirteen: the ability to speak my mind and to walk away. I was vulnerable as everything that I said was included in the assessment of my suitability as a potential member. Although I was not yet ready to stop challenging, I was influenced, subtly persuaded and psychologically coerced to follow the Party line.

During that probationary period, I wrestled with a disturbingly problematic issue. It made me question my sense of ethics as a freedom fighter and those of the whole political party. We were implicitly and explicitly given permission to take things that did not belong to us. It was okay to eat at a restaurant and take away the salt and pepper shakers, the ashtrays or can openers after a meal. The notion that it was our inherent right to repossess what the capitalists had unjustly acquired was accepted. These notions influenced the way we treated resources and energy at schools and in public spaces, as if that was the way to get even with the government. We would leave the classroom lights on as we left school for the day. We wasted resources and energy and behaved irresponsibly toward the future of the same country, resources and generations for which we claimed to fight. For me, the idea was problematic that so-called capitalist-owned properties were justifiably ours because those capitalists had exploited the working class and national resources in order to make its wealth.

There was an absence of moral guidance in the development of a responsible personal and nationalistic identity. There was no effort to create a clear vision of how to develop future generations capable of bringing about change. Eventually, I learned that injustice cannot be cured by injustice; and that the notion of what has been taken by power can only be reclaimed by power does not give permission to steal and/or waste resources. I had also learned that in order for us, the new generation to be truly revolutionary, we must understand such progressive messages within their context. This confusing period was soon clarified through my growing awareness of former misunderstandings and misinterpretations.

Although young and inexperienced recruits, we soon realised that the notion of what has been taken by power can only be reclaimed by power is quite different from "stealing". Such an impotent rationale is not compatible with the teaching or the vision of revolutionary philosophy. There is a vast difference between stealing and reclaiming what are rightful, legitimate national resources. Soon, such behaviours were rejected as we realised that in order to be effective, respected revolutionaries we needed to model exemplary ethics and the behaviours and attitudes of the way forward.

I moved beyond this period of disconcerting dissonance. My commitment grew to extend beyond reading and acting as a cover-up for political meetings. I joined in weekly cell meetings to discuss books, articles and internal and foreign current affairs and events. I distributed the Party's leaflets and newsletters. After dinner, another supporter joined me for the task around the neighbourhood. It was not the norm for a young woman of my age to go out after hours, so I concocted stories and excuses, e.g., I was reclaiming a schoolbook or a notebook from a friend who borrowed it.

These concoctions unnerved me. My heart throbbed in a similar way to that I experienced when I had lied in order to meet Suhail. I feared being exposed, scolded and grounded. In my heart I knew that my mother did not believe these lame excuses. Perhaps she accepted that she could not fight it and hoped that I would be out of harm's way. I started reading the literature of other Arab political parties aligned with the Arab Socialist Action Party.

My father's short family visits to the Eastern Province were intrusions into the rhythm of our lives. To our surprise, in the summer of 1977, he proposed that Ayah and I join him on a holiday to England. We were sceptical, although equally delighted. It was the first time for Ayah and me to travel with our father. I was anxious that Ayah would hint about my political commitment and activities in front of him. Although he is my father, he remained a stranger, an outsider. I viewed my father's work and life in Saudi Arabia as temporary. In my mind, he would eventually return to the US and I would remain a stranger in his life, a transient event.

On that trip, he tried his best to expose us to a new cultural experience. He entertained us at the best and finest restaurants in London. My thoughts were that only bourgeoisie could afford such restaurants. I defined myself as proletariat and had pledged allegiance to the Arab Socialist Action Party. I did not give my father any credit. It did not matter that he was then, and has remained, an Arab Nationalist. It did not matter that he was once one of the pioneers of his generation to promote further education for women among Safwa's educated and open-minded families. I had not realised yet that I had been wearing blinkers. I was as much of a bourgeoisie as he was.

Behaving on the side of caution around our father, Ayah and I enjoyed London and its surroundings. We plotted whenever we could to avoid spending time and engaging with him. We smoked. He disapproved. We loved eating ice cream and burgers. He disapproved.

We giggled and laughed while eating at prestigious restaurants. He disapproved.

My father was patient and tried hard to make us enjoy the experience, to give us an opportunity to explore museums, historical areas and galleries. After his lengthy absence from our lives, it was a strange experience to be with him. His lifestyle was not for us and it seemed totally alien to our ways. His table etiquette was foreign to us; such affectations were for the bourgeoisie.

With our limited command of English, Ayah and I managed to avoid going out with him or to literally lose him while touring the Tower Bridge, London Bridge, the Tower of London and the London Dungeon. Relentlessly, my father planned for us to visit Madam Tussauds, Buckingham Palace, Piccadilly Circus, and Big Ben. He went a step further and introduced us to Shakespeare's literature and theatre. Ayah and I returned to Saudi Arabia unrepentant.

Subsequently, my father announced his intention to send Ayah and me to England the following summer. His reason was not obvious to us. We were to go to Oxford for an intensive course at the Swan School of English.

We did not mind the opportunity, as our gorgeous friend Heba would join us. Living in Oxford with a British family proved to be very different to life in London as tourists. Among the three of us we managed the challenge of communicating in English.

Ayah, Heba and I had a series of cultural shocks. As I look back, I am certain that the host family had no idea or conception of where the students came from. Despite the intensive English course, language proved to be a great barrier.

Staying with the first British family, a mother and her two children, was a struggle. All the bus stops looked the same and we failed to figure out the system or even to notice that there were bus stop names. We managed to get to school in the morning; however, we never made it to the 6 pm dinner time as we would get off at the wrong bus stop and have to walk a long distance. We loathed British cuisine but the landlady had a lock on the refrigerator, and there was no way to get any food other than apples if we missed dinner.

Soon, we complained to our fathers and to the school requesting new rooms. Shortly thereafter, we moved to live with an elderly woman. She had an adequate ground floor apartment with a semi-adequate kitchenette. This proved a good solution for us as it gave us greater freedom to get lost in between bus stops. Ayah and I continued to argue about the bus stops and the correct one to reach our rooms. The three of us continued our adventures, taking a coach from Oxford to London and the train to Swansea in Wales.

Back home, I resumed my political activities. As a potential candidate, it was my responsibility to meet and look after the new recruits for the support group. I coordinated and led the weekly cell meetings. We addressed each other as "comrade" to allude to the context in which this special bond was being created. I was now the one who linked people and books, the cell librarian. I distributed books and kept records of who was reading which book. I conducted the discussion groups and assigned the topics under the supervision of male leaders.

Otherwise, life continued as before. I continued visiting Fatema and spending time at her house. As she went to *elaziyah* every afternoon, I would go to her house after lunch and take my afternoon nap there whenever I could. Fatema seemed frail.

My maternal great grandmother Um Ali had died. I missed having my great grandmother around as she had almost always been there even when all other family members were out. A root of my female lineage had been severed. Part of my history had disappeared. Forever, I would remember Um Ali as she pinched me to get my attention. Sometimes when she was narrating a story she would pinch me so hard, I would have to suppress a scream.

Following her death, my maternal great grandfather Abu Ali died. The winter afternoon narrative and storytelling ended. His voice was now an echo, a distant memory. I was in the 10th grade. He died in the middle of my mid-term exams. As there were no high schools for girls in Safwa, I had transferred to Qatif. I grieved deeply for both of them. I felt confusion on walking into their old room at Um Hameed's house. I remember his voice as he called us to enter his room, as he summoned us to gather around his fire and listen to his stories.

Ayah and I gradually made the transition into our paternal grandparents' family lifestyle. It was becoming more open and relaxed with the influence of freshly graduated young men returning home from the US and France. My activities and interests had changed to accommodate a lifestyle that was out of the context in which I was brought up. I loved Fatema, Um Hameed and I continued to go to her house where I found my refuge.

Despite moving into and out of Suhail's love, I continued to visit his mother Batool. I was confident that she knew that breaking up with Suhail was just as hard on me. I hoped that she understood my circumstances. There was so much that I dreamed of and so much that I wanted to be. There was so much that I did not understand. My intuition was not yet sharp. I was not as mature as I imagined. I was so focused on politics that I simply failed to notice connections and correlations. I continued to read many sophisticated books, yet I remained a novice dependent thinker and continued to pull away from Suhail.

## A fork in the road

When I graduated from high school in 1979, I confronted a fork in the road of life. At that point, I could only meet the Party's criteria for a supporter's role. My uncle Najeeb suggested that I remain home in Saudi Arabia and continue my education. In flattering terms, he endeavoured to persuade me to comply with his wishes. He indicated that I was the lone woman in our household with any interest in politics. I was the last one with a commitment to political activism and with experience in leading support cells. He assured me that it was in the Party's best interest. I was being told to be selfless and to sacrifice my dream of pursuing my education in the US in service of my political beliefs and commitment. He argued that the Party's leadership committee would appreciate my sacrifice. He did not say how I was to be rewarded. I was not to seek a return on this sacrifice, a quid pro quo.

From some mysterious reservoir, I found the strength to say "no". I discovered and exercised my voice. By then, I had completely surrendered my love of Suhail for politics. I had broken up with him to remain with the Arab Socialist Action Party using Suhail's allegiance to another political party as an excuse. I struggled in leaving Suhail; in abandoning my love for him, I was determined not to be in love with him. My heart still throbbed when his name was mentioned and on each occasion that I visited his mother, Batool. I was determined and had convinced myself that this could not be love. I believed that eventually we would outgrow it.

With growing impatience, I had waited through the last two high school years to graduate and to leave Saudi Arabia for the US. I wanted to join the political activist camps organised by the Arab student organisations and other political parties in the US. I wanted to meet all of those interesting Palestinian, Bahraini, Omani, Saudi and other non-Arab student activists referenced by my relatives and friends. I wanted to be part of a different, more liberated world. I wanted to experience a world in which I did not have to fear reading books or carrying a political magazine. I wanted to be a political activist. I wanted to attend lectures, to demonstrate, to write letters to Amnesty International and Human Rights Watch. I wanted to attend functions at the student unions. I wanted to learn the beautiful songs in honour of men and women who died in prisons and under torture fighting for human rights. I wanted to sing for Dhufar in Oman, for Palestine, for Bahrain and for the forgotten political activists in Saudi Arabia. Clearly, my dreams were expansive and idealistic.

Quivering and with great effort, I heard my voice uttering, "*No*, I will not stay behind in Saudi Arabia. I am going to the US." My uncle Najeeb asked if I realised the consequence of saying no. I hesitated briefly before responding. I understood that if I defied the request and went to the US, I would not get any support. I would not be introduced and recommended to any of the political groups. I would go but I would be isolated from the political experiences that I was seeking. Again, I said "no".

That summer at my paternal grandparents' house I had a nightmare of a lion walking into their home. Voiceless and trembling, I stood up and faced the lion. I stared straight into the lion's eyes. The lion left.

Until that time, I had never questioned the liberal, sometimes radical, democratic values and behaviour of the Party's members. I trusted that the Party's leadership was truly democratic and just and that they would not sever all political communication and involvement with me. I trusted their fairness; as I was not yet a member I

## Political Awakening

believed that I was not bound by an official commitment to serve and abide by the Party's rules and requirements.

When I said "no" to the Party's request that I remain in Saudi Arabia, I was under the assumption that my father had already planned and arranged for my US schooling. As he had thoroughly planned the US schooling for Saffiya, I took it for granted that he had done the same for me. When I finally enquired about the arrangements, I caught my father off guard. I learned that there were no arrangements. As I had burned my Saudi bridges with the Party, I proceeded with my plans to go to the US.

I left Saudi Arabia at the end of August 1979 aboard a Pan American airline flight to New York with a connection to San Francisco. Approaching the US, I had to complete an Alien Registration Card. I believe that in that instance not understanding the language was an advantage. I did not question the choice of words; I simply filled in the cards as instructed.

I was eager to get to San Francisco, as Saffiya was getting married on the first of September and a wedding reception had been arranged. As Ayah had left ahead of me for a summer holiday, she was already in California.

My memory of the reception is vague. During my brief visit with the family, I apprehensively waited for someone to comment on my defiance, or perhaps to reassure me that I would not be isolated. Naively, I believed that those who knew me would support me; they would lend me books and introduce me to other activists. I was wrong on both counts.

Immediately after the reception, I left for Houston to live with my father for the first time in my life. I was nineteen years old. My father was almost as complete a stranger to me as I was to him. In every sense, we were strangers; our contextual experiences were different, except for those few brief encounters in earlier years. We had different beliefs, perspectives and convictions.

I was the recipient of multiple shocks. In addition to "father shock", I was to experience the shocks associated with language and culture. At the time, I was only aware of the father–daughter shock.

Up until that time, my emotional ties to my father were based largely on my mother's portrayal of him to me and my sisters. Theoretically, I knew my father must love me, but I did not know how that love should manifest itself. His warm hugs felt just like the social hugs that one receives here and there. I tried my best to behave towards and around him, in accordance with societal expectations of a daughter. However, were those Saudi or US societal expectations? Were paternal similar to maternal expectations? I did not know. Between us, there was an abundant emptiness. He knew nothing about my history. He could not relate to my childhood and I could not relate to his life.

I was nineteen years old. I was a good reader and I knew a few things about politics. I had my own views. I was opinionated. Isolated, I had no access to political activists, to political magazines, newspapers or even newsletters. Thus, opportunities for debate and learning were limited.

The earlier Oxford intensive English course did not make this transition easier. I struggled to speak in English. Shortly after arrival in Houston, I started an intensive language course at ELS, a private institute. In that course we were all foreigners, all second-language students of English.

I was also a foreigner in my father's home. In it, I felt like an alien. It seemed that he simply resumed his role as a father, as if we were resuming life from where we left it years earlier. He abandoned our family when I was age four. For me, our few encounters of the previous fifteen years did not compensate for the lost time. I struggled. I hoped that he struggled also; however, he simply resumed his role as a father.

I was not accustomed to having my father so close and so involved in my life. I did not know what topics were appropriate or inappropriate for discussion. Beyond my political views/commitment, I did not know what to share and what to hold back. While I could speak with my mother about most of my affairs, I struggled with how to talk to him about my monthly period, the pain I experienced and the medication I required. I never told my father about Suhail, as I would not discuss with him the reasons for terminating the relationship.

Although my father was kind to me, that solicitude did not include intervention when I was trying to explain my needs in English to others. Rather, he watched me struggle. Often, I stammered as I ordered food. He observed and listened while I struggled to obtain information and to make reservations. Only when I finished, he would point out my mistakes and correct me. I would cry before I dialled a number and I would cry after I finished talking. It was endlessly frustrating. I wondered why he bothered to correct me. Much later, I realised that my father was doing me a favour, the best he could. He still corrects my English!

Culturally, I struggled in Houston. I felt the Texans looked down on me as if I did not belong to the human race. At the time, I had no awareness of racial discrimination. I failed to make the connection between my appearance and the way people reacted to me. For most people, I was hard to place in terms of race and identity. Some thought I might be Peruvian, Mexican or Indian. I felt unwelcome in Houston.

As I became more comfortable with English, I gathered my courage to greet my neighbours with "Good morning". I received only dismissive glances as if they were asking, "Why are you talking to us?" I didn't know anything about culture shock and those glances would drive me to tears. I was terribly homesick; I was missing Maryam and Ayah.

Daily, I cried on the bus, on the way home, on the way to school and on the way to work. I could not express myself. I could not express my feelings and my ideas. Once as I cried, an American woman approached me to ask if I was a foreigner. Crying harder, I replied "Yes," and "I hate this place." She responded, "You should not feel bad. We are all foreigners in Texas." Human kindness!

I continued to be cautious around my father, especially about politics. I sought a way to get away from him and from my new home. I considered the possibility of a part-time job. He thought it was a good idea, as this would force me to practise my English. I wanted to spend less time at home.

My first-ever paid job was at McDonald's. I was disappointed to learn that I could not join a union, protest or go on strike; thus, my proletarian dream was aborted. For the first time, my friendships expanded to include non-Arabs. I befriended an African-American boy and an American Jewish girl. This was my first experience with these cultures. They were both three years younger than I was. Through them, I peered into the larger US cultural construct.

At the language school, two of the male Saudi students threatened me verbally in front of the entire class. They said they would report me to the Saudi educational attaché because I was working at McDonald's. They argued that it was a disgrace to all Saudis that a Saudi female was working. I was appalled at the idea that work was viewed as dishonourable. I argued that work was honourable even if it was flipping burgers, sweeping floors and taking out the garbage. I fought back and told them to report me if that is what they felt was the right thing to do.

The reality was that I did not care whether they reported me or not. I was not afraid of them or of being reported to the Saudi educational attaché. I knew he had no power over my choice to work or not even if I were on a scholarship, which I was not. Beyond my father, it was nobody's business but mine. Thus, my first public heated argument, the first assertion of my independence and my right to work, occurred in front of teachers and students and was in a language with which I struggled.

A few of the teachers became concerned and felt that I needed their protection. They feared that the Saudi males would harm me. That day after school, one of my teachers waited for me in his car outside the school. He offered me a ride. Initially, I was reluctant. He drove me to my home and assured me that the school and the teachers were all on my side and they would not allow anyone including the educational attaché to harm me.

I was taken by surprise. I was not prepared for such an act of kindness. It was another touching culture shock, a humane gesture of assurance that my teachers and the school were willing to stand up for my rights.

Absolutely nothing happened. The Saudi students did not follow through with their threats. It was my first such public experience. Through it, I learned that some Saudi men are not prepared to confront a Saudi woman with a voice, a woman who would reply to their challenge. These young Saudi men did not expect that I would stand up for myself. The school issued them a warning note that they were not to approach me. They kept their distance. I kept my job.

## Empty politics

Only near the end of my stay in Houston did I finally meet a few politically connected Arab and non-Arab students. Through them I learned about political activities in Houston and in Austin, the capital of Texas. At last, I reconnected to politics. I befriended some Bahraini students and started learning about their activities. I decided not to tell my father, although I knew he was not naive.

My maiden political US activity was to go to Austin under the pretence of visiting friends of friends for the weekend. In Austin, I took part in a student-led protest. I stayed with people who were complete strangers to me, people whom I had not met before and would not meet again. They were kind and generous. As we were strangers, all we had in common was politics. I listened to their stories, to their experiences and the struggles in Bahrain, in Oman, in Kuwait and in many other places. I learned to sort out the relations and connections among them. As I listened, I heard a language so familiar and yet so alien. It was I who was out of context, outside of their reality.

The camaraderie and the kindness were graciously on offer, but it all seemed remote, strange and inaccessible. That day in Austin, many students ended up sleeping on campus as part of the demonstration. There were American, Arab, Persian and many other nationalities. I still remember putting on a brave face and choosing to remain with those who stayed in the cold and hung in there until the next morning.

During this visit in the company of those brilliant Bahraini students, I learned about the Arab Student Organisation camp. I decided that I would attend; I would not allow anything or anyone to stop me. I would have to figure out how to negotiate this with my father later. When I told my father that I was going, he disapproved. I proceeded with the arrangements for the camp, which was to be held near Dallas/Ft. Worth, Texas.

The camp was a beehive of activity. It was set in what appeared to be an old portable conference centre. It was a mini-Arab World with all its conflicting politics and alliances. In fact, diversity was apparent only among the camp organising committee members. Even with my inexperienced eyes I could see that students of each Arab nation clustered together. If they mixed at all, they did so around aligned political views and agenda.

On arrival, all campers could choose a pen name to conceal their true identity. However, most were referred to by their real names; only a few used pen names. This was an interesting level of discipline designed to protect the true identity of the participants.

The camp arrangement seemed peculiar to me. I thought that I would be at ease and less anxious in such anonymous surroundings. In fact, it seemed that I was invisible to everyone around me. To the vast majority, I was just an inexperienced kid, known to no one and barely noticeable. I didn't participate much except to help with arranging and clearing chairs. I enjoyed the adventure, although I felt that my learning was limited.

I returned home with my subscription to *Al Hadaf* magazine, a handful of opposition newsletters and a few cassettes with nationalistic and revolutionary songs. Some of the faces and names lingered in my memory briefly before fading like everything in life. Only a handful made an indelible impression that lingered longer term. That was my first US encounter with the experience I had so eagerly anticipated. I moved on.

As the 1970s ended, major political events erupted around the world. Viewed from Texas, they all seemed remote, unrelated to my reality. As the Islamic Revolution led by Imam Khomeini from his exile in France was approaching its one-year anniversary, militant Iranian students seized the American Embassy in Tehran on 4 November 1979 taking more than 90 people hostage. They demanded that the Shah, Mohammad Reza Pahlavi, who was undergoing medical treatment in the US, stand trial in Iran.

Fifteen days later in Saudi Arabia (20 November 1979) just after dawn prayers, Juhayman al Otaibi led hundreds of militants to seize control of Islam's holiest site, the Grand Mosque in Mecca. That unprecedented act was on the first day of the Hijira calendar – the Islamic New Year – the first day of Muharram. The rebels threatened to dethrone Saudi Arabia's monarchy. It was put down following fierce fighting between the Saudi Army aided by Pakistani and French Special Forces in which 117 Juhayman supporters and a similar number of troops died. Within a month, Juhayman was captured and publicly beheaded, along with 62 captured fighters.

Simultaneously, a political event of less importance to the international media occurred in Qatif, Sayhat, Awamiyah and Safwa in Saudi Arabia. During the peaceful processions during *Ashura*–the annual mourning of the martyrdom of Imam Hussein – the National Guard brutally confronted the congregation. The confrontation resulted in scores of people dead and wounded. The Shia community – a small minority within Saudi Arabia – revolted against the atrocity of the National Guard and the processions of coffins turned to violent demonstrations. This resulted in many more deaths, injuries and mass arrests that included all political groups. The Shia community in the Eastern Province came under siege.

One of the outcomes was that Qatif witnessed the demolition of its historical fort. To the government, it symbolised the spirit of the Shia community's resistance to the atrocity. Other area historical buildings met the same fate. Even though I was thousands of miles away, I felt intimately connected. The changes these incidents provoked were still evident many years later.

In early 1980, *Death of a Princess*, a British drama by Anthony Thomas that documented the public beheading of a Saudi princess, was broadcast on public television in the US and Great Britain. It was considered highly controversial. The Saudi authorities banned all work of any of the actors or artists who participated in the making of this documentary. The Saudi government/royal family held the British government responsible for the airing of the documentary. King Khalid cancelled a state trip to London and expelled the British ambassador.

On the British front, the Thatcher government condemned the documentary. Lord Carrington, the foreign secretary, apologised to the Saudi government. In the US the documentary was condemned during private Senate debates. I watched the documentary free of censorship. To me, it was fascinating to observe how two of the world's leading, self-proclaimed democracies bowed and apologised to the Saudi government for a documentary film. I needed to understand what the apologies and condemnation implied. I questioned, "If the British and the US governments condemn a documentary film, a producer's viewpoint, to what extent will those governments go to maintain their interests?"

Clearly, I was politically naive. I did not have the analytical skills to understand how the Iranian revolution and the seizing of the US embassy, along with the seizing of the Grand Mosque in Mecca, would impact on future regional political developments beyond the local context in which they occurred. I opposed the Shah's regime. The Islamic revolution in Iran was a victory against that regime and in many ways against dictatorship. I knew that I was against coercion in any form. Nevertheless, I had my own reservations about the Islamic revolution's ideology, especially on learning of the mass arrests of socialists, communists, leftists and even Muslim activists. Also, I was disturbed about the mandatory veiling of women. The Islamic revolution compelled me to reconsider ideologies in general. I realised that their biases in favour of the received, i.e., preferred, ideology dictated the absence and the lack of accommodation to different perspectives.

As for Juhayman al Otaibi's revolt against the Saudi regime, I was not prepared for the violent government reaction. Its extreme reaction to Juhayman when he took refuge in Mecca was shocking. The Muslim world stood silent while Mecca, Islam's holiest ground, was assaulted. The Quran, our holy book, testified to Mecca as a place of peace, a ground honoured by Allah, a refuge where no weapons are held or raised and a place where people enter and leave peacefully. Armed, Juhayman sought refuge in this holiest place. The authorities retaliated and the holy ground became a battleground. Little was reported in the international media about this event. At the time, people dismissed the future political implications of it.

## A new chapter – New York, New York

On my father's relocation to work in Manhattan, I struggled less. Quickly, I settled into life with him in White Plains, commuting to Manhattan to attend Hunter College where I enrolled in pre-university intensive English courses.

In Manhattan, I felt alive again. I was no longer in shock or depressed. Every weekday, I commuted fifty minutes each way, disembarking at Grand Central Station. I strolled through the station inhaling all aromas on offer, especially the coffees and pastries.

Each day as I stepped off the platform to climb the stairs to the main concourse, I worried irrationally about fainting and wondered what would happen if I did. It appeared that people would simply step over me and I would die. All passing through Grand Central Station seemed unaware of their surroundings and hardly noticed what they stepped on. Everyone seemed to be in a rush, coming from somewhere or going elsewhere. As I stepped out of Grand Central to walk to Hunter College on 25th Street and 1st Avenue, I breathed again, inhaling the spirit of Manhattan.

At least twice a week, I walked to the United Nations building and sat on the terrace to people watch. My favourite place was the New York Public Library for Humanities and Social Science on 5th Avenue at 42nd Street. I went there almost every day before boarding the train home. I would buy a pretzel and sit on the library steps to read a book, eat and to feed the pigeons. In Manhattan, I cultivated my first passionate indulgence: cheesecake. There was nothing as good as an authentic New York cheesecake. It not only nourished the body but also the soul.

In Manhattan, my political reading was limited to *Al Hadaf* and a few newsletters that I continued to receive. My father and I could have boarded the same train and spent time becoming better acquainted. However, still in my rebellious stage, I would delay my journey to the train station and lag behind him in order that I could travel in the smoking coach. My ability to speak English was improving, but I was not yet fluent. I still had to recite what I wanted to say in my head before I had the confidence and the courage to speak.

At home in White Plains, I started to have conversations with my father on a different, more mature level. Happier that I spoke better English, he conversed with me in Arabic. Our relationship evolved into new but still unfamiliar territory. I remained conscious of what was not between us.

At the beginning of spring 1980, something changed. As we walked in Manhattan, my father put his arm around me and brought me closer to him, expressing interest in my beliefs. In my head, sirens went off and red lights flashed! He asked me about my beliefs in Arab Nationalism and, more importantly, he listened to my responses. Cautiously, I heard myself telling him about my sense of identity and how being an Arab influenced and defined my identity. I told him that I admired Jamal Abdel Nasser despite my awareness of Nasser's political challenges and mistakes. I shared with him my hopes for a better, more just social system in the Arab world. I was twenty years old. This was the first time that I experienced closeness to my father. He was impressed that my beliefs were more grounded than he had expected or thought. I do not think he suspected that I was politically involved, as I had been cut off while in the US. I was careful not to tell him about my political activities and not to mention Suhail.

I completed my English courses and was preparing to file my university applications. In the end, I did not apply to a single university. Rather, I made up my mind to return to Saudi Arabia. I knew only that I wanted to go home, to my mother Maryam and to politics. Between March and June of 1980, my relationship with my father began to change and a bond developed between us. Still, I did not tell him about my decision to leave the US.

Knowing I had made my decision, I paid Manhattan a heartfelt farewell. In the last few Manhattan weeks, I visited all of my favourite places; I ate all of my favourite foods; I went to all of my favourite shops.

As I prepared to depart, I knew with clarity that I was not going to study computer science on return to Saudi Arabia. This was a possible field of study that my father endorsed if I had stayed in the US. I did not know what I was going to do.

When I told my father that I was leaving the US, I am not sure if I expected or at least hoped that he would persuade me to stay. Perhaps I imagined that he might even force me to stay and finish my education; he did not. Why did he not try to stop me? I never asked. As I returned home to Saudi Arabia, my sister Ayah was preparing to leave for New York to live with our father. There she would attend Hunter College for her pre-university intensive English course.

# 4

# Saudi Arabia Options

I did not explore the possibilities for me if I stayed in the US. Similarly, I did not care to know what was there for me in Saudi Arabia; I simply wanted to return.

In July 1980, I returned to Safwa and began to examine my options. Working for Aramco was the only option I seriously considered as it was offering US scholarships to female Saudi high school graduates. My plan was to work for one year, obtain an Aramco scholarship and return to the US for my Bachelor's degree.

Immediately, I sought Suhail again. Still confused, I was in love and still determined not to be in love. We cautiously reconnected. Politics and my aspirations and dreams of a different life pushed us apart again. I had mixed feelings. I wanted him, yet I kept a distance. I desired him, but I fought my desire for him. I was not ready for a commitment. Suhail was never ready to approach, he was always happy to receive.

I returned home still searching for political grounding. I still did not meet the criteria to qualify for full Party membership and remained on the sidelines. I believed that revolutions are the only possible option for changing the status quo, for changing the world. Naively, I believed I could change the world. I had returned believing that I understood better that which I read. I believed change was possible, that my expansive dreams of freedom, democracy and justice could be realised.

I returned to an unanticipated shift in the mindset of Saudi Arabia's Eastern Province Shia community. Young men and women debated the Islamic revolution in Iran. There was an increase in the number of women wearing hijab. Increasingly, people gravitated toward Shia religious leaders and politics. Affiliation had shifted from Iraq's Najaf to Iran's Qum as a new generation of Shia scholars from Iran became more popular. The names and ways of understanding of the new Shia school of thought were being introduced, thus dividing families and friends.

Nationalism was being replaced by Shia political allegiances. Nationalistic songs were replaced by Islamic religious chants. The Shia community around the world received a boost in morale. I did not know much about the Islamic revolution, so I did not engage in the debates around me. Beyond the Shia community, religious sentiments were on the increase as well.

I returned home to witness the first rift within the Arab Socialist Action Party, a rift that would have an impact on my own extended family relationships. Uncle Najeeb and his first, second and third cousins stood in opposition to one another. The dynamics of "comrade" relationships turned into a war of accusation, boycott and alienation. The *Ashura* uprising had resulted in mass political arrests that affected activists across the board. A leading member of the Party became fundamentally religious during his imprisonment. In the first test of its democratic bona fides, the Party failed in living up to its stated belief in the basic human right to freedom of expression and choice. It employed methods of coercion. The rift widened. At the time, I failed to recognise the violation.

In retrospect, I believe that I failed my own re-entry examination on two accounts: the first was my failure to understand the drastic change that led to the rift and how a communist could become religious during such a short period of time; the second was my inability to accept the Party's rejection of people's freedom and right to change.

I questioned, what is it in political prison that changes a person's political allegiances? What happens under physical and psychological torture that suddenly awakens a person's awareness of a religion he had abandoned in favour of liberal ideas? I made a promise to myself that I would not change under pressure and that I would only change out of true conviction and with full awareness of my beliefs.

In view of the stunning religious conversion of the Party leader, I reviewed my oath. I thought that Allah would prefer that I seek the divine when strong, not when weak and broken. The voice in the back of my head whispered, "You do not know. No one can know how they will react until they are in the same situation." I fervently hoped that I would not be in that situation.

The rift in politics resulted into rift within our extended family which brought conflicts without obvious solutions. Our rationale, our political commitment and our assumed consciousness failed in the confrontation with our veiled minds. Those who turned away from Party ideology to religion were proselytised by Party leaders and members to return to the fold; the behaviour copied that employed by religious and patriarchal leaders to enforce their well-defined borders. The Party turned to the same tools it shunned previously: coercion and the restriction of personal freedoms. Willingly or unwillingly, we all failed to accommodate differences. We failed in respecting and recognising the right of others to be free to believe. Accusations were the weapon, the most effective weapon behind which to defend the borders.

Passively, I watched the conflict and the behaviours that contradicted the essence of liberation. I did not question my political beliefs. Like many others, I was on the defence. I wore very thick, opaque political blinkers. Homes of relatives which had once been open and accommodating became out of bounds for some family members. I shifted and adjusted as the conflict continued. I was one of the lucky ones who had access to all sides, to all homes. Nevertheless, it was a difficult journey to navigate.

In September 1980, I joined Aramco after passing my English assessment requirements. I signed up for a typing course to prepare me for work as a data processing administrator in the Public Administration Department. It was my first experience in feeding information into a computer. I was soon bored numb. It was not for me. I needed a job in which I worked with people, not with machines.

Soon, I asked to be transferred to the Aramco Health Service Centre. There I was to rotate between work at one of the many clinical reception areas and one of the wards. I was assigned where there were shortages or needs.

Subsequently, the head of the nursing department called me for my next assignment. I was to work at the appointment desk of the psychiatric clinic for six weeks, as they needed someone to help the secretary. The clinic director, Dr Khairi, wanted to interview me first.

The head of nursing escorted me to the hospital basement to meet him. Walking the long corridor, I wondered why the psychiatric clinic was in the basement. Was it for protection, confidentiality or shame? The psychiatric clinic was opposite the inpatient hospital pharmacy. The head nurse went in to see Dr Khairi first, and then I was called in for the interview.

There I met a tall, elegant, well-tanned man in a white summer suit. I felt short, so small before him that I missed his welcome. I got the assignment and with it a precious gift, a friendship that would last for the next twenty-six years until Dr Khairi died.

Dr Khairi taught me how to practise my beliefs in human rights through simple things such as respect and acknowledgment of every person, irrespective of her or his status. Aramco uses a rigid hierarchal structure that divides employees into senior and non-senior staff. This was not the case at the psychiatric clinic where every patient was important. There were no superiors or subordinates, no well-known people and ordinary people. They were all clients and they all deserved respect, fairness and quality service. No patient was dismissed unheard and all "walk in" clients were interviewed by or at least spoken to by a psychiatrist.

In that clinic, I learned that implementing human rights beliefs requires more than simply reading political tracts. It is about really seeing the person in front of you and respecting her or him regardless of their political affiliation, gender, class, race, etc. I realised I had never seen or read the *Universal Declaration of Human Rights*, which should have been the foundation, the first document to read before engaging with any ideology.

As I approached the end of my clinic assignment, Dr Khairi asked if I was interested in staying on permanently. He said that he would like me to stay only if I really liked and believed in this kind of work. I was thrilled to receive this acknowledgment and trust. It mattered to me that I had proved myself to be good at what I was doing.

Thus, I became the permanent receptionist at the psychiatric clinic and Dr Khairi started educating me about the world of psychiatry. He gave me psychology books to read. He encouraged me to develop an understanding of the psychology of people in order for me to serve them best.

While I appreciated his attention, I was somewhat disturbed by the instant confidence; I was a simple receptionist with filing responsibilities. I worried that he might form the impression that I was going to study psychology. In reality, I was there in pursuit of a scholarship opportunity. I hoped to return to the US on a scholarship independent of reliance upon my father.

However, I had fallen in love with my job. I began to learn as much as I could while working alongside the clinic secretary, Enid, whose British sense of humour was as alien to me as the psychology books Dr. Khairi gave me. I continued with my typing classes. Enid was my unofficial professional skills mentor. She taught me shorthand writing and numerous human relations skills in how to handle clients, doctors and the job itself.

Gradually, I developed a better understanding of human psychology. Dr Khairi asked me to attend the weekly doctors' and nurses' psychiatry ward rounds. He advised, "You need to have a better understanding of the patients' history, diagnosis and treatment to be able to offer the patients more than just an appointment." My hopes and dreams of a scholarship and of going back to school in the US descended to the bottom of my list. My job was so rewarding that I did not resist further work experience.

Then, I was assigned a new role. Dr. Khairi added to my responsibilities an unofficial role as Patients' Rights Officer. He explained that I needed to ensure that all patients were seen by their doctors and that their complaints were listened to and addressed by the doctors, the therapists or another staff member. I was to report to him any patient mistreatment and/or dissatisfaction.

The voice of Shahrazad in *The One Thousand and One Nights* re-emerged to transcend the voices of women suffering mental illness. At work, I listened to and learned about women's suffering and how consciously or unconsciously they had dealt with social pressures, injustice and coercion. I recalled el Saadawi's other books: *al-Untha Hiya al-Asl*, [Female is the Origin] and *al Mara'a wa al Sira' al Nafsi*, [Women and Neurosis]. In her book *Female is the Origin*, el Sadaawi had argued that *"promoting scientific knowledge does not connote idolising it. Scientific knowledge is prone to change, just as a historical and political knowledge. We, then, should realise that some forms of knowledge and facts change as human society evolves. What might be considered true or fact at one time might not be true at other times."*

El Saadawi's *Women and Neurosis* became highly relevant to my work. I re-read it then obsessively. I wanted to understand why the modern Shahrazad lost her voice. El Saadawi had suggested that the problem with the medical (psychiatry) profession is that it is dominated by men and that male psychiatrists are not really different from other men. Clearly, I needed to be cautious and to pay attention to how the cases are spoken of and described.

I made a note from el Sadaawi's observation that *"Psychiatry takes as its point of departure Freud's psychoanalysis, which examines women on the basis of penis envy, Oedipus complex, and castration. Both men and women psychiatrists come from within the same scientific tradition. Women psychiatrists sometimes are more rigid in their approaches to women's problems."*

In her book, el Saadawi argued that at one time or another women desire to be born as men not because of any psychological complex theorised by Freud, but because of the privileges granted to men in society. I agreed that her point was well taken. I was also becoming more knowledgeable of wider mental health and illness issues. I learned about manic depression, obsessive compulsive behaviours, personality and anxiety disorders and much more.

In *Women and Neurosis*, I learned about various types of sexual assaults. Female sexual assault was a totally new concept and I wanted to know more and to investigate it. However, I was sure that it did not occur in my small, kind community, certain it could not happen there.

Away from the clinic, sexual abuse was not an important issue to be discussed; therefore, it was never included on the Party's political agenda. Only the generic "dysfunctionality" issue was addressed and if it occurred, then the revolution – the Party – would take care of it. This was my somewhat naive view.

In the clinic, I listened as women narrated their stories. I learned about their suffering; it ranged from pre-pubescent marriages to childbearing and rearing to being a second, third or fourth wife or to dealing with second, third or fourth wives. Women who came to the clinic were of diverse ethnic and cultural backgrounds. Among them were the poor and uneducated along with the educated, the high-profile, the young and the elderly.

I felt privileged within my own life struggle; it seemed tame in comparison to what these women had experienced as they swerved between sanity and insanity. The real stories of their pain and despair were recorded in confidential files accessible by doctors, social workers and psychotherapists. Despite bearing the responsibility of ensuring that the patients' medical files were updated with their visits and hospitalisations, I had no access to the real reasons for their confinement in the unit. Some women suffered mental illness due to a simple chemical disorder. Some women used their mental illness and treatment as a deterrent to a husband's physical and emotional abuse which in turn gave the husbands more reason to be violent. Other women used it to deter husbands from sexual contact.

Oblivious to my presence, female patients openly talked about their lives. In the multi-bed ward, they spoke as if no one was listening. As I would get the patient's general medical file ready, a woman might start talking about what brought her to the psychiatric clinic. Depending on how she felt on that particular day, she might talk non-stop. They did not necessarily talk to me. The other women on the ward did not necessarily listen. At times, the other women listened without making comments, without acknowledging that they were listening.

In a story like that of Shahrazad, one patient narrated her story as a young bride who was married at age thirteen. She was moved far away from her home in the southern region of Saudi Arabia, and was brought to the Eastern Province. Her life revolved around serving her husband's extended family, and receiving and entertaining other family members who came to visit and stayed for interminable periods. By the time she was in her thirties, she suffered severe depression. She would become immobilised for long periods of time. She could no longer look after her family let alone her guests. When in her fifties, she would sink into depression each time family members called to visit.

From another bed, I heard of the beautiful young woman who graduated at the top of her class with first-class honours who was not allowed to marry the man she loved because he was from a different country. He was a Muslim, but that fact did not matter. Her father would not grant his daughter permission to marry a man from another country. The beautiful young student withdrew from life. It was her loving father who brought her to the clinic, not recognising that his decision was behind her psychological disorder.

Over in that bed was the woman whose husband threatened her with divorce if she used contraception. She bore him nine children, two girls and seven boys. The boys were all born with haemophilia. She was only in her late twenties and had been coming to the clinic since the birth of her third son. She continued to bear children, fully aware that between being divorced and giving birth to children with haemophilia, the second was the more bearable option. She was exhausted. She was detached and totally withdrawn from the reality of her life. She spent her life bearing children.

She and her husband were coming to the clinic for counselling regarding a hysterectomy. She asked, "What is a woman without a uterus?" I did not have a definitive answer. I wanted to say that I believed that women are worthy with or without a uterus. However, surrounded by men, I answered, "Allah blessed you with a wealth of girls and boys. Your boys all have haemophilia and your duty now is to look after the gift you have." The husband dismissed me, escorting his wife out of the clinic. She smiled and meekly followed.

Beyond was the young woman who was traumatised after being sexually assaulted. She immediately checked out of life. She disconnected and slowly became a shadow of a person. In the end, she was continuously sedated.

Near her but far away was the fifteen-year-old young woman who dreamed of finishing her high school degree but instead was married to a fifty-year-old man. She attempted suicide. She failed. She attempted again.

Every day, there was a new woman and a new story. Like parcels, women were dropped at the clinic by male guardians and picked up at lunch time or at the end of the day. They were few lucky ones who had access to Aramco shuttle buses used to transport employees and their dependants.

Men presented their psychological disorders and mental illnesses differently. Their psychological disorders were concealed behind work stress, financial pressures, conflicting personal and family interests and increasing family responsibilities. Behind the dysfunction, there was always a noble reason that was not available to women. Emotional issues were dismissed in favour of the more acceptable or rational work-related issues.

At the clinic, I was exposed to alcoholism and drug addiction as many men turned to them to bury their anguish. In Saudi Arabia, alcohol is prohibited and consumption is punishable. Yet the many cases in Aramco alone revealed how accessible it was to the average Saudi male. Many of the men concealed their faces and their identities, as if psychological disorders breached their dignity. In a community where there are so many identical names, the addition of a face would have been helpful when following up with patients. However, many of these men did not even stop on their way out of the clinic to schedule the next appointment, but rather telephoned later. As a Saudi female, I was brought up to respect these unspoken boundaries of segregation.

I had read *al-Rajul wal-Jin's,* (*Men and Sex*), in which el Saadawi speaks of the absence of women in the world of Arab men. Despite women's increased participation in public life, their status remains relatively unchanged. Women are prohibited from the domains of authority, government and politics.

In her discussion of men, science and sex, she reviews the work of Ibn Seena, Freud, Engels and Marx. In comparing Freud and Marx, el Sadaawi appraised the Marxist analysis as it contributed to the understanding of society because of its emphasis on the socio-economic structure. She explained that men experience significant anxiety when sexually impotent. From her perspective, men's anxiety in regard to their sexuality is a social and psychological problem which relates to the system of patriarchy. She argued that a man's concept of his world centres on his image of the powerful, dominant and aggressive male. That construct constantly requires him to comply with that image. An impotent man surrenders his right to be a man.

In her book, el Saadawi addresses sex, which in the Arab culture is peculiarly perceived as illicit and sinful regardless of the context. As in some other cultures, it causes both women and men to live in conflict between the need for sexual activity to fulfil normal human desires and the guilt of committing such a sin. The peculiarity for me was not the Arab cultural perception of sex; rather it was the societal equation of women with sex that transforms women into the illicit and sinful gender.

Some of the women and men had a simpler approach to life with physical and psychological illnesses. They accepted such afflictions as a test of their faith in Allah. They believed that Allah tests the faith of his worshippers while inflicting illness on them and then seeing them through crises.

Admittedly, I had never before seen the world through el Sadaawi's eyes. Though based on research and true life experiences, her insight seemed to evolve from elsewhere. I had never thought of women and men in complex terms, as my life experiences seemed far simpler. I realised how fortunate my life had been, how fortunate I was, how privileged to have come this close to the suffering of others. I learned how to step out of the clinic, leaving behind me the voices of women searching for those who wanted to listen.

I resumed reading el Sadaawi's *Woman is the Origin* in which she maintained that the liberation of women is fundamentally a political issue. It aims to emancipate women not only sexually but psychologically in order for women to strengthen their mental and social resources.

While working for Aramco, I learned that the political philosophies and analysis of Marx and Engels did not exactly fit life as I observed it. Although I was aware of the inequality within the Aramco corporate structure and how the religious sectarianism between the Sunni and the Shia manifested itself, I had but a superficial understanding of how the gender, race and class divides worked.

Through this work experience, Aramco's inequalities became clearer. Throughout my life, I had heard references to discrimination from my maternal grandfather, my great uncles and other relatives. However, this was at the beginning of the eighties and Aramco was beginning to change, at least superficially.

I naively thought that Aramco has always been a potentially fertile ground for revolution. However, it appeared that the four decades of burning gas and chemical residues in the Eastern Province had extinguished the employees' desire for fair treatment, equal pay and equal opportunities. It seemed to have curbed the workers' will to object.

Within Aramco, a rigid nationality and educational profile determined the starting grade and salary scale which was applied to newly hired Saudi and non-Saudi nationals. Besides the nationality and educational profiles, Saudis were screened according to sectarian guidelines. The Sunni/Shia scale provided Sunni Saudis with greater opportunities for development and promotion within Aramco than that for Shia Saudi nationals. Of course, engineering and science majors started at a higher grade and salary scale than arts and humanities majors. There was a near total absence of equal opportunity. This was Aramco with all of the job security, the benefits and the prestige of home ownership, saving plans and health care. As neither a white American or a Western male nor closely related to an influential Saudi Sunni male, I was deemed a marginal employee. As a minority Shia female, I dropped to the bottom on all of the scales.

The dynamic was fascinating. I began to partially understand how we inherited the superior/inferior dichotomy when dealing with the white Western face. In that environment, it became clearer to me that Marx's social evolution model and the communist manifesto alone were inadequate for analysis. The working class was becoming more diverse with fewer Saudi "coolies", thereby lessening the hope for changes. A large foreign labour force, largely Asian nationals, had replaced the majority of Saudis. The imported force did the 'coolie' work, had no rights, received subsistence pay and were kept in line with threats of deportation.

There was not an intellectual, affluent, progressive middle class of Saudi nationals and no clear capitalists in this skewed semi-industrial context. Saudi nationals had decent benefits and privileges to keep them content. The nationalist secular sentiment was receding while the religious hardliners were gaining ground.

Within Aramco, there was a slight increase in the number of Saudi women at the beginning of the eighties. Still the number of Saudi women employees could be easily counted. The overwhelming majority of Aramco's employees were males.

I worked in Aramco in order to obtain a scholarship. I had become too serious to attract attention. I enjoyed not being noticed. I became more cautious around men. While working there, I became aware of my increasing desire for anonymity. I knew that the desire for invisibility was not because I was finally working in a superficially gender integrated work environment. While I knew what I desired, I was afraid of exploring the true source behind my desire not to be noticed.

Finally, Dr Khairi completed the Aramco scholarship recommendation form that I had requested. I waited with the hope that it would be granted soon and that I could then go back to the US.

While I waited impatiently, Aramco suspended all international scholarships for women. I had two choices: accept a scholarship to one of the seven Saudi universities or work until a miracle happened. Although I did not believe in miracles, I informed Dr Khairi that I would remain in my job.

Those women's scholarships were suspended for a very long time. Within the Party, I was suspended, remaining in my supporting role. Patiently, I accepted my status. I accepted the continued supporting role as if paying penance for my earlier defiance of Party wishes that I should not go to the US. I remained in the background of politics with the same willingness to support and help, but never at the front line of political activism.

At Aramco, I learned many things. There, I experienced my first ever encounter with homosexuality. A Saudi woman doctor, intelligent and kind, tried to test me. Whenever we met in the hospital corridors, she would take the time to acknowledge and to talk to me. She was kind, humble and clever, until one day when she made me very uncomfortable. She came too close, almost brushing her body against mine. It sent me to the wall. Suddenly, I was aware of just how far I jumped away from her. She walked off before I had the chance to observe her reaction. From then forward she avoided me. I welcomed that change, as I was unsure of how I would react if she dared approach me again.

In my ignorance, I thought of sexual deprivation as a cause for such behaviour. Therefore, I reasoned that soon the woman doctor would marry, have children and lead a "normal" life. Inexplicably, I never considered sharing my experience with anyone. A sense of obligation toward women, toward the woman doctor's reputation and to a bond with all women deterred me from sharing the experience. Perhaps I was afraid of my own judgemental bias. Certainly, I was aware of our community's judgemental attitude toward homosexuals. While my view of my community was benevolent, its perspective remained – in every sense of the word – a judgemental view.

Every day at work I was learning professionally and personally. I learned about reporting lines, ethical codes meeting and coordination protocols confidentiality and respect for rules and time, all in accordance with the US business culture. In many respects, those practices were totally alien to the local culture. I had my first experience with workplace ethics, politics and competition. I was influenced by the standards of the psychiatric clinic. For the twenty-one months that I worked for Aramco, I did not miss one day of work. Ironically, I signed my first ever petition in Saudi Arabia while working for Aramco, one of the highlights of my time there. It was a demand for Saudi female employee home ownership loans comparable to those for male employees. More than twenty years later, the petition was realised; Saudi female employees finally obtained a partial home ownership loan programme wherein they were granted a sum of money but not land.

Personally, a new world had opened before me. I observed as other Saudi women employees pushed social boundaries, especially in terms of their relationships with men. My boundaries were still in line with what the Arab Socialist Action Party dictated.

I resumed my friendships with many women with whom I had not been in contact during my ten-month absence in the US. At the time, only a few of my classmates were working for Aramco. I continued to honour my childhood and teen friendships despite Party disapproval, as the majority of my best friends were of the new left ideology. From my ten-month political isolation in the US, I had learned that I would lose much political ground and miss out on many political activities if I severed those connections with my true identity.

Minimally, I resumed my political activities. I participated when I was called upon as the lone option, the only woman for the job. I was content to have access to the books. When other women Party members were sent for their military training, I was excluded and stayed behind. I felt that I was betrayed; nevertheless, there were no negative feelings toward the women who went or toward the Party leaders who excluded me. Eventually, I was invited to write on women's issues for the Party's newsletter, which was now taking shape. I welcomed the opportunity.

It was around this time, in late 1981, that for the first and only time in my life, I was entrusted by the Party with the disposal of a hand gun. I received the gun from a stranger whose eyes were his only distinctive feature. I buried the gun quickly, as if I feared that it would possess me if it remained in my hand a minute longer than necessary. For a long time, I wondered if it was ever retrieved from its burial ground. Was it my sense of duty and conviction that led me to accept my new political role as an amateur or merely my hope that one day I would be recognised as worthy of Party membership?

As I developed the ability to focus on life's rewards, I overcame the nuisances. I focused on my work, my mother and my maternal grandmother. Um Hameed was getting older and becoming frail. She had started exhibiting small signs of weakness and various ailments.

I sustained my ritual visits with her on weekends. There I slept on the rugs that had now replaced the straw mat, resting my head on the hard cushion. I would fall asleep and as I drifted away, I could sense Um Hameed as she covered me with a cool cotton *mishmar* and hear her soft voice reciting *Ayat al Kursi* from the Quran. I felt Um Hameed's hand touching my forehead, reaching to my heart and soul.

Enveloped in her love, I slept.

# Reflection/Monologue 1

*Allah Akbar, Allah Akbar;*
*Ashhad an la Ilah ila Allah, ashhad an la Ilah ila Allah*
*Ashhad an Muhamad rasoul Allah, ashhad an Muhamad rasoul Allah*
*Ashhad an Ali wali Allah, ashhad an Ali wali Allah*
*Hai ala alsalah, Hai ala alsalah*
*Hai ala alfalah, Hai ala alfalah*
*Hai ala khair alamal, Hai ala khair alamal*
*Gad igamat alsalat*
*Allah Akbar, Allah Akbar*

*I followed the Muathen's voice to Fatema's house, crossing the empty space that stretched between our house and hers. The Athan, the call for prayer, soothed me. I knew the Muathen, Abu Jassim. I thought that with such a voice he was fit to be a singer. His call for prayer was far more persuasive than any song. His call was an invitation to be present at the service of Allah for the* Maghrib *(sunset prayer). From the roof of his house, Abu Jassim's Athan reached well beyond the vacant space. As I walked to Fatema's house, men were heading toward the small neighbourhood mosque.*

*While I waited for Fatema to finish her chores, I would take a short nap. In that delicious interlude between sleep and waking, I would feel Fatema's warm breath near my face, as if she were banishing uninvited dreams. I would know that she had placed the light mishmar over my body to cool me. The aroma of riyhaan (Arabic basil) tied at the hem, would lift me up to heaven.*

*On rising from my nap, I would wait patiently for Fatema to hand me the mismatched assortment of soft and hard candies. I then sorted them: some old, even expired; some newly purchased; and some collected on similar occasions. I repacked them in a brown paper bag. Meanwhile, she finished feeding my great-grandparents and my grandfather. Then we would veil ourselves for the walk to the home of her neighbour, a blind woman. She along with other women would be waiting for us almost every Thursday. There, I would read* Halal El Mashakel [The dilemma solver].

*On hearing the call for prayer, I struggled to recognise the Muathen's voice, for it was not that of Abu Jassim. In this reverie, I am walking through a cold void, an unfamiliar road and in a dark hour of night. After handing me the book with care and tenderness, Fatema fades away. I stopped sorting the candies. Defeated, I surrendered my reading.*

Drenched in fear, I was awakened from my dream. I was not thirteen years old. Rather, I was barely twenty-two going toward fifty. I was locked in a small room in a house somewhere in a big soulless city. I was a tiny bird with dented wings trapped in a huge cage. Four male guards marched into my prison room at the call for the *fajr* (dawn) prayer to rudely awaken me. They marched in, silenced the call for the prayer, interrupted my dreams and chased away Fatema, the candies and my reading materials. They turned my bed upside down, searched the small empty room and marched out. I wondered why the *mutawa* (religious police) did not wield their sticks and chase them to the mosque for the *fajr* prayer. I guessed that they were all part of the same conspiracy.

# 5

# Prison Memoirs

### Prison Memoir I

I am awake and overwhelmed by a sudden awareness of my womanhood, of myself as a minority on many accounts: I am a woman; I am a young Muslim Shia woman; and I am involved in politics. I am incarcerated for my short-lived commitment to an illegal political group. Life could not be more exciting at the age of twenty-two years, two months and nineteen days!

This memory is from either the eighth or the ninth of June 1982, Tuesday or Wednesday. Of one fact I am certain: Saturday was the fifth of June. On that day, Israeli troops marched toward Lebanon, invading it on the sixth of June. That was *Al-Ijtiah*, the invasion of Lebanon, or as the Israelis referred to it, the *Operation Peace for Galilee*. Of course, their intent was that the peace was for Israelis.

Who cares to count or remember accurately when imprisoned? I do know that I was left without being interrogated in a temporary prison cell for three nights and three days. During those long hours, I confronted the possibility of not having a return address for the next three to five years.

In the early dawn hours of the fourth morning, I was driven to a two-storey villa in a residential area of the capital of my country. There was no way to identify the streets, as the vehicle had no rear windows. *Years later, I endeavoured unsuccessfully to find the villa.*

On that fourth morning, I was ushered upstairs and led into a room adjacent to a bathroom. As I looked around the small room, I thought that living with the minimum requirements of daily life would suit me well. I looked through the handbag I had prepared before they came for me. My uncle Hasan had to return home to retrieve it as I left it behind under the assumption that I was only called for interrogation, rather than incarceration. I counted: three underpants, two nightgowns, one knee-length dress, one pair of sandals, one Kotex box and one pack of red Marlboro cigarettes. I had included no bras. In the room, there was one bed, one sheet and one pillow.

A male guard entered the room. Standing beside the bed, he turned his gaze away as the Sharia code mandates that an unrelated man and woman cannot be in seclusion. Pathetically he said, "I hope you like it here." I made no effort to respond. Purposefully, I veiled my unvoiced response. His body revealed the anxiety that his lips concealed. Without permission, he took my handbag and searched it. I wondered what would become of me in this isolated, soulless place. Curtained with black plastic bags and a few old newspapers, the room's window resembled an art work in progress.

I marvelled at my body's chart of vital signs. The head was on its own, as the brain seemed dysfunctional. The heart was invisible on the chart; the veins revealed no blood coursing through them. I found no evidence of me anywhere. I lost count of the times that I simply slipped away. As a dispassionate bystander, I watched myself as my life passed before me.

I found myself recalling the last few months' events since they came for my uncle Najeeb in March. In the three months that followed, I sensed that the last decade of political activism was all coming to an end. While I sensed it then, I was more certain of it on that Thursday night, 3 June 1982. Without protest, I too was coming to an end.

On that Friday morning of 4 June 1982, I was lying awake when I heard someone sobbing in the living room. I recognised the source but I did not move from my bed until after she left. I could not move. Then I rose and left my bedroom.

Casually I asked if it had been my great aunt Um Taha's voice that I had heard. Collecting herself and choking back her frozen tears, my mother replied: "They came after Kawthar last night. They collected her from her apartment in the Aramco compound where she lived and worked. They brought her to her mother's home and kept her in the car outside while they searched first her room and then the whole house. They turned your aunt's house upside down. Your aunt said that they took things with them. Who knows what things?"

A few hours later, my uncle Hasan returned for lunch. For some time, I had been staying with him, as it was more convenient to get to and from work from his house in Khobar. Avoiding my eyes he said, "We should go to Bahrain today. I will accompany you. You will stay with friends there. Then you will go to the United Arab Emirates where you will stay with my family until things clear out." "Clear out" was nicely put.

Silently, I indicated "No." No one could understand why I chose not to leave, why I chose the "no option" option. I believed fervently that I was making the right choice. My family thought that I was mad. I believed that it was a realistic decision. No one wanted to listen or to try to understand, so I did not bother to explain. Lying in bed that night, I thought: Why would they come after me? I was only twenty-two years old at the time.

The fifth of June came too soon. I was scrupulously clean. They would not find anything on me, so what was the worst thing that could happen? Earlier that day, a cousin who was staying with us knocked at the bathroom door while I was in the shower. She told me that a man had been enquiring about the house and its residents. She told him to whom it belonged. As she related the incident, my heart sank, the water froze and goose bumps erupted all over my skin as my body went numb. I felt a powerful, grasping hand reach for my heart. The hand stiffened while tightening its grip around that beating muscle.

When they finally came, it was around two in the afternoon. I was still in my housedress, as I was staying home that hot summer day. I had not had lunch, as we were waiting for my uncle when the doorbell rang. A white four-door sedan was parked in front of the house. Four men dressed in white *thobes* stepped out of the car.

I chose to greet them at the door. I knew what awaited me and I wanted to be there. I opened the door. Without permission and without any warrant, they entered. I guided them to my room where they searched the drawers, looked through my underwear, shook my handbags and looked under the bed and carpet. I rested my head against the door panel while trying to register every detail of what was ahead of me. I stared vacantly while they searched the room. We were both empty. The emptiness was comforting.

I watched myself as I accompanied them in my housedress. I asked if I could change my clothes. "No need," was the reply. "We need to ask you a few questions and then you will be free to return." I looked at the small handbag that they had already searched. It was the same one I had prepared. "Return." The word echoed inside me. Suddenly, I realised that to them I was but a piece of goods to be borrowed and then to be returned. I packed one short dress, two nightgowns and three pairs of underwear.

The four men in white *thobes* escorted me to the waiting sedan. Following a script written for me, I sat unresistingly in the back seat of the white car. The strict segregation law of the country was violated: I was a single woman with no male guardian under escort by four males, none of whom was even remotely related to me.

As the car sped out of the neighbourhood, their supervising officer said they would like to see my office. I heard "search". The car was on its way to Aramco's Dhahran Health Centre where I had worked for the last two years. He made it sound like a friendly request that I could refuse. I complied without complaint hoping that the security officers at the Aramco gate would not grant them entry; my political naivety was profound.

They searched the office. They found a notebook that belonged to the secretary. It had shorthand notes, a list of my duties and directions for how to do things in case of her absence. It was not mine. Nevertheless, they took it. I did not complain.

In a white four-door sedan on the hot afternoon of the fifth of June, I left behind my life, a life that I had believed I knew. I gazed out of the white car window. I lifted my eyes toward the sky. That day, I registered in my memory that the sky in my country is grey not blue. There were no birds in sight. I thanked the birds as they protested my violation with their absence.

As the car drove through another city, I recalled the headlines from the daily newspaper: "*Israel invades South Lebanon.*" The story indicated "*The Arab League protests the Israeli invasion and appeals to the UN for action. The Israeli government says the army will stay until borders are protected from Palestinian attacks."* I counted one, two invasions. I judged that the Israelis would never leave. My mind was paralysed. I recalled a sad song, a poem by Mahmoud Darwish.

> *Allahu asbah gha'iban ya saidie*
> *Sader ithan hata busat al massjidi*
> *Wa bia al kanessata fahya min amlakeh*
> *Wa bia al muathen fi al mazad al aswadi*
>
> God is absent
> Confiscate the mosque's rug
> Sell the cathedral, as it is his property
> And sell the prayer caller in the black market

God! What if they asked? Would they want to know what I thought of God? At the secret police headquarters, I was escorted to an office where a senior officer waited. Trying to be kind, he offered me a seat and a cup of tea. He did not offer me a telephone call. I thought tea sounded good, hoping that it would cool me a little. Unexpectedly, my uncle Hasan walked in as I was sipping my first cup of tea. The senior officer was assuring me that they only needed a few answers from me and that the process should not take long.

As it did not suit them to do so, the officials paid no attention to our strict local customs. In our community, the Islamic Sharia code requires that women must be accompanied by a male guardian at all times while out of their homes and work. There I sat among unrelated men casually sipping tea. We were taught that Islam prohibits entry to a house without its resident's permission. I wondered what religious code these men followed.

Two hours later, the senior officer addressed my uncle suggesting that it might be a good idea to bring a change of clothes for me. He explained that he had just received orders to transfer me to the capital. With those words, I divorced my body.

At eight o'clock that night, I was escorted to the airport. My escort was one of the four men who came for me earlier. His concealed gun announced itself as he passed through the security system. Although it sounded loud and long, no one paid any attention. Clearly, it was a conspiracy in which all the participants were complicit. I marvelled at the smoothly oiled police machinery. I was escorted to the office of the secret police at the airport. I was paraded before all the personnel in order that they could identify my face. I sipped more tea, storing caffeine for the long road ahead.

Only royalty or criminals would be escorted in the way that I was. Frantically, I scanned each face I encountered. I sought someone to recognise me, someone who might tell Maryam, my mother, that I had been seen leaving the airport. I checked to see if anyone noticed. Dressed in my nightgown, I was certainly not mistaken for royalty in that airport. I was invisible.

No one asked for my name, address or telephone number. No one cared to ask how old or how young I was. No one asked if I wanted to call Maryam to say good-bye. Of course, I wanted to call her – they should have known. Of course, they knew. I wanted to tell her how much I loved her.

She would have said: *"You do not love me. If you did you would have chosen differently."* I know that I would have answered, *"I did it for you, for me and for all of us. I will give you wings and we can all have voices."* She would not want to understand. She would not accept my gift and she would have said, *"Who told you I want wings? Who told you I want a voice?"*

For almost a decade, Maryam had worried about my increasing political activities and radical views. When I was only sixteen, I read the Party's yellow (Chinese) and red (Russian) covered political books. At that time, I had been angry with Maryam for loving my father after he abandoned us. For ever, he left her and he left us. She watched but chose not to stop my reading. She would look under my pillow after I napped looking for forgotten books. She looked for the red covered ones and put them away. She read the titles and questioned me, but only displayed nods of disapproval and a short supplication. She feared for me. I was always able to soothe her, momentarily. But a mother's heart knows.

At the end of the flight, the black van waited on the tarmac. This time there was no security process. As if I were a parcel, my police escort handed me over to two new officers and then he disappeared. He had been sent from Riyadh to the Eastern Province to detain me. It was around midnight and the streets of Riyadh, the capital, were empty of people. As now, missions like this one were executed when darkness rules. In that capital, there would have been no protest even if it had been carried out in daylight.

The black van drove into the garage of a large building. I was led to a room on the second floor. I learned that it was the guard's room. For the first time since I left home, my guard was a woman. Clearly, her worn-out body did not appreciate being roused just when she had begun her rest. I restrained my voice. She motioned to a worn-out mattress covered with an equally worn-out sheet. I sat wrapped in my veil, enshrouded in my fear.

It was not persecution that I feared. Rather, I was afraid to confront the real me. Terrified of what I might find, I had successfully resisted this confrontation with the person within for twenty-two years. This is where I would confront what I feared most: my beliefs, my courage and my identity. Everything would be exposed. This was where the journey began. This was where I started my journey without a map, without a compass. A tremor quivered inside me. What if I got lost? I judged that in that case I would be lost for ever.

The soft sounds of snoring filled the room; then the volume was amplified. I heard screams. I imagined that my fears were being broadcast on a loudspeaker. Again, I heard screams, painful and altogether real. They must have belonged to men – surely not women? – who were being tortured. I wondered if I knew any of the prisoners. Certainly, I knew of many who had been incarcerated.

Dawn lost track of time and arrived late. I prayed for it not to be on strike. I remembered to recite Mahmoud Darwish's poem, to sing a song for Maryam:

> *Aheno ela khobz Umy*
> *wa qahwat Umy*
> *wa lamssat Umy*
> *wa takbur fia al toofulat yauman ala sadr Umay*
> *wa aasshag omrie lani itha mutto*
> *Akhjal min dame' Umy!*
> *Khuthini, itha udtoo yauman wishahan luhdbuk*
> *wa ghati idhami be ushb taamad min tuhre kaabak*
> *wa shudi withagi*
> *Bi kheslate shaer*
> *Bi khait yloih fi thaiyl thaobak*
> [...]

Here is the poem in full in English:

> "I long for my mother's bread
> My mother's coffee
> Her touch
> Childhood memories grow up in me
> Day after day
> I must be worth my life
> At the hour of my death
> Worth the tears of my mother
> And if I come back one day
> Take me as a veil to your eyelashes
> Cover my bones with the grass
> Blessed by your footsteps
> Bind us together
> With a lock of your hair
> With a thread that trails from the back of your dress
> I might become immortal
> Become a God
> If I touch the depths of your heart
> If I come back
> Use me as wood to feed your fire
> As the clothesline on the roof of your house
> Without your blessing
> I am too weak to stand
> I am old
> Give me back the star maps of childhood
> So that I along with the swallows
> Can chart the path
> Back to your waiting nest

I thanked Allah for Mahmoud Darwish, for his poetry and for Marcel Khalife's voice singing Darwish's poetry. It kept me alive, positively inspired and floating with lightness.

In front of me, the woman guard placed Kraft cheese, jam and honey, along with *tameez* bread. There were five plates: one for each of the three other prisoners, the guard and myself. Mechanically, I did what seemed the only thing to do: I put one piece of bread next to each plate where I had put cheese, jam and honey. The guard brought a big tray and stacked the plates on it leaving one. She looked at me. I looked at the plate and continued sipping my tea and smoking my cigarette. I ate a piece of bread. I liked the bread. Later in the morning she brought back the cheese, the jam and the honey.

I remained. Three nights passed. No one took my name. No one asked. I smoked only a little, as I feared that if I smoked all of the cigarettes they would not allow me any more. The steel bars clanged endlessly. They clanged all night and all day. With each clang, my soul shattered. Every night when the lights were switched off, I relaxed. Then the records office was closed. As I lay in bed in the dark behind the bars, I heard the screams, the sobs and the heavy footsteps climbing the stairs. There was a knock at the door. I heard my name. I heard, "The end."

They came for me at one o'clock in the morning. It was time. I heard something echo. I experienced numbness. A jeep was waiting. In the jeep, two new officers and the woman guard accompanied me through the streets of the sleeping capital. Into eternity, the road stretched. Time stopped. We were swallowed into a quiet building, one with which I would become familiar. A few guards were scattered around armed with machine guns on their young shoulders. I wondered if they knew my identity. I wondered if it mattered.

On the third floor we waited. This time I registered the details. I wanted to be numb, and yet I wanted to remember. The tiled building was largely empty. I was summoned. My heart contracted while the angry fist squeezed harder.

Behind the two desks were two men and before them a woman, me. All believed they loved their country. One of the men apologised for the inconvenience. I thought he had acting potential. The other observed quietly. I was offered the chair closest to the desk. The room was dim and full of cigarette smoke. I wished they would offer me a cigarette and a ticket home. Then we could all go home. They offered neither.

They handed me a notebook with a name on the cover. I had forgotten the way the name looked and how it sounded. The man who apologised continued, *"I only have a few questions for you. Answer them and you will go home."* I hated, "you will go home". The fist squeezing my heart extended to encompass my lungs, my stomach and my brain.

Suddenly I felt sleepy, overwhelmingly sleepy. If they were to give me a pillow and a blanket, I would go to sleep. I wanted to sleep until it was all over. Terrified and trembling, I seated myself on the chair. The urge to sob nearly overwhelmed me. I wanted to cry for my mother. I wanted to cry until they got tired of my crying. I wanted my mother.

The two men concealed their smiles as I confronted the notebook before me.

Page One:
Name: Muna
Case: Arab Socialist Action Party
Offence: A recruit in an illegitimate political organisation

My first thought: There are no legitimate political organisations in my country. The official's voice returned, forcing me back into the dim room. The questions were already written and all I had to do was to provide the desired answers. I had no answers, acceptable or otherwise. I remembered the composition assignments at school: Describe how you spent your summer vacation; write about what you liked or disliked.

Just as with those compositions, I wrote in a stream of consciousness. I wrote and then wrote more. I handed the notebook back and waited for my failing grade. I waited a lifetime.

The not so agreeable officer read my notebook. He read every letter, every word, every sentence, every phrase, every paragraph and every word I did not write. I watched him as his blood slowly boiled over my words. I watched as he reached into his drawer to retrieve something. He placed the object on the table and snapped at me, "Is this what you meet around?" I realised then that he had a full bottle of black label whisky. I was relieved. The voice snapped again, "Are you a virgin?" I trembled.

I guessed that the question might be an invitation, a request for permission to rape and an automatic failing grade. Abruptly, the possibilities were enveloped in a notebook flying toward my head. I was unsure of whether to answer the question or to avoid the slap. Maryam's face came between me and their question, between my answers and me. She forced her face into the scene, although she would not have wanted to be there. I knew that she would have hated the lie I considered. I resolved to finish with pretence.

I sat alone. I was brought alone. I was left alone. Then in a conspiratorial tone he cajoled, "You are smart. All we want you to do is to give us some names so that you can go home afterwards. This will make it easy on you and on all of us." He spoke softly. Names! What sort of names did he want? I chose to recall none. I was mystified before a notebook that had been thrown at my face. All at once, my tears, my weakness and the ultimate betrayal surfaced.

I held an exhausted pen between my fingers. I had to fill in those blank pages. I had to empty my life. While I deliberated, another notebook with my name on the cover was suspended before me. "Do not play dumb, do not play nice and do not play with us!" the senior officer raised his voice again. "Someone told on you. Everyone tells on everybody else."

I do not remember how and when I surrendered to the torture. Perhaps I started where the numbness stopped, or I might have finished where it started. "Someone told on you," echoed like no other words had or ever would again. I saw it: my name was staring back at me. I withdrew to a place where I ceased to exist. I languished, suspended over hell entertaining images of the things that the two men could do to me while I was trapped, while isolated. Waves of anxiety washed over me. I dropped the pen. Betrayed. Dawn had arrived. Anger and smoke had blurred the vision of the two men.

They left me alone while they followed the moves of my pen. It pacified them. Unlike ancient dictation mistakes that could be revised hundreds of times, these mistakes could not be altered. I chose the failing grade. I had decided that it would be the passing one in the end. The senior officer smiled at me while holding my new notebook. He suggested a deal. Now he spoke softly, "You are very young. If you help us, we will help you." He paused. "We need to question two other women. Women you know. We want you to make the contact for us. On behalf of the secret police, I am giving you our word that you and the women you name will not be imprisoned. All of you will be released as soon as we finish questioning them." I knew then that I was alone and totally isolated.

For the first time in this experience, I felt *alone*. I was left completely on my own to figure out that I was not prepared for this. I was left *alone* to face the truth, not about what could really happen to me here, but the possibility of it happening. I observed myself sitting in the strangest of places, being questioned by strangers about others. It seemed that the strangers were conspiring to prolong my anguish for as long as I lived. I was helpless, powerless and felt worthless. I do not know how I found the answers that satisfied them. Apparently, I did. For the moment, the books were closed.

Back on the road at dawn with no knowledge of the destination, I was engulfed by terror. A guard who knew how to leave traces of disgust that lingered for a long time further intimidated me. I was locked in. The guard's taunt, *"I hope you like it here,"* hovered in the air. I did not respond to his senseless, cruel taunt.

The room with the black plastic and newspaper curtains was dim. They took the key, of course. It was narrow, dark and cold despite the rising June heat and dryness.

A few days passed. The only voice I heard was that of the guard advising me that my meals were behind the door. He would open the door and I was to reach out for the tray. One day the senior guard returned unannounced and told me that I was to be moved to another room. This time they moved me to the main foyer where there were only two rooms, one of them for me. Diagonally across from my room, the steel bar-barricaded stairway repelled, secure with its big metal lock. The guards kept the lock's keys.

The room into which I moved was smaller than the first one but decorated with the same black plastic and newspaper curtains. There was not much luggage to move and I quickly settled into my new space. Soon I lost track of the days. It should not have mattered. I was more concerned about how many days were left of my life and with how many days I had already lost.

Abruptly, life became slow and quiet. The sweet supplications of my mother faded away, no longer following me as I entered and left home. I surrendered myself to being cut off from all human communication and to the absence of newspapers, radios, television and people with whom to converse.

I felt deserted knowing that Suhail was already in the US. Although we had no longer been in a relationship, I missed his presence in my life. Knowing that he would be concerned about my well-being brought some comfort in my confinement. At the same time that I missed him, I felt guilty as I recognised the need to let go of my feelings toward him. I was no longer sure about my love for him. Thus there, I completely let go and determined to move on with my life. In my mind, I set him free with the hope that he would find love again.

The boringly monotonous days were all the same. The prison guards gave me a box of Lipton tea bags, a jar of Nescafé instant coffee and a container of sugar. I began collecting tea bag labels to mark the number of days passed in confinement. The hours clicked by slowly and heavily. Time became part of the torture routine, as insurance that I was keenly aware of my confinement. On a daily basis, I knew that I was alive when one of the guards knocked at my door to announce breakfast, lunch or dinner. Otherwise, I was numb for long stretches of time.

As time advanced, each day became slower than those before it. Although numb, I was determined not to distort my circadian rhythm, not to confuse day and night. I felt hollow. The room felt hollow and I was swallowed within its walls. It was difficult to remain alert, consciously and physically alive. Determinedly, I willed normality into my confinement; I forged a pact with myself to wake around six-thirty every morning and to turn off the lights at eleven in the evening. It did not matter if I was sleepy or not; I always switched off the lights at eleven.

To pass the time and to remain active, I began to walk around the room as many times as possible. When boredom arrived, I would swirl and dance. I proceeded to stretch and hang my body off the bed backwards. My final routine involved standing on my head as I leaned against one of the walls. There was a lot of time to pass; there was a finite number of activities for such a limited space.

For some time, I found comfort in sitting behind the locked door to listen to the sounds of stillness, of silence. For long periods, there was no sound except that associated with doors opening and closing. The soft steps on the stairway and the clicking sound of metal announcing the opening of the barricaded metal door leading to the first-floor foyer signalled life behind my confined space. The humming sounds of the air conditioner muffled the sounds of life. I imagined that I heard the guards talking. Later, I learned that they were talking to a woman guard in residence of whose existence I was unaware.

Every morning the guard on duty would bring in the breakfast tray and a flask of hot water. Except for the bread, I left the food untouched. I did however retain the flask of hot water.

Soon, the month of Ramadhan approached and I sank deeper into my solitude. I missed home and Maryam. I missed fasting and preparing for *iftar* (breaking the fast at sunset) with the family. To me, fasting while in confinement epitomised torture. Compared to Maryam's heavenly cooking, the food was dull and I was indifferent to it. I suspected that the cook was either an Egyptian or Sudanese national because of the cuisine and the particular dishes served. Fortuitously, I did not need much food to survive. During Ramadhan, I ate the soup and a few *luqaymat* (flour dumplings served with date molasses or home-made syrup). I kept the fruit and biscuits for later.

During Ramadhan my numbness was momentarily disturbed when the senior guard marched into my room to question my failure to rise for the *fajir* (dawn) prayer. In his presence, I remained silent. He left only to return soon with a copy of the Quran and a few religious books. In my heart, I knew that when I prayed it would be for Allah, not for the senior prison guard.

Late one evening, the senior guard came to tell me to get ready to leave. Again, the officials came for me in a jeep similar to the first one. It was waiting at the front gate of this prison villa. In the jeep, familiar officers and an unknown woman guard waited. They accompanied me through the streets of Riyadh. During that Ramadhan period, those streets of the capital were not sleeping; everything was alive. Again, we were swallowed into the same quiet familiar building where a few guards seemed busier than on my last visit.

This time I knew we were heading to the third floor. As I was already numb, I did not bother to take note of my surroundings. Behind the two familiar desks were two familiar men; meanwhile, the woman guard stayed behind the closed door. One of the men asked how things were going. The question got lost. The room was not as dim as I remembered. This time they offered me a cigarette, which I declined. This time I realized the futility of wishing for a ticket home.

This time they did not hand me a notebook. This time they made their request clear. The senior officer smiled. "You know why you are here." I responded, "No, I do not." He asked if I would be willing to call my paternal grandfather and persuade him to have my aunts repatriated from the US for questioning. He suggested, "You could be released after we question them." I was to blindly accept this offer on behalf of the secret police? What more did they want? I was already confined. I had already been interrogated, tried and sentenced without the courtesy of a trial. I looked at them and asked, "Can I go back to my room?" With my fate sealed, I reluctantly confronted the mornings. Counting the days was useless, so I threw away the tea bag labels that I had initially used as markers.

From that point forward, silence ruled. In that interval, I existed in an impervious void, an empty, hermetically sealed vacuum. I was alone, in solitary confinement, for eight and one-half months. Once a week, I was presented with an attendance record book. I signed next to a name that once was mine. During those few seconds, I would scan the record searching frantically for familiar names. None matched my vague memories of those I had known in another life. From one week to another, I endured life to glance at a name that was once mine. With that glance, I confirmed that I was still alive.

And once a week when silence and darkness colluded at the day's first prayer call, a key turned, opening the door. The male guards would come in and search the room for I don't know what. This perverse routine stripped me, leaving me terrified and hollow. It always transpired after the dead of night had passed. It submerged me in pain and filled me with fear that lingered. For eight and one-half months, this weekly ritual was never to be missed. To survive, I had to lure myself into sleep. Coincidentally just as I was on the verge of drifting into sleep, the key would turn. It turned between consciousness and unconsciousness, between wakefulness and sleep, in that twilight between light and darkness. I named these incidents "terror crusades of darkness . . ."

The events of the fifth of June 1982 passed unremarked until much later when prison officials decided that it was harmless for prisoners to read the local news. Eighty days after that fateful June day, when I obtained the first newspapers in my incarceration, I found the front pages were anything but benign. There were photographs of Palestinian fighters being evacuated from Beirut; a home they loved to ruin, and which in turn loved them to death and exile. Also unsettling were the photographs of Palestinian fighters forced to leave their women, children and elders as they boarded ships to another exile. The headlines read, "The Israeli Army refuses to withdraw from Beirut to its pre-Lebanon invasion borders unless all Palestinian fighters are exiled from Lebanon." Swiftly, the Palestinian fighters were exiled from Lebanon as the Israelis withdrew slowly.

Darkness prevailed. Subsequently, I was momentarily stirred from my numb state to witness the slaughter at Sabra and Shatila. Death was acquitted. I wept for myself, for the last Palestinian who witnessed the killing, for the last fighter and for Lebanon. I wept for the slaughtered.

## Prison memoir II

Confined, helpless and numb, I witnessed Beirut under the Israeli siege. Lebanese and Palestinians were blockaded for eighty days with Israeli military forces attacking them from air, land and sea. Beirut stood as the last hope for Arab dignity. The whole world watched, including the Arab world, while Beirut was burned in the name of border security. I watched from prison as Lebanese and Palestinians stood up for what remained of us, what remained of Arab dignity. After eighty days, a decision was reached. The Palestinian fighters were deported to Cyprus under UN care. Protection was guaranteed for the safety and security of women, children and the elderly Palestinian population who remained behind.

Then the whole world slept while the Lebanese Phalange (Christian) militia entered Sabra and Shatila under the protection of the Israeli Army. There they slaughtered Palestinian children, women and old men. The Israeli Army denied responsibility despite their barricade of the two camps while the Phalange raped and killed hundreds of Palestinians. They did so under the pretence of eliminating terrorists in the making.

Why does the world lose its voice when it comes to Palestine and

Palestinians? This was the Arabs' final *Nakba* (catastrophe) and *Inkisar* (breakdown) – the dream of a dignified, united Arab nation had been utterly shattered.

For me, the world went dark. The slaughter and deportation of countless Arab minds and souls had been in process for some time. Noble ideas and dreams were abandoned. While I languished in a Saudi prison, a nation and the dreams of many generations ended in helplessness and hopelessness. Hopes and dreams of a better future were aborted while the whole world watched.

What is to become of the Arab nation? What is to become of Arab women and men? What is to become of a humanity that stood by as Beirut was violated in the light of day, its tribes mute and deaf? For all of us to remember and sing, Mahmoud Darwish wrote "Beirut":

> *Beirut Tufaha, wa al qalb la yadhak'*
> *Wa hesaruna waha fi alamin yahlek*
> *Sa nurages el saha wa nozawig al lailak*
>
> Beirut, an apple
> And the heart does not rejoice
> Our siege is an open oasis in a dying world
> We will dance the square
> And we will marry the lilac

In the grand scheme of life events, my incarceration in that small prison room from 5 June 1982 to 4 July 1983 was insignificant compared to the burning siege of Beirut. For the many who have suffered longer and more brutal prison terms and conditions, my experience would appear like a beautiful day's stroll around the Eastern Province's sandy beach.

At age twenty-two, those 13 months proved a turning point in my life. It is where I began life fully conscious, where I met myself unedited for the first time, with no internal or external boundaries except that of imprisonment. Then, what I was to learn and what I was to become were totally unexplored territory.

Although I fought fiercely to remain true to my code of ethics, I learned to behave both as prisoner and simultaneously as the prison guard. I learned how to blackmail. Further, I learned to use that split second in which I could steal a look at another woman prisoner. By learning something about them and their appearance, I might be able to match them with the names I saw once a week when signing the prison register.

I successfully bribed one of the four women guards with my first-ever gold necklace and locket. It was a gift from my maternal grandparents, Immy Fatema and Abwie Hajj Ibrahim. I was emboldened by that success.

Initially, I thought that I could blackmail and emotionally manipulate all four women guards. Soon, I was to discover that I could not buy the influence of all of them. Each of the four worked a one-week per month rotation. Thus, I studied them intently, observing their quite different personalities and circumstances.

Um Ali was a no-nonsense woman who genuinely believed that she was performing a great service to her country. She was truly loyal to her job and fiercely clear about her duty toward protecting the country and the government from people like me. Um Ali is a widow with only one son who had joined the National Guard. I perfectly understood why she, although tender and kind hearted, disapproved of, and at times, despised all prisoners. She was a slender woman with a face adorned with traces of the desert's sand dunes. In it, I saw Bedouin tents and a life of nomadic travels. The lines in her face are the signature stamp, the tribal trademark of her desert legacy.

During one of her rotations, I turned my face directly into the sun after four and one half months of deprivation. Months after the door was first locked behind me, I was permitted to leave the room for the first time. On that glorious winter day, I went to the only place a woman political prisoner was allowed to go: the rooftop. Um Ali took me there where I wept as my face stared back at me from an abandoned, filthy mirror in the washroom. I wept on seeing a shadow of the former me staring back through the abandoned mirror.

At that time, I did not understand why I had been allowed such a privilege after such a lengthy isolation and I did not choose to ask. I had resolved that I would ask nothing. Little did I know then that the requests of the other women prisoners had secured the privileges and the basic needs such as the daily local newspapers, radios, the television set and then fresh air and sunlight that we enjoyed.

On that day, I looked at myself and wondered if I was dead. My skin was as yellow as myrrh and a distinguishing mark of grey hair at the front of my hairline greeted me. I searched for my soul!

During one of those weekly outings to the sun, Um Ali casually confessed that we had met before. I had no recollection of any such encounter. She indicated that she was the woman guard who had accompanied me when I was interrogated. I was shaken to realise that I had been so distressed that I could not recall the lone woman who escorted me to the interrogation. In the entire world, she was the only witness who could verify and testify to my interrogation in the middle of the night.

Then Um Ali told me about Wedad, the beautiful Palestinian woman who was kept in the master room. She had to share it with the women guards, as it was their workstation. The room was isolated from the other main floor rooms that hosted us, the other four women prisoners. Wedad's room had its own en suite and she was the only one isolated from all communication with the rest of us.

Of course I knew Wedad; however, I did not show any interest in her story. I made it a rule not to offer unsolicited information. I knew of Wedad's reputation, although I had never had an intellectual or political conversation with her. The few times I had met her had been in Riyadh or Dhahran. On those occasions, I was still viewed as a novice, someone perhaps not yet capable of conversing with someone of Wedad's intellect.

Um Ali spoke about Wedad with respect and compassion, as I would have expected. Among us, Wedad was revered as a Palestinian woman freedom fighter who had put her life on the line for the Palestinian cause repeatedly. I was not surprised that Wedad had captivated Um Ali and merited her respect and that of the other women. I imagined how Wedad spoke respectfully to the women guards reinforcing their own self worth. I was confident that she expressed her appreciation for whatever they did for her.

Wedad was sick, according to Um Ali. I did not know what kind of treatment she was offered. I did not ask, as I was not supposed to know Wedad's identity. At times, the instinctual selfish protection of oneself carried a high price tag. I appreciated Um Ali for the comfort her updates brought me.

The guards Sharifah and Um Abdallah were of the "take pity on me" character. With ease, they became victims of my blackmail and emotional manipulation. Eventually, I summoned all the courage I could muster and used them to transmit brief notes to Wedad. Through them, I let her know how much I respected and admired her courage. Also, I transmitted my sorrow that I could not communicate more openly and support her more.

While Sharifah and Um Abdallah had endured their share of hardships, they – unlike Um Ali and Khaltie Mabrookah who worked loyally – sought petty rewards. Sharifah and Um Abdallah were willing to use and be used. To Um Abdallah, I gave my gold necklace in exchange for writing to Wedad. For me, it was worth every word that reached Wedad's hands and found their way to her soul.

The women guards' rotation pattern varied among us five women prisoners. Whether they did it out of pity for us or on instruction was unclear. Sharifah, while smoking a cigarette after dinner one evening, abandoned caution to question me recklessly: *Were we imprisoned because of our involvement in a major drug smuggling scheme?*

Stunned, I simply did not know where to begin. My response was trapped between my brain and my throat. I could not think beyond how to take my next puff of smoke. Futilely, I watched the cigarette I had wasted on Sharifah go up in smoke. Numbly, I searched within myself for a non-response or a question to divert her. The shattering realisation of how we were portrayed forced me to question the purpose for which I had put my life on the line. How was it possible to be labelled as a drug smuggler, rather than a freedom fighter?

Each of the four women guards had a distinctive story. Each had accepted her place in society and her fate in life. I suspected that none of them had ever questioned authority. I suspected that none had found her voice. Perhaps they never discovered that they had the right to choose. Of course, they simply might have made a conscious choice to live in the shadows. In my now distant memory, I recall the many beautiful women's faces and voices that marched before me.

Of the four, my favourite was Khaltie Mabrookah. At age 60, she was of African origin and had a smile that reminded me of that of my maternal grandmother Fatema. Daily, she exhibited contentment and a smile and eyes that spoke of compassion. In addition to the physical resemblance between Khaltie Mabrookah and Fatema, they shared a similar vibrant spirit. In Khaltie Mabrookah, I felt Fatema's presence and saw her smile. I felt that she was blessed.

As a child, Khaltie Mabrookah had accompanied her parents to Saudi Arabia as slaves. They belonged to a Jeddah-based merchant family. Khaltie Mabrookah was a free slave, as she proudly repeatedly reminded me. Each time that she boasted of this status, I would smile, as it made no sense given the contradiction inherent in "free slave".

Unperturbed, she would dismiss me and continue with her story. Her eyes beamed as she spoke of her only son who is now happily married. She would add, "Unlike us, he chose an independent life away from the family." Khaltie Mabrookah chose to stay with the merchant family as the senior nanny of their youngest daughter. With her husband, who worked with the merchant in the market place, she shared a room in the servants' quarter at the merchant's house.

When the young daughter came of age, married and moved to Riyadh with her husband, Khaltie Mabrookah shifted from Jeddah to Riyadh to be with her. With the move, her role changed. While she continued as the designated senior nanny to the girl's children, in reality she was the supervisor of younger caregivers. Khaltie Mabrookah smiled as she talked about the educated young Filipina nannies and the English language they spoke, a skill that she did not possess. She realised that she was being guided gently into involuntary retirement.

Given the marginalisation that she must have felt after a lifetime of service to that family, perhaps taking a week off to guard complete strangers served as a welcome break. Quite selfishly, I longed for Khaltie Mabrookah's compassion in this place where I chose not to mention my own family. Indeed, I had chosen not to ask for the right of family visitations or indeed the right to anything. Rather, I chose passivity and numbness. I accepted the consequences of a path I had chosen at age thirteen and a decision I had made at age nineteen.

Among the guards, Khaltie Mabrookah was perhaps the only one who understood what brought us to this place. Perhaps that is why

I was able to persuade her during the *Eid al Idha* celebration to open all of the doors to the women prisoners' rooms. She then allowed me out to the washroom for a few minutes. There, I stood at the door and had a glimpse of the other women. In the midst of despair, I performed a belly dance to bring a smile, a laugh, or a tear to the faces that peered from behind the barred room doors.

I felt sorry for all of the women guards. Nevertheless, I pursued my attempts to bribe them to defy the rules, defiance which could have resulted in their reprimand. At times their rigid, blind obedience to the rules provoked me to question whether they were ghostly apparitions of women or perhaps ghosts of the living dead. In retrospect, I believe my expectations of them were unrealistic.

As I observed the guards' behaviour, I realised that at age thirteen, I had begun to be aware of what it means to be a woman with a strong opinion. Then, I did not fully understand the impact and the consequences of having strong opinions. For example, I had an opinion about my father's decision to reject a job offer that would have brought him closer to home, closer to us. Not knowing him well, I wrote my first letter to him. In it, I told him how selfish I regarded his decision. He was not angry. My father responded to my assumptions with admiration to a daughter who hardly knew him; he admired my ability to express myself in writing to a man I hardly knew.

I kept my father's letter like my mother had kept all his letters to her. My allegiance, support, and commitment belonged to my mother, my sisters, to women. And as I became aware of my primary allegiances, I became aware of how critical I am of women. I believed that they all could and should have strong self-esteem and should aspire to be free without being clear myself of what it all meant.

Confined, I recalled how between the ages of thirteen and sixteen I read everything I could obtain including the newspapers that came wrapped around the freshly baked bread. Fortuitously for me, my paternal grandfather had an excellent, although narrowly focused library, with religious books, poetry and few novels. There, I read a series about the Prophet's wives. Afterwards, I was impatient to share what I had read at my great aunt's house where women gathered in the evening. Later, I realised that I was a source of some amusement to them.

Ironically, in that small prison – one of the most heavily censored environments in the world–a new, beautiful world of poetry, music and art was placed at my door. Prior to my imprisonment, I had regarded those realms as time wasters, as only red (Russian) and yellow (Chinese) hard-covered books with incomprehensible words were deemed worthy of the limited young mind of a sixteen-year-old girl. Here in my small prison room, I lived for Thursdays, as the newspaper culture and arts supplements arrived that day.

Strictly confined, I had the world's literature, music and art at the tips of my fingers. I was introduced to new poets and discovered old ones. I learned about classical music and was introduced to painters and sculptors from both East and West. In my confinement, literature, art and music proved agreeable companions.

Through those supplements, I discovered the poets Fawzia Abu Khaled and Muhammed Jabr al-Harbi. Prior to prison, I had read only carefully selected material and I was not familiar with the wider literary scene in my own country. In truth, I read only politicised literature that was pre-approved as aligned with the Party's philosophy and leadership. Al Harbi's poem *"Nakhlah lil Reeh"* [Palm Tree for the Wind] was a godsend, a salvation to my heart and my spirit. I was selfish in that I ripped out the page and kept it before passing on the newspaper supplement to the next prisoner. Repeatedly, I read it until I had memorised it word for word. Then, I could not anticipate that I would meet al-Harbi and that he and his wife would be among the few who witnessed a beautiful experience and a 1984–85 milestone in my life.

This is my translation:

> Palm Tree for the Wind
>
> Let's agree
> the beginning is difficult
> the ending is bitter- or sweet if we may
> the road is a pale cloud – if we wish – or an open sky
>
> Let's agree
> on the relationship between us
> to weep for history – or to weep because of history
> or to count our ships and sail
> into the wind – against the wind

We sail
from the boundaries of despair,
toward an ultimate horizon,
Despair that consumes us
away from our images – we sail
toward a new entity
to begin
free of boundaries or sky

Let's agree
On affairs
to love; to sing; to say; to repeat
to add to your years – an eternal smile
to friends
A palm tree – an offering to the wind
to dwell without a past that throbs on your forehead
to be my forehead
to fight as you wish – and to ally as you wish

Let's agree Sir
Let's agree
On the colour of this universe;
how? how could it be bleak?
as women are derived from its origin – a desired dawn
how? how could it be bleak?
and Birds an extension of women

Let's agree
that my dissimilar fingers
my life's seasons
don't set me apart –

My life is like yours
an instant
a candle
an insensible dance
a limitless forest
and the sun is singular
and water is water

Let's agree
on the fingers and the seasons

Let's agree
finding the answer is possible – if you are the first to wish
Sir
Let's differ – and concur
Beginning is hard
People are masquerades – and passages
And the key to the Truth exists between your hand
and twilight
Let's agree

"Palm tree for the Wind" filled my heart with a glow that defied my own despair time and time again. From that day, whenever despair appeared at the door of my heart I recited "Palm Tree for the Wind" with joy in my heart.

In solitary confinement, I read Fawzia Abu Khaled, never imagining that one day she would be one of the most inspirational lecturers of my life. She was one of the many brilliant professors who would teach me about Saudi society in the Department of Sociology at King Saud University in Riyadh. Through those weekly newspaper supplements, Fawzia Abu Khaled's poetry graced my life:

A Pearl
This Pearl
was a gift of my grandmother – that great lady –
to my mother
and my mother gave it me

And now I hand it on to you
The three of you and this pearl
Have one thing in common
simplicity and truth
I give it with my love
and with the fullness of heart
you excel in

> The girls of Arabia will soon grow
> to full stature
> They will look about and say:
> 'She has passed by this road'
> and point to the place of sunrise
> and the heart's direction.
>
> (Translation by Salma K. Jayyusi, from *Literature of Modern Arabia, an Anthology*, 1988)

The censored and strictly controlled newspapers not only nourished my mind and my soul, they became my salvation and a bridge that connected me with the other women prisoners. Thus, the newspapers were recycled intellectually and practically. The carbon used in newspaper advertisements became our ink. The newspaper margins became our writing pads. Our hairpins became our writing implements. One of the women prisoners, Ahlam, told us how to do this, and I thanked her as she put her knowledge and expertise in science together to show us once again that "necessity is the mother of invention".

Between Thursdays of the newspaper supplement cycle, I slept and woke to write and discuss the newspapers, the poor food quality and the incredibly bad religious books that were imposed on us. Each of us was given a copy of the Quran, and a few books of the Hadith and Sunna. I was convinced that anyone with the slightest knowledge of Islam and the Prophet Muhammed (pbuh) would be repelled by the material in those Hadith and Sunna books. They purported to reveal the Prophet's sexual practices with his wives. In disbelief, I read of the lack of respect shown to our Prophet. I was impatient to write to my next-door neighbours to learn their reactions. Many years later, I understood how those inaccurate, misguided religious books served an ideology that has no relation to the true essence of Islam.

Writing. This act of defiance to the strict isolation became my sanity. Before prison, I had little direct experience with variations in human spiritual strength. Some are strong and some are weak and what makes someone strong breaks another person. I had a conscious choice to avoid this test; rather than escape to Bahrain with my uncle, I chose to endure the prison experience in search of my essence, my spiritual strength. I was shocked and dismayed to learn that the other women prisoners regretted their chosen path of liberation.

I began to question my own reactions and my understanding of the truth. Did I know the truth or was I simply oblivious to the world around me? I had no regrets. For me, life is about the journey and not about regrets. I believe that we choose, even when we believe we have no choice. The selection of "no choice" is a choice in itself. Therefore, I decided that I should reflect, learn and become better acquainted with myself. In essence, I journeyed to learn my identity. I decided that I would take my chances and make the best out of what was before me.

I was the last of the five women prisoners to receive a copy of the Quran and the Hadith and Sunna books. I returned to reading the Quran with an open mind and heart. I practiced memorisation and recitation of the surahs and the verses that I have always enjoyed reading. Before receipt of the Quran and the other books of Hadith and Sunna, I had lulled myself to sleep with mental gymnastics. I counted from one to infinity or alternatively compiled lists of all the female or male names from A to Z to exhaust my brain and invite sleep.

From memory, I recalled fleeting images of book titles and authors that I had read since the age of eleven. They nourished me through the monotonous diet provided by my warders. The prison administrators hoped to rehabilitate me by giving me nothing but religious books. They lost the war upon my admission.

Arbitrarily, the religious books were chosen. There was no logic to what was written about the Prophet (pbuh) and his followers. Although I had no credentials as a religious scholar, I could immediately discredit the alleged prophet's sayings and practices as they contradicted the essence of the Quran and the way of Islam. In my solitude I wondered how the Muslim council keeps silent and why the Muslim world does not defend the Prophet (pbuh). I can only attribute the silence to the power of what is alleged to be the religious word.

I was far better served by the eight and one-half months of solitary confinement than the four and one-half months during which I shared a room with another prisoner. In my solitude, my voice developed its own tone and it grew stronger and more robust. There, I debated issues about women, freedom, politics, religion, life, love and principles.

In that solitude, I recognized that the choice of passivity and numbness was for the protection of my sanity. The senior prison guard could not understand why I was the only one among the other women prisoners who did not ask about or for anything and also why was I the only one who smoked. Later, I knew that he was not only offended by my smoking, but also puzzled by the fact that I never rose at dawn to pray. He was extremely confused not only that I didn't ask for my family, but I didn't ask about the direction of Mecca (Qiblah), nor did I ask for a copy of the Quran. Much later, I understood why he once asked if I was an orphan.

During the thirteen month confinement, I experienced little punishment or deprivation. I was first censured when the prison guards found my toothpaste and soap writing on the bathroom mirror; there, I wrote poetry and song lyrics to uplift the spirits of the other women prisoners. Therefore the prison administrators removed the mirror. Thus, I continued writing on the bathtub. The senior prison guard directed a junior officer to deliver a verbal warning to me.

The torture was not what I had anticipated; it was nothing in comparison to what I had read of the experiences endured by other political prisoners. Yet it was at times almost unbearable even though it was mostly limited to deprivation. Once family visits were granted, the core punishment was the total deprivation of time with them and any personal human contact. According to the degree of mischief I had committed, I was deprived of newspapers and/or of cigarettes. So I learned that every time my voice echoed in a request, I would be deprived of something, be it cigarettes, the newspapers, and not being allowed the outing on the roof.

One constant torture arrived in the darkness of night. It was an annoying pounding sound of a spice grinder (*hawan*) that would reverberate within the walls of my small prison room until the early hours of the morning. I was never certain of the sound's reality or if it was only inside my own head, a far more worrying possibility. When eventually I had the courage to ask the other women prisoners if they heard the same pounding sound, I learned that I was the only one who could hear it.

This routine annoyance continued to define the rhythm of my otherwise quiet prison nights. On numerous occasions, I considered reporting the pounding sound to the senior prison guard. As I doubted its reality, I continued to resist that option, as I would not offer them a golden opportunity to torture me more or accuse me of insanity. As I contemplated the pounding sound, I thought that someone was trying to drive me insane, to drive me to despair.

Although the fear of the torture techniques served largely to keep me safe in my passivity, I was driven to mischief by my curiosity on one occasion. On that day, I was particularly restless; endlessly, I had wondered about what was concealed behind the black plastic-covered windows. Overtaken by my curiosity, I peeked out hoping to recognise the street. Nothing was familiar the first time. On the second occasion, I caught a glimpse of children playing before the guards stopped me. With that discovery, I decided that someone who worked at the prison must occupy the building beyond my prison room. It is possible that all the villas around the prison were owned and occupied by the Ministry of Interior's secret service employees.

There in that small prison room, I experienced for the first and last time in my life what it feels like to kneel and beg another human being, to kneel for other than Allah. I kneeled and begged the senior prison guard when my pen and ink were confiscated. I kneeled and begged only to discover that no one has the power to confiscate my voice. That was when I discovered the beauty and power of owning one's own voice – not a mimic, an echo or a shadow of a voice. Kneeling, I found my own voice.

Kneeling, I thought of the songs we sang for all the liberation fronts around the world and for Palestine, Bahrain, Oman and the Arabian Peninsula. Yet we never sang for ourselves. We never sang for women. We never gave our voices a voice. Women as freedom fighters took only what men allowed them to take. I asked myself for the first time what it means to be a woman freedom fighter and what role women play in liberation movements. Although I was detained in the name of politics, it was not about politics. I began to question the status quo, i.e., patriarchy.

While in solitary confinement, we prisoners staged a hunger strike. Mysteriously, the long strips of newspaper margins found their way again into the hems and folds of my dresses and nightgowns when they were returned from the drying line. On those strips were the instructions for the strike. I was instructed not to accept food until all demands were met. The simple demands were to allow family visitations, to house two prisoners together and to allow us to share a group meal once a month during Ramadhan and the Eid holidays. On one of the notes, I was told of the extra supply of biscuits left for me in the bathroom. The other women prisoners thought I was too thin to hold up during the strike and they did not wish for any of us to collapse. Soon after my release, I learned from a dear friend that members of the US Central Intelligence Agency in Dhahran were involved in monitoring our hunger strike. He had been casually informed of the women political prisoners' strike by his friend at the Embassy, maybe to check if any news was leaked. My friend enquired if it was true that we went on hunger strike.

Shortly after they moved me into a shared room, I realised the catastrophic potential of co-habitation. For four and one-half months, I was to share with Kawthar the en suite room formerly occupied by Wedad. I remembered Kawthar as confident and strong. In prison, I met a broken woman, a mere shadow of that person. In her voice, I heard anger, resentment and contempt. In contrast to her, I was a phoenix. I would not crash and burn as she did. Rather, when pushed to near breaking point, I would pull myself up and rise to face any adversity. Consciously or unconsciously, she played a passive aggressive game of "voice and silence", choosing when to talk to me. When I disagreed with her, she shut me out.

Locked in with Kawthar, I learned what it means to live with depression. I had no way out, no escape exit. I was confined in that small room with a manic-depressive. I would not ask to be returned to solitary confinement, as I had promised myself to show no weakness, no desires and to have no requests. I judged that the core punishment was the deprivation of any contact with my family and any other normal human begin.

Incarceration with a mentally ill person goes well beyond "core punishment". Solitary confinement was a walk in the park by comparison. As if locking me up was inadequate punishment, I was further penalised by Kawthar's unremitting depression and I simply did not know how to cope with it. I did not realise then that life was testing me, preparing me for what I would one day confront at my front door. For four and one-half months, I slept and woke to the smells, tastes and sounds of depression.

In that singular space, I was forced to endure the imposition of a woman's manic depression. My eyes remained wide open until I heard the sound of her soft snoring. Only then would I drift into sleep. Fearing the unknown retaliatory nature of manic depression, I slept fitfully, waking regularly to ensure that she was still asleep and I was still alive. Inside the prison room, everything functioned according to the severity of her depression. My prison companion determined whether and when we would listen to the radio, who would read which newspapers first and the menu for our dinners.

Apart from my companion, I was actually content in my own confinement. I was neither angry nor resentful. I was frustrated and unhappy, but I had accepted the consequences of my political activity. Everyone who walks the path of political opposition knows sooner or later that a price has to be paid. I was definitely not dancing and singing, but I had perfected a routine to protect my sanity that worked, so far.

However with her arrival, I had to navigate cautiously around my thoughts and my responses. When she launched into her list of resentful and angry remarks, I was never sure of an appropriate response, one that would not further fuel her fury.

Quickly I realised that I was not allowed my voice, my opinions. As she perceived that she was a victim, she viewed me as her adversary. She blamed the leaders of the movement and scorned those who were abroad and therefore not imprisoned. At age sixteen, I had accepted the consequences for my choices and actions. I understood the risks. It did not make sense now that someone nine years my senior was blaming others for her own choices. It was a relief to me that at a young age I had accepted responsibility for my choice.

In disbelief, I listened as she charted her transformation into a faithful believer in Allah and observed her reading the Quran. I wondered why some only seek Allah when they are in need and fail to love him and have faith when life is placid. I wanted to find Allah through love, not through despair. I reasoned that if she read the Quran perhaps she would come to accept her responsibility in what happened to her. As true believers, we are required to do so.

In those months, I had to practise self-censorship of all my thoughts and feelings. I could neither speak of the political experiences nor discuss the books, philosophies, ideas and beliefs that shaped us and led us to share that cell. How could it be possible to ask someone to erase eight years of one's life, to deny that experience?

Then, I felt that I was imprisoned in every sense of the word. It was then that the walls of my prison room were transformed into a tight cell. It was then that I had difficulty breathing; I suffered anxiety attacks brought on by my fear that an unguarded word would irritate and ignite the anger of my prison companion. Was this the last attempt by the prison administration to break my defences? They must have known of my companion's depression. I knew that without intervention, they would have been successful. My goddess smiled on me. I was fortunate.

Shortly after moving into that shared room, visitation privileges were granted. I hoped that family visits would improve my companion's outlook. To my disappointment, those privileges did not lessen the depressive episodes. Indeed, they became more intense and frequent. I feared to acknowledge her deteriorating condition and to point it out to her. Similarly, I was reluctant to report it to the prison administration fearing their reaction. In that room, I was with someone who endorsed the silence of the prison room. I was incarcerated with someone who while aware of my presence was totally unconscious of my existence in the space we shared.

Those bi-weekly family visits saved my sanity. Seeing my family strengthened my defences. Receiving poetry collections and samples of my mother's heavenly home-made food nourished my soul. It was the sustenance I needed to persevere. To them, I complained about the food and made references to the rigid security and strict rules around the prison villa. I dared not implicitly nor explicitly reference what I was experiencing with my prison companion for fear that my family might report it to the prison administration.

My father's visit was the most difficult encounter during my imprisonment. When news of the visitation rights reached him in the US, he returned to Saudi Arabia to see his daughter imprisoned. In that encounter, words were lost between us. Our last conversation in

March 1982 served as a harsh reminder of my mistrust of my father. At that time, he was on his annual visit to Saudi Arabia. That was immediately after my uncle Najeeb was arrested. I saw that question of mistrust on my father's face then. He did not have to mention it. At my uncle Hasan's house, my father looked me in the eye and asked if I feared for myself and if I was involved or could be implicated in any way. At that time, I said "No."

Now here we were across from each other under the guard's observant eyes. My father was graceful. There was no need for words. In that prison, he embraced me, holding me tight to his heart. I listened to his love for me through his warm chest and the music of his fatherly heartbeats. From that time and forever after, I had a father and a best friend.

As the anniversary of the first year in prison and the fasting month of Ramadhan approached, my companion's depressive episodes intensified. Then, silence was the only possible language. I swallowed my voice. Sleeping at night became more difficult as I still woke when she did. To her, it did not matter whether I slept well or not. She turned on the lights and woke me. I watched as my strength and resistance began to crumble. At a moment of acute despair, my companion attempted suicide by slitting her wrist while bathing.

Luckily or intentionally, she had left the en suite bathroom door unlocked. Perhaps she wanted me to save her. She took longer than usual so I called her from behind the door only to receive an echo of my own voice. There was no response to my call. I knocked at the door, and there was no response. I opened the door to find her unconscious on the floor with a trail of blood leading to her wrist.

I broke down and my tears gushed out as if it was my lifeblood flowing onto the floor. The shock and pain disoriented me, as it was a few days later I realised that I had been moved yet again to a different room away from the scene of the incident.

I recall tying something around her arm to stop the bleeding before rushing to the internal alarm bell. I leaned on it resting my hand there until the guards rushed in. They lifted her away from the blood and into the car, away from the prison, away from me. No one looked back or stayed behind. I was left behind alone where I spent many hours cleaning the floor and her nightgown of her blood.

I felt as if I was being punished for my strength. This strength of mine was becoming my curse. I did not deserve this. No one deserved this. I wept to expunge the blood and filth, to cleanse my memory and my soul. I wept as if my life was taken away from me. I wept as my world went even more silent. I wept for a long time and for a life yet to be lived.

My companion was brought back to my new room after a week and a few days of hospitalisation. We were not allowed back into our old room. Silence remained the only language we shared. I understood that I had no right to ask why she attempted suicide nor did I have the right to mention it to anyone. We remained solitary in our own worlds. There was no remorse, no apology. There was her right alone to force her experience on me.

I had decided to request a return to solitary confinement after the Eid holiday, which was approaching at the end of Ramadhan. I decided that I would take my chances, but I was not going to be consciously or unconsciously victimised. I had decided to defend my soul and protect it from being shattered. I was aware of how close I was edging toward the borders of sanity.

# *Reflection: Monologue 2*

On the 4<sup>th</sup> of July 1983, stripped of all powers and rights, I was driven to the familiar, tiled-floor building. There I signed off my right to speak out about what had happened during the past year and thirty days. It was a pre-requisite for release into a larger prison.

After the signing, I – along with my fellow inmates – met with a religious man. He lectured us on faith and the dangers of political activism. He reminded us of how lucky we were to be citizens of this country. He assured us that if we had been in any other country, we would have been dead; perhaps he was correct. It was an interesting exit from one prison to another. I wondered if this religious man and the many others I encountered in this odyssey really believed in what they said and did. Did they really believe in the concept of citizenship in a land where citizenship equals tribalism, in a land where the right to citizenship is bestowed by royalty? I believe they did.

Leaving the smaller prison for the larger one made little difference to me. I did not know what awaited me. I was a stranger re-entering the life of another, reclaiming her role, her space and most of all her memories. Then, I wondered what would become of us, my country and me. On that brief flight back home, no one cared to look at me. However I was looking, searching intently for something familiar around me. Scrupulously, I examined those about me and the world I was re-entering. It would take a decade to re-establish my identity.

Fighting to rescue my memories, I struggled to hold on to what had happened. For the moment, I stopped trying to make sense of *it. Then, I craved to understand how I had made my choices and, more importantly, why I had made those choices initially. I was not as afraid of what might become of me as I was terrified of finding that I had been chasing someone else's vision.*

*Intuitively, I knew that things would be lost between the smaller prison and the larger one. I felt different, hollow in my numbness. I feared exposure, more profound than any I had previously experienced. I left the small, solitary prison room behind more confused than when I walked into it.*

*I walked away empty, with no trophy and no scars. Was that what I had sought? A trophy? A scar? At least the other women prisoners left with something tangible. One left with a slash on her wrist as a reminder of her attempted suicide. I was left to wash her blood away, letting the water run over her nightgown and onto the tiled floor until her blood absorbed me. It was a nightmare I wanted to recount over and over in order that I would not forget the details, the smells, the tastes and the sounds.*

*I exited prison with memories that belonged to someone else. I wanted to remember how a woman decided to die with a witness to watch her journey through the experience. I wanted to remember what had brought me to that room at that moment. I needed to understand what had nurtured me to serve as a witness to another woman's attempted suicide.*

*A scar or a trophy? It did not really matter. At that moment, I knew exactly why I did not leave the country when I had the choice and the chance. I recognised that it was not just my belief in the political party and all that it represented, including its imperfections. I had been driven by my own stubbornness and pride – or naive belief – that I could change the world.*

*I did not understand then what I was seeking. Was it acknowledgment and recognition from the male members of my family? Did I simply want them to admit that my strength and courage equalled or excelled theirs? That they did not have the strength to make the hard choices I made? I made the choice that I was not going to run away. I chose politics at sixteen. I was not then ready to confront my inability to act on my beliefs. I did not understand then that freedom of choice is valid only when one takes responsibility for living with the consequences of one's choices.*

## Reflection: Monologue 2

*I had never questioned whether going to prison had really been my choice or simply an angry, ill considered, perhaps naive reaction. Perhaps it was all that and much more than memories can reclaim. Thus, I passed a year and thirty days in prison. I lost my job, a potential scholarship, Suhail's love and a possible lifetime partnership, but not my life. The voices, the vision of life yet to be lived and the knowledge of what I had seen and did not want to forget created a new strength in me. I exited the smaller prison to confront an unanticipated crossroad, waiting for my life to resume.*

# 6

# Transition: From Prison to Prison

On 4 July 1983 and accompanied onto the plane by a male relative, I boarded with the intelligence agency officer's voice still ringing in my head: *"Congratulations! You are released. You are lucky that you have been pardoned this soon. We are happy to see you go as you kept us worrying and guessing when you might burn the whole place down."* Foolish me! I did not know that I had the option of torching the prison. What a powerful afterthought! I felt defeated for some time to come.

With defeat, I chose to continue my passivity, as I found it a useful barrier. It served as a good defence mechanism while I tried to internalise what had happened. I needed to regain my balance, my own sense of being. I was drained and somewhat delusional from the events of the previous year. I was beyond defensiveness in responding to allegations that women who seek political affiliation are prostitutes. In the small minds of the prison personnel, prostitutes and drug smugglers were all the same. I had no energy for contempt and it did not matter at that point who had turned me in.

I did not merit a prison exit or welcome home celebration. I arrived home almost at midnight to silence. My mother, Khaltie Anisah and a few of my mother's best friends greeted me at the door. My paternal grandparents had moved to their new house during the time I was in prison. My mother continued to live with them while my paternal great-grandmother stayed behind living in the old traditional Arabic home. As I entered the house, the lights were dim. Motionless, my paternal grandmother sat in the middle of the room. As no sign of my uncle Najeeb's release had reached home yet, there were no signs of joy or relief. As I bent over to embrace her, she greeted me. I felt as if I was a distant relative, not a grandchild with an unmerited prison sentence on my back. I had to accept that celebrating my release would have to wait. It was the end of Ramadhan. I hardly slept; I was prison lagged.

News of my uncle's release reached home the following morning, but it was not until my uncle arrived late that evening that the mood of the house shifted. After his arrival, my paternal grandmother blessed my release and that was that.

I was grateful without knowing why or to whom I should be grateful. I urgently needed to allow my voice out, but something stood in the way. That something was beyond my control. Numbed, I could not feel my heart and my soul; thus, I continued to deny my feelings. I avoided that confrontation under the guise of needing to sort out my life.

Although I sensed my mother's pain and suffering, I never apologised to her for the pain I caused her. I felt that I did not need to justify my choices in life. It seemed unreasonable to apologise to her for serving her and my country. At the time, I directed my energies to cleansing body and soul of the smells, tastes and sounds of depression.

My world changed directions as Suhail's mother, Batool, moved to her new home closer to my paternal grandparents' house where my mother and I lived; nevertheless, it was more distant than we had ever been before. Although Suhail and I were no longer together, I had her love. Through her, I was always in love with him. I sought to nurture my love of Suhail through Batool and thereby bind myself to what we had known.

In the end, I had traded our love for politics. I traded our love for a noble cause, for freedom; that was my rationalisation. Much later, I realised and admitted that I traded Suhail because I did not have a voice with which to defend my heart. I did not have a voice to defend my freedom to choose the man I loved. Therefore, I avoided Suhail and everything to do with him, except Batool. He moved on to other relationships.

When I exited the prison room of that residential villa at age 23, I re-entered the larger prison of life within the Kingdom. That day, Suhail had an engagement ring in his hand. However, it was not intended for me; his engagement ring was for a relative.

Suhail had moved on while I was in jail. He followed his heart with another woman. She was ready and willing to make a commitment to him without any obligation to a political agenda.

In the transitional period between the smaller and the larger prisons, I withdrew into my inner secluded world. I avoided Suhail's love. I convinced myself that he had moved on in his new relationship, an engagement with a wedding planned in the near future. I convinced myself that our relationship was over and that I should get on with life without him.

We lost track of one another. Did I love Suhail because of Batool or love Batool because of Suhail? There was everything between us to give strength to our relationship; however, we would never be lovers or have a life together. Our love survived, sustained by a code of unspoken boundaries that instinctively enabled us to keep our distance from one another. I required a further fifteen years to learn the truth. It is a truth that yields no comfort, except the knowledge that comes with the truth. Now, our lives have moved too far apart to ever have any chance to be together again.

Disoriented, my world was still spinning. I needed to get my life back on track. I was emotionally battered. While I felt defeated, I was not completely broken. For me, looking back and trying to work things out with him was not an option.

I needed to look forward, to reconstruct my life, to regain my sense of reality. I had no passport and was on the political activists' blacklist. I was certain that I had lost Suhail forever. I felt that I had been deceived, trapped and sacrificed. I had to make the best of it; I had no choice except to summon all my strength and endure.

On being released, I was still a political prisoner. The thought of being in love was the last thing on my mind. I was relearning my own truths. I was learning in the only way a woman like me could learn, by taking risks and making sacrifices.

Confused and drained, I had no energy to challenge the status quo when my uncle Najeeb started bringing home X-rated and pornographic movies. When I questioned his choice of these movies, I initially accepted his justification. When I refused to watch them, he accused me of being a backward thinker. I was still able to see my uncle as a liberal, political activist apart from his desire to watch porn movies.

A profound and alarming event then occurred that ruptured my trust in him irrevocably. My confidence and comfort in being with him alone in the same place evaporated. One evening, he initiated a discussion that at the time I took as his way of provoking a re-examination of the boundaries of debate. He said, "Women should first have sex with someone they know well." I took the statement as an implicit examination of the possibility that I had experienced sex with someone I knew well. Later that evening, he came to my room and offered me a back massage, which I declined. I was overwhelmed with an uncomfortable feeling at the way he made the offer and about other observations of his recent behaviour.

This incident marked the beginning of the end to a relationship that had been founded on respect for political ideals. In the end, I realised that the respect, which had blurred my judgement, had been misplaced. Unconsciously and slowly, I distanced myself from him. I permitted only the bare minimum of encounters, those that I could not avoid. I was still incapable of articulating my feelings and failed to see beyond the impressions of what I had noticed and experienced.

My sisters and my aunts were away and my intimate women friendships were in the formative stage. I did not know to whom I could turn for help with making sense of these confusing observations.

My life was changing rapidly. I had acquired a different awareness of life, of people and relationships. I began to examine and re-examine all the relationships in which I was engaged. I realised that for the last seven years most of my relationships had been bound by and linked to my political affiliation. For the first time, I questioned what I valued about my family, friends and acquaintances and why I wanted to sustain a relationship with each. I had very few non-political male friendships; they continued to diminish as my female friendships evolved and flourished.

As most of my female friendships were of family or political connections, it was not possible to distance myself from them; they existed within the context of my everyday reality. I perceived that I was engaged in various complex relationships, including that with Kawthar, my prison companion. While I desired to disengage from her completely, my mother insisted that I sustain a minimally courteous relationship. In our community it was not going to be easy to break away from Kawthar especially when the assumption was that we would be inseparable after sharing an experience. Separation was imminent. Our relationship or what remained of it was fading away. I remained courteous.

In order to go forward, I had to look back at my life in relation to others. I also had to acknowledge that I had changed. My sisters were far away and we could not know the length of our separation. They were my sisters and had been my friends. I hoped that at this age and after this experience our friendship would grow into a unique bond of wanting to be together, rather than of being obliged to be together.

In sifting through those relationships, I realised that life takes its own course. In my case, some of my former friendships evolved and some faded away. What do relationships mean? I had never before examined what they meant to me. Now I sifted everything in my life through a new filter and examined everything minutely. My female friendships seemed to suffer fewer casualties than those with males. Is this unique to women? Is it a feature of my culture? Perhaps it is related to age? I am unsure.

Between my 1983 release from prison and 1989 my life was suspended along the coastal strip between the Arabian Gulf and the desert. In that borderland between my past and my future, I wrestled with my demons while shielding myself from my pain. I armoured myself behind a hard shell of anger and bitter resentment toward everything masculine. I could not and did not want to conceal my bitterness. At that point of my life, it did not matter. I was inflamed with resentment and anger. The inflammation was exacerbated by the knowledge that I did not know why I was angry or at what, i.e., I was unable to articulate the cause of my rage.

In a quest for understanding, I retraced my steps and returned to reading. I asked friends and acquaintances for replacement copies of books as most had been destroyed. I had a voracious need to re-read, in order to confirm my beliefs. My quest was for validation that I did indeed understand the "Big Picture". I now had a better understanding of political activism.

Quite by chance, I stumbled on Nikos Kazantzakis' classic story, *Zorba the Greek*. I parted with Zorba with great reluctance. As I approached the end, I mourned his ecstasy and his spontaneous will to live. On finishing the novel, I cried. My reading spanned the classics, non-fiction, fiction and all that came into my hands.

In mourning Zorba, I also mourned the reality of the politics in which I had believed. In those bitter years, my heart was filled with sorrow, as this was also the time of my parting with Suhail who moved on with his new life. Had I covetously wished for him to wait for me with no hope of being with me and with no commitment from me? Perhaps I had wished that he would take the risk and wait. The reality is that I was inaccessible and he did not wait.

What options do women have as they exit prison? I was unemployed and with no real sense of future direction. Returning to school was the only available option for me. I had been fired from Aramco, never to be re-employed again. My very wise mother insisted that I pursue my degree, the only way forward in her view.

As I reconciled with this decision, I was suddenly overwhelmed by a compelling desire to cook and to be in the company of women while preparing meals. Until then, my cooking experience had been limited to a few simple cake recipes and the preparation of eggs, salads and two traditional dishes: *elgaymatt* (a traditional Ramadhan dumpling served with date molasses) and *sagoo* (a sweet starchy dish made of tapioca pearls).

Now, I found myself yearning for the warmth of women gathered around my mother's kitchen. I implored my mother, a renowned cook within our small community of family and friends, to teach me to cook our traditional dishes. At age twenty-three, I could not perfectly steam white rice, the most basic culinary trick.

This discovery, my love of cooking and of feeding people, proved a therapeutic miracle. Many years later, I realised that it was a major component of my healing. Through food, I found a comfortable, enjoyable way to be with people. Food and cooking were therapeutic for my soul and body. I was stunned by the strength of my desire to become a lady of the kitchen, a chore I had until then shunned.

My mother's first reaction was dismissive. She questioned my intent asking, "Are you serious or you are just going to waste my time?" I assured her that I was keen to learn to cook that I was very serious.

My mother explained, "I do not do measuring cups. If you wish to learn how to cook, you have to spend time with me in the kitchen and observe. I will have you do things. That is the only way you are going to learn." By observing her, I learned how to cook. She used a stirring spoon to measure the water needed for cooking the rice. Arbitrarily, she scooped flour and mixed it with water to make the bread dough. She made traditional desserts using her eyes to measure quantities of flour, sugar and oil.

On entering the culinary world with my mother and her friends, I discovered a passion for cooking and for feeding people. In particular, I had a passion for making dough, pastries and desserts. In the company of women, the act of creation was healing and therapeutic in that kitchen. I was surprised and delighted with my own self discovery.

The kitchen became a sacred place for the restoration of my sanity. Indeed, there is a sacred quality to cooking centred on the act of creation for others. I began to understand the purpose of the kitchen and the benefits of women gathering around my mother while she was cooking. Much of our time with friends and loved ones is savoured as we cook or eat. Very importantly, many difficult topics are discussed and problems resolved around food and in the kitchen. Cooking has remained an integral part of my healing journey.

## University

Perhaps in those kitchen hours with my mother and her friends I saw the wisdom of pursuing further education. Thus with the blessing of my mother, I relocated to Riyadh; there, I enrolled in the sociology department at King Saud University at the end of 1983. As I feared that I might have been blacklisted, I was delighted to gain entrance.

I continued to sense that I was being monitored, that I was still being kept in check. My friendships, my choices, my experience of being a Shia woman amidst the Sunni majority made my university experience most interesting (only about 10% to 15% of Saudis are Muslim Shia). I felt that I was maturing, coming into my own. Gradually, I was evolving into a woman with my say in how to shape my life. In that environment, my sense of shaping and reshaping a mind of my own was possible. Among intelligent, educated women, we created many voices and beautiful bonds.

The currents of life propelled me forward. Seif, a well-known journalist, who was involved alongside me in political activities, captured my heart. He was a member of a well-known tribe and of the mainstream Muslim Sunni population. As a Muslim Shia, I was in the minority with no tribal lineage. In prison, I had learned that radical politics is the only one way to advance change. I had gained a new perspective on how to remain mentally and politically active. I believed fervently then and now that change is inevitable.

Nevertheless, I knew that our relationship would be problematic for both families. I dismissed it, as I was in love. Perhaps I imagined that our love would overcome the challenges of a complicated relationship and social reality. I was so naive in my love that I thought that with a progressive intellectual man I could defy the tribal mindset.

Seif sought to return to journalism after his release from prison. At the time of his arrest, he was the youngest chief editor of one of the major daily newspapers in Saudi Arabia. We served our prison terms concurrently, although certainly we were not incarcerated in the same facilities. We were both imprisoned for our affiliation with the Arab Socialist Action Party. We did not know each other that well despite having met intermittently. Our social and political paths had never connected. He was something of a celebrity, a rising star and the gifted child of the political movement. I was a young woman, a marginalised member within the larger political groups; largely, I remained unnoticed.

I met Seif during the university registration week. In early 1984, we began seeing each other at my uncle Adnan's house where I then lived. Soon afterwards, my father returned from the US for his new Riyadh-based job. Thenceforward, we primarily met at our Riyadh home with parental knowledge and permission. We shared our friends, more precisely, Seif's circle of friends.

I visited his family home on only one occasion; I entered under the guise of being his sister's friend. Seif's mother – whom I met only on that one occasion – never knew that I was a Shia or that I was in love with her son. Although Seif knew my world in its most intimate details, I only entered his world once. I was prepared to enter a world where as a Muslim Shia I might be rejected. At that time and place, both Sunnis and Shias accepted the marriage of their men to Christian women, yet they obstinately opposed mixed Sunni and Shia marriages. These double standards fascinate me.

By the time we met in Riyadh he was making good progress in regaining recognition as the fine journalist he was. Through Seif, I was introduced to new circles of his friends and acquaintances, poets and novelists. To my delight, the first poet I met was Muhammed Jabr al-Harbi whose "Palm Tree for the Wind" had lifted my spirit during my incarceration. Beyond my immediate family, he was the first person from Seif's circle to witness our relationship. Muhammed and his fiancée welcomed me into their life. I continued learning about the literary scene in Riyadh meetings and became acquainted with many creative artists of my country.

My relationship with Seif was filled with debates about our political experiences, their impact on us and the way forward for our future and us. Seif and I shared a love for reading and listening to classical music. We exchanged books and savoured our time together listening to symphonies and watching videos of famous ballet companies. We both found that being free of political allegiances was what we then needed to heal and to grow into our own.

I never doubted Seif's love. We were disciplined, as I needed to focus on my study. When we talked about a further commitment, we decided we would have to wait until I graduated from university.

In my relationship with Seif, I confronted the hypocrisy and double standards that govern the attitudes of Saudi's liberal intellectual elite toward relationships between women and men. My uncle Najeeb, the self-proclaimed leading intellectual of the dissolved political party, openly advised me not to have sex out of wedlock. He explained that, irrespective of Seif's love for me and my trust in him, having sex out of wedlock would destroy me as a woman.

I did not respond to his advice. Astounded, I did not know how to respond. In the presence of my uncle with his silent lover who sat intimately holding onto his arm, I was mute. She appeared immune to a judgement that was as much about her as about every other woman. I longed to know what went through her mind. Did she really not question my uncle's statement? I was appalled, disgusted. I swallowed my words.

This was a powerful new learning experience. On that occasion, there was no possibility of claiming that the remark was a joke, or a test of my ability to take a joke. I knew that my uncle was not joking and I knew that I was on the road to a new discovery: the hypocrisy of the liberal intellectual! No matter how liberal and radical men appeared, they played the roles simultaneously of the protectors and the violators of women's rights. I saw that they would always determine what is best for women.

After a year and nine months, Seif ended our relationship abruptly. That September of 1985 I was in my second year of university. I informed my father of Seif's request to speak to him openly about our relationship; a month later, Seif walked out of my life. With no explanation and no rationalisation, Seif brought the relationship to a close with a four-page letter handed to me by his sister. The relationship ended with a few polite words of appreciation – *Thanks for the memories* – and a vague promise to meet some day. I made one futile attempt to telephone him for his true reasons. Seif refused my call and thus ended the relationship. The consequences for him were negligible.

His letter was vague and illogical. I had no part in the terminal decision. In that culture as in many others, woman has no say when being abandoned or exchanged. I did not fight or resist the end. I judged that if I had ended the relationship, Seif would have demanded my reason for his rejection. Men have the exclusive right to demand. My open, liberal, progressive views were of no import. The fact that my relationship with Seif was within the protection of my family was of no import. Unilaterally, he determined the outcome of the relationship.

I had faith in the woman I had become. I was determined not to allow a man to drive me to a breaking point. Prison did not break me and I was not going to have a man, no matter how much I loved him, break me. I was worth much more than a four-page letter. I was worth too much to break down for a man who walked out of my life without a reason. At that time, I knew what I could and could not handle. I believed in fate and I found comfort in the fact that Seif, like Suhail, was never meant to be. My belief in fate ensured sanity for my rational mind.

I had one option and that was to deal with my reality. I had a university degree to finish, exams to attend. I had to regain my ability to concentrate on my lessons and my books. I was alarmed upon receiving a "C" in my introduction to psychology midterm exam.

It motivated me to seek professional help. I sought my former boss, my old medical friend in Aramco, Dr Khairi. I knew that I needed assistance. I called him and briefly explained my symptoms and the cause. At the end of the call, we made an appointment.

In that October 1985 appointment at the Dhahran Health Centre psychiatric clinic, I did not need to go into much detail. I summed up why I needed help. Dr Khairi handed me a small bottle and instructed me to take one tablet, once a day. There were thirty tablets in the bottle. Dr Khairi asked me to look at him. He said he did not think I would need to finish the medication.

Besides members of my family, Dr Khairi was the only witness to my political arrest, as he had to grant clinic access to the Saudi intelligence police to search my workstation. From his office window, Dr Khairi had watched me as I got out and back into the police car. Dr Khairi told me that as he watched me being escorted by the four men he had faith that prison would not break me. He continued, "If prison did not break you, a man leaving you will not."

Battered and exhausted by grief, I went home to my sister Saffiya who resided in Aramco's Dhahran senior camp. My mother could not conceal her relief at the conclusion of the relationship. In our small Shia community, this meant that the family would not have to justify my marriage to a Sunni. My mother would not have to battle the criticism of a mixed Shia Sunni marriage and would not despair because of my decision, one supported by my father. I still remember the pain of a broken heart and the stream of tears burning my face.

I entered Saffiya's house where she and my mother were waiting for me. As I saw my mother, I felt a lump in my throat and I felt the pain. I looked to her for comfort, seeking refuge. My mother was the only one who knew how to touch my pain. I knew also that she was afraid in doing so that she would inflame her own still open wound.

All I needed was to cry on my mother's shoulder. I did not. I could not. I now understood the meaning of my mother's words – *"It felt as if I were being burned alive"* – in the aftermath of my father's abandonment. She too had experienced abandonment and rejection, accompanied by pain. She was the only one capable of soothing my pain.

That evening my eighteen-month-old nephew touched my heart as he wiped away my tears. With the few words he could utter, "*Ah-wa-wa* [ouch!] Khala Muna," he made the pain even more intense. I was intensely grateful at that moment for the presence of Allah in the grace of a child. My nephews were natural healing charms throughout the process. I refocused all my energy on them, other relationships and my education. I returned to Riyadh more determined to resist heartbreak. I knew that somehow I would see myself through the pain.

While I had felt on the verge of a breakdown, I forbade my heart from breaking or shattering. I had been defeated in my unrealistic expectations and hopes that people would fight for and embrace change. My liberal ideas came face to face with the reality of our slowly changing society. I struggled to revise my unrealistic expectations and to accept the difficulty of change for some people. Intuitively, I sensed that my being a Shia might have had something to do with Seif's decision to leave me. I loved him and therefore I did not deny him the right to choose what was best for him, but that was far easier said than done. My heart hardened; slowly, it shut out any possibility of love or the prospect of a relationship.

In reflecting on my relationship with Seif, I wondered why he had never tried to make love to me, or even to persuade me to explore that aspect of our relationship. Unilaterally, he drew the line and rationalised that it was better for us as neither had passports; therefore, we could not leave the country in case of an emergency. I did not accept his argument. I felt I was ready to explore that aspect of the relationship. I never pushed it further and Seif was too careful and too determined not to allow it. After his exit, I speculated that he did not want to make love to me because he knew our relationship was temporary or that he did not want to risk marrying me out of obligation.

I recognised my emotional fragility and endlessly struggled to hide it. I ferociously concealed my devastation and my disappointment as I lost confidence in progressive, liberal men. I believed that I would lose control if I revealed my emotional fragility. I locked away my heart and my emotions. I burned from the rawness beneath my skin. In the face of so much pain, I was inaccessible.

In my pain, I realised that there was one person I did not have the courage to face: Suhail. With this experience of rejection, I realised what he must have felt when I walked out of his life. Clearly, I could not open my wounded heart to him. I dared not ask. It helped that he was married and living abroad.

At first hand, I came to understand how other women and men dealt with failed relationships, how they managed to move on to the next one. I admired the ease with which others seemed able to dismiss the past and embrace an unknown future. Through the experience, I had learned of my limited ability to move beyond the pain. Increasingly, I became dismissive of love and of the interest expressed by some men around me in the possibility of a relationship. I was processing my feelings and my life without Seif. I knew that I had to heal before I could move on to another relationship.

Gradually, I learned to accept that our humanity is far more complex than the simple questions we ask. Life was not fair and simple, and it was never going to be. There were no simple explanations. I was moving away from my unrealistic idealistic vision of life to becoming more realistic in my hopes and aspirations. I learned that relationships are complex and have little, or nothing, to do with the ideology a woman or a man holds. I consciously pushed myself to expect and accept life's disappointments. I had to accept life for what it was. I needed to mature, to grow beyond my pain. I recognised that Seif left a void in my life. However, I was determined to move on. I believed that in order to fall in love again I would have to be whole, balanced and free. I occupied myself in the best way possible: I embraced a life of learning and women's friendships.

Free of contempt, I opened my heart to heal itself from loving Seif. That blue four-page letter marked the end of a beautiful relationship. From it, I extracted these things to remember: 1. He loved me but could not marry me; 2. He believed that for a career in journalism, freedom from entanglements was required; and 3. He was certain that if this was genuine love, it would not matter how it ended, as we were clearly going in different directions. In closing, Seif wrote that he hoped one day we would have a cup of coffee and talk. Within the first six months after we parted, I dismissed the first two items from further consideration. *Fourteen years later, we had that coffee and chatted.*

## Transition: From Prison to Prison                                149

I journeyed back to sanity. I re-centred my heart and re-aligned my life. Free from political allegiances and the affairs of the heart, I found my way to friendships with women. I was free to embrace the beautiful women of my country with their unique experiences. I formed friendships with women who accepted me without regard to my political activism, my imprisonment or my religious affiliation as a Muslim Shia woman. I gravitated toward women friends for their intriguing personalities and experiences, for their humanity. I was welcomed into friendships with Muslim Sunni women. I rediscovered the beauty of simple humanity, undistinguished by religious affiliation or political backgrounds. I rediscovered the simple beauty of being myself and of accepting others free of pre-judgements.

I was born and raised within the Shia community and traditions. Nevertheless, it was at King Saud University that I came to understand what it means to be a Muslim Shia and what it meant for me to be a Muslim Shia woman. Within the high walls of a deteriorated old university building in Olaiysha, Riyadh, I fell in love with the Muslim Shia philosophy and school of thought. From reading the sociology of knowledge and the sociology of religion, I learned that it was the Shia philosophers who introduced the first radical school of thought in the history of Islam. At King Saud University, I initiated the intellectual rediscovery of my religious community and myself.

At the same time, I was confronted daily by the Wahhabism practised by the majority Sunni population within Saudi Arabia. The attitudes of this majority toward minority Shia Islam are not generally benevolent. Wahhabism is attributed to Muhammed ibn Abd-al-Wahhab, a conservative theologian, Hanbali jurist, scholar and ideologue founder of this austere reform movement. He was born in 1703 in Uyaynah and died in 1792 in Ad-Diriyah, both now in Saudi Arabia. He proclaimed the necessity of returning directly to the Quran and Hadith; promoted strict adherence to traditional Islamic law and a return to the "true" principles of Islam; and advocated a return to the practices of the first three Islamic generations. That interpretation excludes recognition of Ali ibn Abi Talib – regarded as the first Shia Imam – thus provoking antagonism toward the Shia communities worldwide. Ibn Abd-al-Wahhab formed an alliance with ibn Saud in 1744 that ceded control to the latter over military, political, and economic matters; Ibn Abd-al-Wahhab claimed responsibility for all religious concerns. The alliance resulted in the foundation of the first Saudi dynasty and state and remains the basis for Saudi rule today.

Largely sheltered within a like-minded Eastern Province community, I had known and lived a Muslim Shia life. Previously, I had rarely encountered the contempt that some Saudi Wahhabi Sunni hold toward Shia. Until my university studies, I was unaware of the magnitude of Shia thought and traditions and their influence on mainstream Sunni philosophy and practice. My Sunni classmates would graduate without ever acknowledging those contributions.

Through my studies, I discovered the degree to which Wahhabism influences and controls the minds of mainstream Saudi Sunni. There, I met countless women and men with liberal, even radical, beliefs and convictions who were more dogmatic about Wahhabism than the most fanatical Zionist. They were utterly unwilling to consider any other point of view. In Riyadh, I became more critical, more intellectually rebellious and more independent. Still, beyond proclaiming my Shia heritage, I lacked adequate courage for argumentation and debate. Other Shia students disapproved of my assertion of Shia identity, judging it irrelevant, unnecessary information.

At King Saud University I was privileged to be taught by brilliant Saudi and non-Saudi women who excelled in their expertise. It was liberating to learn from women professors who accepted me for who I was, irrespective of my religious affiliation. There, I had a second chance to learn what I had read during my years of political activism. With brilliant tutors, I studied again the social and political theories and philosophies that had influenced my developing ideology since age sixteen. Ironically, it was there that I first truly understood Marxism, as I became more knowledgeable and aware of the history of social thought.

I re-studied Arab-Islamic history, its diverse thought and philosophies. My love for books and learning encouraged me to examine and to learn from different, often contradictory, philosophies. I discovered the brilliance of the Arabic heritage through the work and contributions of ibn Khaldun, ibn Rushd (Averroes), al-Farabi, ibn Arabi, Mohammed Abdo and Jamal el-Din al-Afghani. Through the work of Auguste Comte, Emile Durkheim, Max Weber, Charles Wright Mills and many more, I learned how Marxism evolved. Despite strict government censorship and the extreme control over thoughts and ideas, there existed within the university an oasis for learning. A cornucopia of books was accessible in the library to those who were curious to learn. Early on, I discovered that treasure house where I was not limited as to which books I could or could not read. With this new access to knowledge of how societies and institutions work, I expanded my awareness of the factors that influence and advance Saudi society. Scholars such as Halim Barakat (*The Arab World: Society, Culture, and State*) and Tim Niblock (*State, Society and Economy in Saudi Arabia*) provided me with a new critical lens through which I could examine the influences on our society; they also served as a counter-balance to my previous Party indoctrination.

Books were also available through publishing institutes such as al Majlis Alwatani lil fenoon wa al adab (The Kuwaiti National Council for Arts and Literature) in Kuwait, and Markaz Dirrasat el wehda al Arabiya (Center of Arab Union Studies) in Beirut. The library at King Saud University itself offered a wealth of old literary publications that I doubted had been discovered by hardline Wahhabi faculty and staff. I suspected that they would have been banished, if not burned, if discovered.

Those were the golden years of King Saud University. We were enrolled in classes within a flexible unit and semester system. We were trusted and treated with respect as mature adult university students who entered and exited according to timetables. Years after I graduated, the university enrolment system was changed to reflect a rigid schedule that the conservative Riyadh community demanded in order to control female university students. The new system made it easier for parents and guardians to monitor female student conduct on entering and leaving the university. This daily monitoring ensured that university enrolment was not an outlet for young Saudi women to explore unsupervised freedom.

Riyadh was the first Saudi city I lived in where I experienced quite different community norms and traditions. Until then, I had lived in a small town, attended high school and worked in various cities in the Eastern Province, home to a large, progressive Shia community. By comparison, Riyadh seemed a hothouse of oppression.

Women in Riyadh were far more restricted in their movements. There, I first encountered the *mutawa*, the Saudi religious police, whose duty is to ensure strict adherence to established codes of conduct. They may detain offenders indefinitely. This includes foreigners in spite of the Quran's injunction that there be *"no compulsion in religion"* (*surah al-Baqara*, 256). Within Riyadh, the *mutawa* became a daily engagement, as they were everywhere – even at the university gate. Their over-arching presence was an additional, unwelcome adjustment to life in Riyadh.

In my small hometown, the religious police had a low profile. Within our small Shia community, more relaxed norms and traditions reigned. In comparison, it seemed less restrictive, far freer than Riyadh. Additonally, a minority of families, including my own, had more relaxed rules for women. I knew very well that my family was an unconventional exception.

In Riyadh, I became aware of a different way of life in which women capitalised on being at university. Some women used the university to taste freedom with prohibited relationships. Daily, they were dropped off at the university gate by their drivers or guardians and subsequently picked up by their lovers. Women friends formed protective shields around them and offered safe passage to a world of choice: a risky choice, but a choice nonetheless. Observing these conspiracies and the level of support that women with limited resources demonstrated to each other amazed me. Within my small circle of friends and acquaintances in Riyadh, I was impressed and awed with the courage of young Saudi women and the risks they were willing to take for a limited degree of freedom. They decided where to go and what to do with their time while ostensibly attending university classes. As I listened to their stories, I knew that I would not take such risks. Indeed, I felt privileged that I did not need to.

I felt safe and well protected living with my father in the suburb of Olaya. He knew what I was doing and whom I was with at all times. As I was free of any commitment to political activities, there was nothing to hide from him or from others. I was envied for what seemed to be freedom at its very best. My father is a genuinely liberal man. In our home, we had an open relationship and when he disagreed with me, he left it to me to decide. Even when he disagreed, I always had his support. I went where I said I would go, knowing that I would not have to prove it.

As I listened, I was fascinated that women disguised themselves in men's clothing and vice versa in order to have access to each other. The majority of the women and men got away with their subterfuges, but there were those who were exposed and punished. Under the pretence of a sudden sickness or a family crisis, students dropped out of university, never to be heard from again. There were no reports of honour killings in the local newspapers, nor did I expect them to be published. Of course, honour killing does not need to be physical; there are many ways to kill women.

I loved the defiance of those women while recognising their vulnerability. In that society where they would pay a very high price for their risky behaviour if caught, they made the decision to be where they wanted to be. Whether I agreed or disagreed with the behaviours and the risk taking was immaterial.

Rigid, unyielding communities such as that one in Riyadh created the conditions that drove those freedom seekers to use the university. In Riyadh – the stronghold of Wahhabism – women did the unthinkable; they dared to take risks and defy the ultra-conservative family and religious prohibitions. The creative narratives of those women were like the stories woven by Shahrazad. Every day, each wove a new story to save herself from the sword of Shahriyar and to save the community of women. In Saudi Arabia, every woman is a Shahrazad and every man is a Shahriyar.

At that point in my life, I believed that I had the right to claim my identity as a Muslim Shia woman and a citizen of my homeland. I had a right to my own narrative, a Shahrazad with a different voice. However, my purpose was not to save my life from the sword of Shahriyar but to be the woman I am among the thousands of Shahrazads. While it is a challenge for a woman to have a voice when in the company of men, it is a thousand times harder for a woman to have a voice in the company of women. This proved a challenge to my fellow students, especially those who perceived the Shia tradition as not only an undesirable school of thought, but also an illegitimate one. I did not conceal my religious affiliation, nor did I want to.

Many of my fellow students tried to show me what they considered to be the right path. They endeavoured to prove to me that I was more like an atheist than a Muslim. They felt it was their duty to convert me to the right path. It was an interesting experience to discover the degree of their ignorance and the power that Wahhabism had over so many people.

Other students tried to convert me to Wahhabism in the belief that the Shia school, the oldest and one of the five major schools of thought, is illegitimate. They seemed blind to the influence of the highly respected Shia Imam Jafar Al Sadiq on the mainstream Islamic schools of thought. They seemed totally ignorant that Shia Imams have the honour of direct lineage to our Prophet Muhammed (pbuh). It is an interesting paradox that Sunni Arabs honour their own tribal lineage and yet dismiss the Shia community's honour of its Imams' lineage to Prophet Muhammed (pbuh). As a Muslim Shia woman with only a small voice within her own community, I had little hope of having a voice in a Muslim Wahhabi community.

Fellow students would stop me as I passed by the mosque to ask why I did not join in the prayer. I was taught that praying was never for show but for Allah. To me, Islam was being interpreted in a very narrow way, losing its uniqueness as the middle way, the moderate path. At times I wanted to scream that I had a choice and that I chose to pray at home between the noon and the sunset prayer. I was labelled a *"Rafidhiyah"*, a derogatory term for a member of the Shia community. Idealistically, I imagined that I could reason with my fellow university students. As I would begin my disquisition, I would quickly realise that the students were completely unwilling to listen or reason. Naively, I had hoped that at university, students would be more open-minded, more critical and more independent in their thinking than mainstream society.

For me, this was not about Islam; it was not about Shia and Sunni. This was about resisting the hegemony of religious ideology. It was a struggle against centuries of Wahhabi brainwashing. It was as narrow and intolerant as any political ideology. In one of the most religious countries in the world, religion remains a taboo topic. Discussions around the Islamic schools of thought and of other religions were not permitted. There is only one correct religion in

Saudi Arabia and it is not Islam; it is Wahhabism and it was the beginning and the end of all discussions. The vast majority of students did not recognise nor acknowledge the five major Islamic schools of thought and the many ways of understanding, interpreting and applying Islamic values and principles. Their minds were firmly closed.

During those university years, I became more open in expressing my ideas and allegiances, whether it was during a class debate or elsewhere on campus. I wanted to be with people and to have friends who knew and accepted me for the person that I was rather than for my religious affiliation. It seemed that freedom of thought was only for the books.

As I studied social theory, I soon realised that Marx had never directly addressed gender, or the woman question. I decided to challenge the Marxist position on women. Thus, I chose for my sociology of theory research paper the topic of women in Marxist theory. I submitted a critique of Marxist theory that substantiated the absence of women within the discussion of the class struggle. In that critical analysis, I found my voice as I challenged my own belief in Marxist ideology.

I did not anticipate the reaction to my paper from the liberal intellectuals in my circle. My uncle Najeeb was highly critical of my attempt to challenge and critique Marx's failure in addressing women's issues. My critics simply dismissed my effort. Clearly, I remained delusional about the meanings of freedom of expression and democracy as practised within my circle. With equal clarity I realized that I was meant to believe in one thing while accepting quite different, even contrary, real world applications.

My rational voice knew that this was not the Quran, only Marx's social theory. I recognised also that it would have been no more difficult to criticise religion. Within that closed circle, I could not criticise Marx and other Marxist thinkers and I could not criticise religion and the interpretation of the Quran. Freedom to dissent was non-existent.

For the first time since I was sixteen, I questioned my belief in Marxist theory. I questioned what it meant to be a liberal thinker and what it meant to have freedom of thought. What are they worth if I am unable to say what I think and think what I say? Is this their true value? Am I to learn about schools of thought and philosophy that I must accept blindly without challenge, without question?

Something was wrong; something felt very wrong. I had to break out of that stranglehold. I didn't get involved in politics nor did I go to prison to hand over my voice to others to speak on my behalf. I had two choices: the first was to accept the answers men provided without challenge; the second was to challenge institutions where men were the only legitimate authority, institutions where women simply echo the voices of men.

I chose to challenge the authority invested in men. During that transformational phase, my relationship with my uncle Najeeb continued to deteriorate. Simultaneously, my relationship with my father was growing stronger. I had to navigate carefully, as the relationship between my father and his siblings was sensitive. I realised that within that paternal culture my father was relatively more liberal and democratic than my uncles. My father was not attached rigidly to his ideas or to being right. If I put forward a strong rational argument, he would respect it alongside his own.

My commitment to study and to living with my father allowed me to become more independent. Slowly, I created my own circle of friends and became more independent of family relationships. Gradually, I drifted away from political affiliations and in time that became a thing of the past. Some of my ex-political associates continued political discussions with the hope that I would change. Others left the experience behind and went back to a conventional life. Many – like me – had lost faith in the power of movements to change society.

In that period, I began to invest many nights in discussion and debate with my father. The debates nurtured and nourished my mind. They allowed me to voice my opinion. While listening to my own reasoning, I would discover that it did not make sense.

While my father was very helpful to my intellectual development, he was not good in dealing with emotions and pain. I concluded that it was a male thing. He navigated our conversations away from any topic that might lead to my relationship with Seif. My father and I rarely discussed it beyond its immediate impact in September 1985. He regularly reinforced the idea that I should be strong and get on with my life. Thus, I mirrored that projection of strength and the rejection of weakness.

Between 1984 and 1989 my father and I were intellectual companions. My relationship with this man that I first knew at age sixteen grew deeper and deeper. We were both self-sufficient and we respected each other's way of life. We compromised and yet in many ways did not compromise.

During this period, I nurtured my love for cooking. My father entertained and I happily cooked. I found that I enjoyed planning his dinner parties. I had one cookbook and I tried most of its recipes on the guests. While my mother had a dismissive glance, he employed an "I am not so sure" look. I could hardly blame him as he was entrusting his invitation to a woman rebel. He limited his question to my level of confidence in the result. Knowing that I was experimenting with a new recipe for the first time on his guests, my father must have had either an alternative plan or real faith in my cooking ability. Cooking and baking were therapeutic in consuming the energy that love and grief required. They helped me regain my centre. I was able to give and love in a new way.

I knew that I was not yet over Seif; therefore I avoided everything that would remind me of him. Only I knew how long I despaired over losing him. I knew that I was still in love with him.

Shortly before graduating at the end of 1987, I found the courage to re-connect with Seif's sister Husna who had recently married. I collected myself and went to see her, to congratulate her on her marriage and to explain that I needed to distance myself from them until I regained my strength. Being with Husna, I realised that at last I was over Seif, as my heart had lost that beat. That distinctive beat that had jumped out of my heart every time Seif's name was mentioned was only a memory. It was time to return home to the Eastern Province. It was time to begin a new chapter.

## Returning Home to the Eastern Province

Disillusioned, at the beginning of 1988, I returned home to the Eastern Province to rejoin my family. My father and Sara, his American girlfriend of over a year, had married at the end of 1986 upon his job transfer from Riyadh to Al-Khobar in the Eastern province. I returned to shuttle between the homes of my mother, my two sisters and the home of my father and stepmother Sara and brother Nawfal. While Nawfal is my half-brother, we never and we do not use such half-measures in our family. Thus he has always been our brother. His mother Anna had agreed for Nawfal to live with my father and Sara for the 1989 school year in the Kingdom.

Eagerly, I anticipated the freedom to think aloud and to being accepted by family and close women friends. As for social duties and obligations toward others, they were fragmented in a world to which I no longer belonged. Something inside me was clamouring for freedom. I was convinced of an alternative way of life more compatible with my worldviews. I often felt that I was born at the wrong time.

On returning to the Eastern Province, I attempted to rejoin Aramco knowing that it was possible that I was still blacklisted. Despite that possibility, I thought that I should give it a try. After a few silent Aramco months, I visited the government employment office where I was told there were no jobs for sociology graduates.

By the summer of 1988, I was employed by a Khobar-based private school as a social worker. My role was to look after the students' well being, monitor their academic performance and also to coordinate with parents in case of persistent social and behavioural issues. The school enrols students from nursery and kindergarten all the way to high school. As it is a private school, only children of middle and upper class families were able to afford the fees.

In my personal life, I resumed the few close intimate friendships that remained from my childhood and schooling prior to 1979. I resumed my full involvement in my sisters' lives as I waited for the birth of my two nephews: Saffiya's third and Ayah's first son. At work I established new work friendships with Saudi and non-Saudi women colleagues.

At work, I reviewed the school texts and the Saudi ministry of education teaching material with despair. Recitation and memorisation continued to dominate and there was no recognition of critical thinking skills. As nothing had changed since my schooling, I realised that the current and future generations would be as ill prepared as I had been.

On my return home, I noticed an increased visibility of the religious police. The *mutawa*'s presence and control were pronounced, especially in major cities and town centres. Their influence reached Safwa and all other major Shia community centres. Now, shops were forced to close during prayer times. The civil police united with the *mutawa* and now patrolled the streets and joined in forcing the shopkeepers to close for prayers. In the past, the shopkeepers would pray while children and adults shopped. The customers left their money on the counter or returned later to settle their accounts. Now, people were ordered to pray. Instead of praying to Allah, people prayed to escape persecution. The Wahhabi extremist religious sentiment was increasing. My life seemed a constant battle with its reinterpretation of Islam and its negative attitudes toward the Shia community and specifically toward women.

My first confrontation with the official religious police occurred during the weekly Thursday market in Qatif. I was to meet my two sisters (both, of course, Shia Muslims like me) and my stepmother Sara and aunt-in-law, uncle Adnan's wife Louise (both US nationals and Christians) for shopping for local products. Before their arrival, I began to examine the hand-made local products.

While browsing, I heard a commanding voice, "Cover your face – woman." Initially, I did not pay attention to the voice and continued shopping only to hear the voice again, this time louder, "Cover your face – woman. I am addressing you."

I looked up to find myself face to face with a member of the committee for the promotion of virtue and the prevention of vice – the *mutawa*. Those who have read of or have knowledge of the religious police in Saudi Arabia will understand my consternation.

At that moment, I heard my small but firm voice reply "Recite". The religious policeman looked at me as if I was speaking in a foreign language. I quickly continued, "Recite the verse in the Quran that orders women to cover their faces." I added, "Listen, I am willing to cover. I am not rejecting your request but I will only cover under the condition that you recite the Quran verse that commands it." I knew too well that I was in no position to bargain. I must have waved to my women companions to keep away as they watched the scene unfold before them. I was oblivious to the consequences.

Confidently and quietly, I continued to address him: "I am sorry if you cannot recite or do not know the verse; however, you have no right to order me to cover my face. The Quran, the word of Allah and Islam do not mandate that women cover their faces. It may be compulsory here in this country but it is not compulsory in Islam."

At that moment on that day and for the first time in my life, I gave myself the permission and the right to access directly the Quran and Islamic teaching. I had claimed my right to access my holy book – The Quran. It is the book of divine guidance and direction for mankind (and womankind), which all Muslims – including the religious police – are expected to follow.

From my study, I knew what the Quran said, the religious police did not. I had learned that knowledge is power. It was a powerful lesson in which I learned that a woman's voice is a strong asset.

With my forceful response, I created silence. I had no idea of how it would be received or what would happen next. On the rare occasions when I had witnessed women speaking up for their rights, I observed that men and society at large were taken aback. I also knew that the odds were going to be against me. Quite freely, the religious police happily humiliate Saudi and non-Saudi nationals because they are protected by the institutionalised power invested in them. As I had not planned or intended to provoke such a confrontation, I could not imagine how the situation would be resolved.

Irritated, the *mutawa* walked away initially. I was about to resume shopping when I saw him walking toward me accompanied by two ordinary policemen. Raising his stick at my face and with a reprimanding tone, he commanded that I cover my face or I would be arrested. Something snapped; I must have been possessed, as I momentarily lost my sense of reality. Furiously, I responded, "Put that stick out of my face before I break it into pieces on your body." He and the two policemen must have been stunned. I continued, "I said I will cover if you know and can recite the Quranic verse that commands women to cover their faces. If you do not know or cannot recite it, then you have no right to demand that I cover. The verse in the Quran addresses women's modesty. As to covering in the way you religious police dictate, it is not mandatory. It is your preferred religious interpretation, not mine. Go learn the Quran first and then return to order women around."

I gasped, "My father knows where I am and he knows that I do not cover my face." Then I turned to the two policemen and said, "I will not only hit the religious man, I will fight the three of you if I have to. I have nothing to lose. I am already in prison." I referred them to verse number 59 in *Surah Al Ahzab*, "*O Prophet! Tell thy wives and daughters, and the believing women, that they should cast the outer garments over their persons (when abroad): that is most convenient, that they should be known (as such) and not molested. And Allah is oft-forgiving, most merciful.*" I included also verse number 31 in *Surah Al Nur*, "*And say to the believing women that they should lower their gaze and guard their modesty; that they should not display their beauty and ornaments except what (must ordinarily) appear; therefore they should draw their veils over their bosoms and not display their beauty.*" When the beauty of a woman is revealed, the Quran instructs men to lower their gaze. Clearly, this proves that covering is a preferred option; it is an argument that the religious police will never accept even if they know it is the truth.

I walked away, rejoined my women companions, opted out of shopping and returned home. I know that I got lucky that day; the only possible reason that I was not detained is that I was in Qatif. The grip of the religious police on the Shia community is less tight than that in the Sunni dominated cities. If the situation had escalated, the religious policeman and his colleagues might have been outnumbered.

Although I understood my father's disapproval of my behaviour that day, I was disappointed that he was upset. My father said, "I would not bail you out if you had been detained." I understood that my father had the right to avoid being humiliated by the religious police if his daughter was charged with indecent dress. I knew also that without standing up to such institutionalised abuse nothing would ever change. I told my father that I would always stand up for myself even with the knowledge that he would not bail me out. If the Prophet himself (pbuh) was instructed by Allah to advise people and leave them to choose, why is it that the religious police assign themselves to be Allah on earth? The word of Allah to his Prophet as cited in the Quran's *Surah Al Nahl* (verse 82) says, "*but if they turn away, the duty is only to breach the clear message."* There is clearly no recommendation in the Quran for beating women with police batons.

With my realisation of the power of knowledge, I sadly recognised just how poorly educated the religious and secular police are. They are ordered to enforce rules that they do not understand and which often have no basis in the Quran. Few of them will have studied the Quran and even fewer will be able to relate the laws they are to enforce to the Holy Book. In the Mutawa, as in the majority of the Muslim population, the essence of Islam is poorly represented and too often misrepresented.

As if it was not enough to have men with sticks humiliating people, some women adopted this bullying behaviour. Soon after the Qatif incident while shopping in Al Khobar, a woman in niqab instructed me to cover my face in order to avoid burning in hell. I cannot fully explain what happened; I only know that I lost it. I was furious. The religious police are financed, fully supported and endorsed by the government. The last thing I needed was for a woman, a complete stranger who had assigned herself to be Allah on earth, to command me to cover my face.

The only sound I heard was my angry voice. I literally went after her and followed her around the store asking her to recite the verse from the Quran that instructs women to cover their faces. I said, "If you cannot recite it then you had better shut up and mind your own business." I continued: "You would be the one to burn in hell. I do not want to go to heaven if that means being with people like you."

Finally, I calmed down when her sister grabbed her hand to lead her out of the store while criticising her for interfering in other people's business. I was sorely tempted to follow her. I did not feel that I had said all that I wanted to say. I stopped half way to the door and breathed deeply. I wanted to cry out with an echo throughout the whole country that this is not Islam and it has to stop. Something was wrong. Something has been wrong for a long time.

It seemed that detention in the large prison was inadequate punishment; complete strangers were to be permitted to suffocate me. During that same period, when I returned to Riyadh to obtain my transcript and my degree, a flight attendant approached me on board the flight to Riyadh with a request that I change seats. Surprised, I replied, "I did not request a change of seating." Politely and quietly, the attendant pleaded that I keep my voice down; the man who was in a seat two rows ahead of me was not happy that my face was not covered. I thought to myself that he couldn't even see me unless his eyes were placed in the back of his head.

I changed the seat after telling the attendant that I was not happy to do so and that the airline should establish a seating code that would ensure that males were not offended. On the return flight, the flight attendant approached me with the same request: the man sitting next to me was not comfortable with my uncovered face. I quietly looked at the man next to me with his face full of malice. I asked him if he had looked at his face in the mirror that morning. I continued, "I would not want to look at you if you were the last man on earth."

I turned toward the attendant and refused to change seats. I said, "The man should change seats as I am very comfortable where I am." I was not going to change my seat. As we were already on the runway, movement within the aircraft was prohibited. The question was moot. I felt at peace with and respect for myself for having refused to change seats.

What else could I lose? Freedom? I was in a large prison where members of the religious police and ordinary people have assigned themselves the right to unlawfully detain us under the pretence of the promotion of virtue and the prevention of vice. Within their eyes, I am discredited because I did not cover my face or wear the hijab. They totally discount, reject, the validity of my knowledge and understanding of the Quran and Islamic teaching.

The official and non-official religious police know that religious mediators – institutionalised or otherwise – are not required between Muslims and Allah. The religious establishment accepts that it cannot deter punishable violations and crimes in our civil society; therefore, it punishes matters in which Muslims have a choice. Despite their knowledge, both the religious police and ordinary conservative Muslims conveniently forget that there are no intermediaries in Islam. Thereby forcing Muslims to worship Allah denies ordinary believers the right to discipline themselves in their commitment to religion. Thus some have assigned themselves the role of Allah on earth. This is what has become of Islam in Saudi Arabia and in many other Muslim countries.

The hometown to which I returned was not the one I had left; it was a strange place indeed. As a child I had experienced Islam in its simplicity; now everything seemed to have been invaded by a religion that I did not recognise. The gentle, tolerant, simple religion with which I had grown up had disappeared; it had been hijacked by the counterinsurgency. The more I resisted and refused to submit, the more my sense of being a minority intensified.

# 7

# Walking Away – Walking Back

Near paralysed, I endeavoured to balance on the continuum between a leap of faith and a leap into insanity, suspended between what might have been and what might be. Of course, there were various possibilities: to remain suspended; to be shattered utterly; or to land on my feet with a few wounds and minor injuries.

During the decision-making period, I experienced wide swings along the emotional continuum. Exactly six years after being released from prison, I made the decision to leave my country. At the moment that my passport with its five-year valid period was placed in my hand, I mentally exited.

The memory of my February 1982 trip to the US tempted me to consider immigration. I shuddered as I recalled endless conversations and my earlier judgements of people who entertained the idea of immigrating. Hypocritically, I believed in freedom and yet I judged negatively those who wanted to journey toward a new future. With the receipt of that passport, my perspective changed.

In the summer of 1989, I left Saudi to travel freely in France, Spain, the Netherlands and the UK. I viewed the work of artists, listened to symphonies and bought the books that I had read about while incarcerated. I chose those I wanted to read. I chose freely and independently for the first time as an adult.

The 1989 Tiananmen Square protest, known as the June Fourth Incident, was the focus of conversation and debate. Hungary dismantled its barriers, which signalled the collapse of the Berlin Wall. That, of course, presaged the collapse of the communist league of countries. At that time I had re-read Marx's work from my new perspective as a student of sociology. I understood his writing much better as a theory of social evolution.

In Paris, I was able to hear for the first time my authentic thoughts about a world I knew previously only through political ideology. I began to listen to my own voice. I no longer defended Marx's work as an ideology, but debated it as a social theory and criticised its lack of a well-defined perspective on the role of women. I listened to people as if for the first time. With these new perspectives, I was now challenged to understand why people could not foresee that the communist experiment might falter or fail.

From Paris, I observed France and the French celebrating the 200th anniversary of its glorious revolution. In the midst of the great spirit of achievement, I found myself thinking of freedom. What ideology had driven a nation with a great history of enlightenment and revolution to subjugate and colonise other nations and deprive them of their inherent human right to be free? What ideology leads the human race to be simultaneously the freedom fighter and the tyrant?

Ideologies – social, political and religious – all belong to men. As long as the human race feels the need to raise arms, to imprison or silence others in order to advance their narrow self interests, those ideologies are doomed to evolve into an oppressive regime, regardless of their essence. Increasingly, I was critical of ideologies that dictate one right way of thinking, one right way of looking at the world. While recognising that the world has a wealth of ideas, beliefs and philosophies, I no longer felt attached to or bound by any of them.

In my restless wandering, I missed the solitude of my 1982–83 prison experience. The need to reconnect with myself was strong. Therefore in exploring new boundaries, I sought to fulfil that promise to re-engage with myself. Repeatedly, I heard my father's voice telling me, *"You won't be able to stay away for long. Soon, you will return home,"* but the word "long" correctly defines my four and one-half year exile. Once back in Saudi Arabia after that exile, I grew restless and within eighteen months, I left again in search of a homeland. Nineteen years later I am still searching.

At the end of 1989, I departed for California where I was planning to pursue an advanced degree (MA) in sociology. I went in search of the woman I met briefly while incarcerated in 1982–83 somewhere in Sulaimaniya, Riyadh, Saudi Arabia.

In 1990, I settled in California. There, a different sense of loneliness invaded my heart. When I dreamed of freedom in America, I had not anticipated loneliness. I expected that all my dreams would come true. Within the confining boundaries of my self-imposed exile, the freedom and justice I sought seemed illusory. Aimlessly I wandered around California's San Francisco Bay. With an anguished heart, I woke one morning to hear a voice singing:

> Morning has broken, like the first morning
> Blackbird has spoken, like the first bird
> Praise for the singing, praise for the morning
> Praise for the springing fresh from the word
> Sweet the rain's new fall, sunlit from heaven
> Like the first dewfall, on the first grass
> Praise for the sweetness of the wet garden
> Sprung in completeness where his feet pass
> Mine is the sunlight, mine is the morning
> Born of the one light, Eden saw play
> Praise with elation, praise every morning
> God's recreation of the new day
>
> (Cat Stevens/Yusuf Islam)

Tears flowed to soothe my pain and it became possible that one day I could return home. With that epiphany, I discovered that I was a woman in the making. I became aware that I yet endured pain, interspersed with numb periods. "Morning has broken" stroked me spiritually.

Life returned to more normal rhythms. I still had faith in Arab Nationalism; I still had faith in justice and a belief that the world will be a better place to live for all people. That summer my sisters and their families visited California. I knew going home was possible but it was not an option I wanted to entertain at that time. For me, the only option was to be me, to reclaim my identity.

At that time prospects were bleak with the invasion of one Arab country by another, initiating the first Gulf War. I struggled to retain my hopes for a better future for the Arab world, to sustain belief that we will learn from history and walk away from the region's vicious, divisive political games.

From my distant perspective, I watched documentaries, discussion panels and television interviews of prominent Arab-Americans, as if the Arab world had been newly discovered, as if it had just been created. Objectively focused, balanced programmes were hard to find. Largely, the programmes spoke about the Arab world in a way that seemed foreign to me. My hopes and dreams for a better Arab world, for a homeland, were slowly dying.

I followed most carefully the news about the courageous women who protested in the heart of the Saudi capital, Riyadh. There, they took the steering wheel, sent their drivers away and drove, sending a message that it was time to change, to move forward. I heard of Seif's arrest for coordinating the international media coverage of the women's driving protest. Saudi women who were involved were detained, some were publicly humiliated and some were harassed. The majority of the traditional and liberal public alike decided that it was not the right time to stage such a protest. It is never the right time when women choose.

To me, the Saudi reality seemed distant. My reality was far removed from that of the women and men of my country. In Berkeley, CA, my reality was the experience of students staging protests against the Gulf War on the grounds of the university campus. Free of their fear of being detained or humiliated, students boycotted their classes to rally against sending American troops to the Arabian Gulf and delivered speeches against the war. One day I walked toward the campus through coffins with mock bloodstained corpses in front of the main campus building.

As much as I wanted to be part of what was taking place in the Arabian Gulf, I knew that it was not my reality and that I could not relate to war any more. However, I had not lost my revolutionary fervour. I had learned that revolution could happen without the need for bloodshed. I knew that war was going to breed more war and I no longer wished to be part of it.

I knew that this was not a war for liberty or democracy; it was a war to protect US interests and its control of the region. I marvelled at the ordinary men and women who genuinely believed that they were sending their children to die in order to protect someone else's liberty. I wished for a turning point in the history of the Arabian Gulf; a wake-up call for all ruling families, governments and all the Arab nations. To my disgust, the flame of hope and change awakened by the Gulf War was quickly extinguished again.

I boycotted all the major news stations. I followed the Gulf War in the *Christian Science Monitor* and in selected articles by Noam Chomsky, Edward Said and others who presented a balanced view and in-depth analysis of the crisis. Aware of their biases, I avoided major newspapers.

On the whole, I was concerned but detached. In despair, I watched as petty, despotic dictators with self-sustaining political egos frittered away any hope of a united Arab world. I wanted to immerse myself in the study of the 60s and 70s revolutions in the Bay Area, i.e., the student movement, the civil rights movement and the feminist movement. Although I was knowledgeable about the Vietnam War, the Watergate crisis and of US interests in Saudi Arabia and the Arab world, there was another realm of new experiences and new boundaries to transcend.

In Berkeley, I reconfronted my prejudice about same-sex relationships; in retrospect, I realize that it bordered on bigotry. At last, I summoned the courage to push myself to understand and to accept a different way, motivated by my attraction to a man who was not open about his sexuality. I liked Paul enormously. Thus, I was profoundly shocked to learn that he was a homosexual. Did I want to understand with the hope of changing him, or did I want to understand in order that Paul and I would remain friends? I invested four years and hundreds of discussion hours in becoming comfortable with my homosexual friends.

In California, I learned that we choose our friends for their goodness as people, because they connect with us morally and spiritually. Paul was my first gay friend. Later in Sacramento, I met April whose homosexuality helped me to understand not only the decision about choice or no choice, but the psychological and emotional struggle of being homosexual in the US. With April, I was able to discuss and question what I am comfortable with and what I am uncomfortable with about homosexuality.

I was brought up in a religion that like most others forbids homosexuality and considers it a sin. Putting my imagination to work, I considered the possibility that one of my beloved nephews, nieces or friends was homosexual. The possibility of rejecting one of them because of his/her sexual orientation motivated me to overcome my bias toward homosexuality.

I learned to accept their differences without having to lose their friendship. It was from my friend April that I learned that the reasons and causes behind homosexuality are unimportant. We are all humans and humanness is not about our sexual orientation. It is about how we best serve our humanity.

Gradually, I became more comfortable with homosexuality and interested in understanding more about a culture that was alien to me. I conquered another prejudice and learned more about sexual freedom in Berkeley in the 60s and 70s. As I analysed heterosexual relationships and potentially unacceptable sexual practices that go on behind closed doors, I realised that simply because a man and a woman are involved, it does not make it right or okay.

To me, every issue and every movement in California seemed interlinked. I observed, I read, I listened, I debated and I learned. Until then, I had been educated primarily in the Arabic language. As I sought to pursue a master's degree (MA) in sociology in the English language, I had to demonstrate adequate linguistic skills in order to be accepted at that level. Thus, I enrolled in intensive writing courses for one year at Armstrong College in Berkeley. In addition to English, I attended general education classes in order that I could expand my academic vocabularies.

In 1991, I moved to Sacramento to begin my MA degree. I was interested in the sociology of knowledge and in the women's liberation movement. My heart was in the Arab feminist movement and in the work particularly of the Egyptian Nawal el Saadawi whom I had read since the age of sixteen.

## On becoming a woman

In 1991, I was thirty-one years old. Finally, I had a place of my own, a one-bedroom apartment. There in that apartment I became acquainted with my body, while bathing or showering. I learned to look at, accept and love my body. For the first time I was not afraid of or uncomfortable with my body. Belatedly, I came to terms with my menstrual cycle.

I started to notice the changes at the various stages of my menstrual cycle. I began a new relationship with myself as a whole – body, soul and intellect. I began to connect with my spirituality, my emotions and my biology. I was thirty-one years old when I dared to sleep naked for the first time in my own bed. My body resisted nakedness as if it embodied the whole of the cultural memory of prohibition. It was no longer about the cultural memories of norms and impositions; it was about what my own body experienced and what I imposed on myself. Nakedness represented a violation of everything I had learned about the cultural gender code. I was thirty-one with a virgin's body and an insatiable mind. I not only noticed my sensuality, but also acknowledged it, and embraced and liberated my imagination to transcend the limitations of narrow, culturally imposed norms about the illicit.

For the first time, I had become curious about my body only to discover how unsymmetrical it is. The right side of my body was slightly larger than the left side. I was taken aback by the fact that I had never paid close attention to my body before. I had been oblivious to my own physicality. Now, I had nothing with which to compare my body, as I had never noticed what it looked like when I was younger.

Quietly, I celebrated my discoveries and my contentment with my body and myself. It is a combination of what I was born with and what I had accumulated through the years. I had started to discover and to accept that my body, my facial features and even the acne scars are all part of my identity. With ease, I embraced total peace with my image.

In that process, I realised that I had no concept of an ideal look. To me, beauty is a mystery, a mysterious combination. Femininity is an essence, is in the nature of womanhood and is every woman's birthright. That is why femininity cannot be quantified or qualified.

Despite my imperfections, I felt privileged within my femininity. I recognised that my sense of femininity and my bodily shape and look are unique, non-exchangeable. It was not physical. It was within my sense of wholeness and completeness that I felt both my beauty and my femininity. It was also in the recognition of my desire to be healthy and to age gracefully. The fine lines that had begun to define my face testified to the years in which I had built up my credit.

Thus at age thirty-one, I began to relate to my body. Learning how to care for and to nourish it became a ritual celebration. I consciously decided to develop a positive relationship with my body, particularly during my menstrual cycle. I was determined to conquer the culturally acquired attitude of disgust and the genuine physical discomfort that I experienced during my monthly period.

Even today, I do not fully understand the basis for the feelings of disgust, discomfort and shame that I learned to associate with the menstrual cycle. As I was growing up, references to women as impure when menstruating influenced how I related to my body. However, I received no explanation for this supposed impurity. The menstrual cycle was not a conversation topic even among friends. It was referred to surreptitiously as my "friend" or "companion". We were not even taught the correct terms for the menses, i.e., the periodic flow of blood and sloughed-off tissue from the uterus.

At that time in my culture, women were not seen as normal during the menses. This sense of abnormality is what I experienced during my own monthly periods. The menstrual cycle, particularly the absence of the menses, was a source of anxiety. When it did not arrive on schedule, it was viewed as a sign of trouble and possible misconduct for unmarried women. The monthly cycle was never revered as a symbol of life and the power of reproduction. To me, it seems one of those true love–hate relationships that poses a controversial issue physically and mentally.

Regardless of the old residue, boundaries and limitations imposed on my emotional–physical relationship, I was mentally ready to work on it. I began by re-reading Feras Al Sawah's *Ishtar: the Goddess and the Origin of Religion and Myth*. The goddess, mother earth, the lunar cycle and the symbol of fertility were a positive starting place for an examination of my body's cycle. Gradually, I began to think positively about the menstrual pain. I determined to welcome it and to disempower it by discontinuing the pain relief pills. I would train my body to tolerate pain.

Gradually, I approached my cycle in a more relaxed and welcoming attitude, despite the hormonally fuelled emotional roller coaster that I rode every month. When advised to take calming herbs and medications, I refused, although I consciously knew of the impatience and irritation that accompanied the pain. I accepted that I had a right to be impatient and irritated. I was entitled to experience the emotional roller coaster without feeling that I had to be calmed down. Gradually I gained control of the menstrual pain; when it arrived, my body tolerated it. While I continued to experience the roller coaster, it slowed and my emotions mellowed. Gradually, I experienced my body as more natural during my cycle and I no longer permitted it to limit my activity. Very importantly, I was no longer sick and did not need to stay in bed.

Reluctantly, I decided to see a gynaecologist for the first time in my life. I had never considered it before, nor had anyone, including doctors and health professionals in Saudi Arabia, ever suggested that I have a gynaecological examination. Such examinations were traditionally limited to married women or to cases of major health issues. Despite my liberal thinking and my promotion of women's rights; despite having worked at a hospital; and despite being keenly aware of women's health issues, I had never considered an appointment with a gynaecologist. Today, that seems curious indeed.

In making the appointment, I specifically requested a woman gynaecologist. The clinic receptionist explained that my appointment was with a male doctor and that was all that she could offer me at that time. She assured me it would be okay. I was not happy with that and I felt uncomfortable with the idea of being checked by a male doctor.

I was torn between my intuition and the voice of reason. The voice of reason prevailed. I should have known better and gone with my intuition. I hated every second of my visit to the gynaecologist. My anxiety was such that I experienced considerable pain from the examination. That male gynaecologist was totally insensitive to the fact that this was my first ever examination, that I was tense and that I was from a culture for which such check-ups were outside the norm for a woman like me. The examination instruments seemed like instruments of torture. I wanted to disappear under the examination table. Thus, I covered my face in order to avoid the whole process.

I left doubting the necessity of ever again seeing a gynaecologist. I convinced myself that any future visits would have to be warranted, and that there would be no male gynaecologists in my life. I felt exposed, as if I had been opened up and dissected. I resented the examination and the fact that a complete stranger now had a better picture of my entire reproductive system and had seen more than I was able to see. I resented the fact that the doctor did not sit down with me, explain the procedure, what it would entail and what I should expect. That insensitivity toward me as a woman having such an examination for the first time ensured the remote possibility of returning for further routine examinations. I judged that even if this had been my tenth or one hundredth visit, I would have expected the doctor – male of female – to have a high degree of sensitivity.

For some time, my negative feelings about the clinic visit lingered. As I reflected on it, I thought of my mother and of all the women in my home community who have no language with which to respond to medical questions. This would be true even if asked about general health issues. They would have frozen if asked to respond to questions regarding their reproductive system and sexual health. I wondered how they would have felt in their struggle to respond to such questions. Even with my education and progressive experience, I felt near tongue-tied there on that gynaecological table.

That visit focused me exquisitely on women's physical and mental health. Until then, my perspective on women's issues was largely centred on their political, civil and legal rights. Thus, the positive outcome of the distasteful experience was that I was provoked to think of all areas of women's lives that I had not considered before. I realised that I had limited myself to issues of socio-economic and political roles, which while important are not the totality of women's concerns.

Gradually, I began to expand my reading to include women's health, well-being and spirituality. I began to converse with my own body whenever I observed changes. I felt the oneness of me: body, soul and mind. For the first time, I inhabited my body, listened to it and paid attention to how it monitors and rejects food, people and sensations, including my own desires. My body has a voice, one that I could now hear. I was no longer dependent upon my rational mind and morals for restraint from what might be legally illicit or socially and culturally prohibited. With this new awareness, I could trust in the signals that my body, soul and mind share. This collective ensemble transformed my life to wholeness, to a balanced unity.

At last, I was free from external influences, free of all the voices that manipulated or exploited me. Although I believed that I was also free of all the internal voices that manipulated and exploited me, I was not. Indeed, I was at the beginning of my journey into the most terrifying battle of my life: the battle with myself, with my inner voice. I hurled myself into the struggle, beginning with my body.

I had never been more aware of my anger, my antagonisms, as I was at this stage of my life. I became acutely aware of my life, my body and my age. At last, I had adequate courage to love my body, to love its delights and its imperfections.

As I made peace with my body, I remembered how fearful I had been of it and of how it could betray me. I remembered my mother's panicked eyes when around age fourteen or fifteen, my menstrual period simply stopped. I remember the hot pads, the daily massages of my lower abdomen and back and the hot cinnamon drinks.

What induced my body to play that game? Eventually, my mother and I were rescued by the arrival of the pain and nausea, followed by the red spotting. Then my mother relaxed. She had suffered for almost three months. The burden of shame and the fear of a damaged reputation weighed heavily on her. The possibility of being proved unworthy of bringing up girls properly must have added to her suffering.

Along the road to maturity, something changed. I became more realistic. As I recalled memories of my mother through hard times, I remembered how insensitive I was toward her fear as a mother, as a woman. For me, admission of defeat is difficult, regardless of the issue.

I first surrendered when I admitted that my mother would have been better off if she had one son along with her daughters. She needed male support, that extra acknowledgement, the affirmation that only a son could have provided. In our small, insular community, a son would have made her life as a single mother infinitely easier. That was a bitter pill for me to swallow. It was as if my feet had finally touched the ground of reality. Among my community of friends and relatives, I was challenged to make this admission.

I had become more realistic about the rhetoric of women's

aspirations for a more just and fairer world. I recognised that the world was organised around enabling men as the centre of the universe and the disabling of women. Although there were families in which women were enabled to optimise their limits, the patriarchal system was organised around limiting women's ability. Thus far, I had enjoyed living in a different world to that I had experienced in my own country. I was thinking more freely, seeing the world through different perspectives. And yet, I confronted limitations. I had discovered the beauty of the voice that I command and of my will to command it.

Since Seif left me, I had feared intimacy. I had considered that to be in love, to be intimate in the way I was with Suhail and subsequently with Seif was a weakness. I had made a conscious decision to avoid love. I was tired, exhausted and hurt. I did not want to risk the experience of pain. I did not want to invest my emotional energy in a relationship. The discovery that I was capable of loving and having a relationship had frightened me. Therefore, I shunned love and feared it, as it challenged my peace and solitude.

I had much to learn and relearn about my weaknesses. Life is full of the temptations of love. I wanted to live and defy a world that conspired to deform me and mould me into a copy of another woman. I was terrified of looking at my face in the mirror, afraid of seeing a deformed stranger rather than a true reflection of myself. I had come to appreciate the truce that I made with the world, one that allowed me to breathe between fighting and fighting back. I realised how tired I was of fighting myself.

I experienced an epiphany: a blinding moment of absolute clarity when the pieces of my life merged into a complete whole. With total clarity, I realised that I wanted to be complete and to have a healthy body, soul and mind. Further, I was clear about wanting to live and enjoy life free of contempt, free of judgements and free of the pain of the impositions of others. In addition, I wanted to be more open to others and to accept differences. Finally, I wanted to eliminate all residues of ideologically restrictive thinking that dictated how to see the world. I had embarked on a new journey of learning and it took me a long time to fully appreciate the new path I was paving.

So far I had forbidden myself the intimacy of love relationships. I wanted to focus all my energy on rediscovering myself, my new interests, my likes and dislikes and on determining what to do with my life. Berkeley was generous in offering me two opportunities to fall in love again. One was a true love of the person, the woman I was; the other was the pure physical attraction to the body I inhabited. I believed that I was doing the right thing by refusing both opportunities. During this time and for many years to come I truly believed that the rational mind could overpower the temptation of love. It helped to be detached. My intense focus on learning was a powerful aid in the avoidance of love. Thus, I entrapped myself, and as much as it might not have been wise or fair, it served my purpose for the present.

In California, during the 1992 summer holiday of the second year of my journey to independence, my uncle Najeeb apologised to me. He admitted that he had stood in the way of my relationship with Suhail and the possibility of marriage and a family life of my own. I had never considered asking about his motives, so it did not matter why the apology now. I never asked if he had stood in the way of both relationships or just that with Suhail. It was too late for an apology, too late for me. By then, I had managed to piece together my own truths.

I knew that my uncle had been responsible for the break up with Suhail. It had not been my choice. Indeed in the emotional intimidation of those circumstances there were no choices. But did he also motivate Seif to abandon our relationship?

Boldly, I replied, "I made my choices. I could have had other relationships. I did not choose to do so." I wanted to deny him the credit of his influence on my life at that time. My uncle failed to notice that I was no longer sixteen, nineteen or twenty-two years old. I was becoming a woman on my own. I was an independent person and no longer needed men to validate my feelings, my choices or my life.

My view of the traditional codes of relationships between women and men in my family had changed. I now understood that the presumed liberal and democratic attitudes advanced particularly by my uncles were but abstract concepts. They were ideals, not a reality that they wished to live. I had learned that if I challenged the status quo I would be viewed as being inflexible, as lacking a sense of humour and incapable of having fun. For uncle Najeeb, the only possible way forward was for me to comply with his emotional coercion and manipulation.

I realised that the unspoken code demands that love is interpreted to mean support of family members blindly, without question, regardless of wrongdoing or of personal disagreements. It became clearer to me that such blind love required the dismissal from consideration of all violations and all contradictions. Love became equivalent to the absence of critical thinking. The strength of love was measured by the degree to which one defended the paternal bloodline as articulated by uncle Najeeb.

This realisation had made being with my family more difficult. It was no longer an option to dismiss the independent voice inside my head. I had become more aware and more sensitive to coercion and manipulation. I had watched how ideals were replaced by no less than tribal sentiment. For better or worse, the bloodline had become the exclusive ideal.

During this family gathering in California, the traditional gender segregated roles were becoming more pronounced and the future of gender relationships within the family was unfolding. Women accepted their traditional roles as caretakers of children, of adult men and the home. I struggled to remain silent.

In this brief family gathering, the seeds were sown that led to my breaking away from my most limiting boundary, my extended family. I realised that there was no middle way. I either had to accept the status quo or to start mapping a new road, a new way forward. I had not and did not intend to spend my life following an illusion. Rather, I had journeyed through life learning and growing as a person.

I accepted that to believe in and to relinquish ideals are parts of the maturation process, part of the complexity of being human. I was not suffering insanity. I knew that I was not the only one in my family who could hear and see the hypocrisy and contradictions. The difference is that I chose to pay attention. I chose to address these difficult issues realising that it is much easier to have an emancipated voice among strangers than among family and loved ones. I realised that my quest to own my voice had just begun. I write now knowing that for the others my writing may sound like an exaggeration. This however is my reality; it is my daily experience of life.

It had taken me fifteen years to realise that I had been manipulated and exploited by men both in the name of religion and in the name of freedom. Working through the residues had been painful! Trapped in defeat, I had to start again.

I embarked on my MA degree in sociology by immersing myself in books and meeting hundreds of women through their writings and/or their social and political activism. I wanted to remain apolitical. That, of course, is impossible if I want to live a full life with reason, passion and purpose. As life is so intertwined, issues of health, society and the economy are intimately connected with politics. My small apartment was filled with books, hundreds of them. I enjoyed postgraduate student privileges, a status that permitted me to borrow up to fifty books. I was allowed to keep some of them for up to three months. After the year of incarceration with only the Quran and a heavily censored newspaper, this seemed a miraculous bonanza.

In August 1992, I finished my coursework and embarked on the research and writing of my thesis. In my advisers, I had the best from two worlds: Professor R. Kloss with his considerable knowledge of the sociology of social movements and Professor Al Qazzaz with an equal knowledge of the Arab world.

I devoured the feminist sociological literature and I re-examined el Saadawi's books within that context. I traced the history of the women's liberation movement in the Arab world. In that eye-opening journey, I read about women activists of what the Western world classifies as third-world countries, the underprivileged and the exploited world. Quickly, I realised how influenced I had been by the Western notion of feminism. I pursued my quest in search of a voice that is distinctly mine. I adopted the Marxist/liberal/radical view of the feminist sociology of knowledge as my starting point.

I had chosen an eclectic approach for my master's thesis just as I have chosen an eclectic approach to life. I was no longer bound by or limited by preconceived ideas. Now, I could read and learn from the world's feminist literature – Eastern and Western alike. I re-read C. Wright Mills' *Sociological Imagination* in a quest to understand the role of mass media in manufacturing the consent of women and men in US society.

Until then, I had read mostly Arab male sociologists. Thus, I started to read and concentrate on Arab and Western women sociologists and researchers. Through feminists' literature, I was introduced to the literature of pioneering Arab women writers that I had never heard of before. I learned of the contributions of many Arab women who devoted their lives to the promotion of women's rights in Islam and the Arab culture alike. Women's names, words and beautiful voices were my companions. My head, my life and my small apartment were filled with books written by women about every conceivable topic. I studied women's views of Islamic, communist, capitalist, radical and liberal philosophies. My mind was now filled with different voices. While each voice resonated with my own, none was mine. I knew that I had to find my own voice. I turned again to open myself to this new fascinating world of ideas, of different perspectives.

The reading and the learning was not just for a degree, it was for me. It was for my own sake that I chose to write on the feminist movement in the Arab world. I chose to use the feminist sociology of knowledge as my framework. I had not anticipated the liberation that accompanied my study of feminist literature.

I began to read about women in the modern Muslim world. I was introduced to Fatna A. Sabbah's *Woman in the Muslim Unconscious* (Athene series, 1984). Sabbah shows through religious texts that the ideal woman's image is judged by silence, immobility and obedience. Sabbah examined the relationship between the domain of order represented by the legal discourse and the domain of disorder represented by the erotic discourse. Woman is viewed as an omni-sexual creature, *"a voracious crack ... whose most prominent attribute ... is her sexual organs"* (p. 24). The ideal woman silently follows the path of obedience and seclusion. Women are exclusively sexual beings; economically and politically they are obliged to remain subservient to men. Sabbah asked what evokes the female body as an object of love, desire and male concern. Further, she questioned what places women in the submissive role vis-à-vis Muslim men. Sabbah demonstrates that what underlies these perceptions and expectations of male and female sexuality is an "official" view of the universe, one that is organised hierarchally according to sex.

The more I read, the more I realised how little I knew and how much I had been deprived of knowing. I had become familiar with

Fatima Mernissi's extensive research. Through it, I discovered that I had deprived myself of my right as a Muslim woman to access my own religion. Mernissi called on all Muslim women to claim their inherent Islamic right to equal access to the Quran. Having access to my own religion resonated with me.

I started reading the Quran with a new perspective, without the authority of male religious scholars and with an open mind. On this occasion, a prison guard did not force the Quran on me. I sought a copy in Arabic and an English translated version.

Mernissi's book, *Beyond the Veil: Male and Female Dynamics in a Modern Muslim Society*, is a study of sex roles, sexuality and sexual inequalities in Islam. The study is useful in understanding the conflicting trends and values Muslims must navigate.

In examining the role of women in Islam and in modern Muslim societies, it is important to understand the differences between theory and practice. When traditionalists claim that Islam does not teach that women are inferior, they have a point. Islam does indeed *"affirm the potential equality between the sexes"*. Thus, in theory women are not inferior to men

In practice, Islam does not start from the premise that women are inferior. Quite the contrary, Islam recognises that women are powerful sexual beings. Thus the actual social inequality which women experience does not stem from inferiority, but rather from fear of their superiority. Men fear this sexuality and thus must control it. Because woman's voracious sexual impulse represents a threat to the order and stability of the community of believers, it must be controlled.

Keeping an open mind, I continued to read about women and the Western manufactured conception of womanhood and femininity. I started with *Good Housekeeping* and then journeyed to *Woman's Day* and *Family Circle*. I even explored *Playboy* and its portrayal of womanhood and femininity. However, the only subscription I had was for *Ms Magazine*, which was devoted exclusively to feminism.

Along the way, I read Naomi Wolf's *The Beauty Myth: How Images of Beauty are Used Against Women* (Harper Collins Publishers, 1991). In this book, Wolf examines how modern conceptions of women's beauty impact the spheres of employment, culture, religion and medical issues such as eating disorders and cosmetic surgery.

In her book, Wolf questions why so many women feel that they do not measure up when it comes to their looks. The book explores how images of beauty are used against women. It provides an understanding of the dynamics of the power of the media in shaping women's views of their self-worth. Wolf demonstrates how the media manipulate women (and men) into feeling insecure and unhappy. Further, she documents how Western culture cultivates the stereotype of women as sexual objects and men as success objects. Wolf explores the relationship between female liberation and female beauty. She uses research and statistics to demonstrate that as women succeeded in breaching the power structure, eating disorders rose and cosmetic surgery became the fastest-growing medical specialty.

Wolf attributes this phenomenon to a cultural backlash against feminism that uses images of female beauty to keep women "in their place". She argues that there are many women (and men) who believe that the stereotypical "ugly feminist activist" is only a feminist because she's too undesirable to get a man. Wolf shows that, throughout the years, there have been forces in the patriarchal culture that attempt to punish women who seek more control over their lives and their environment. The "beauty myth" is dangerous because it has succeeded in distorting women's internal sense of self worth. It has created a standard of femininity that is impossible for women to attain.

It was Mernissi's sociological research that provided me with a new lens, a counter-balancing view for re-reading el Saadawi's complete research, "Studies on Women and Men in Contemporary Arab Society", 1990. My life was engulfed in papers, pens and books. Within my car, I created a mini workstation. Thus, as I drove to and from the university, I would stop on the roadside to write. Often as I drove, ideas, arguments, hypotheses and debates flowed like a river inside my head. Often, I spent sixteen hours daily writing, deleting, editing and rewriting. In search of an Arab feminist sociology of knowledge, I summarised all of el Saadawi's research and translated it into English. I sought an epistemology, a way of understanding the nature, origin and scope of knowledge through the lens of an Arab feminist.

At last, I allowed myself to live with the spirit of the many women writers and researchers who had influenced my life. Out of the books, names, faces and words came to life. In my imaginary mental world, I have asked many questions and have engaged in long conversations with Malak Hafni Nasif, Huda Sharawi, Doriyah Shafiq, Nawal el Saadawi and Fatema Mernissi as I studied their work. Each day I would hypothetically engage one or more in a lengthy debate and ask numerous questions.

Then I would turn to Western feminists including Sandra Harding, Dorothy Smith, Catharine A. MacKinnon and others. Each day was a celebration of minds and souls. Every day was a dance, a symphony. The viewpoints spanned the spectrum from extreme liberal to extreme conservative. I danced with, engaged, ideas, perhaps for the first time. I consciously developed the ability to read and listen without the need to develop a counter argument. My ability to accept new perspectives without being on the offence or defence was slowly developing.

I had as much satisfaction as disappointment. I triumphed and despaired as I researched the history of women. As I researched past solidarity conferences and examined the worlds of the privileged and those who are not, I found women crippled, disadvantaged in one way or another in both the East and the West. With every book review and with every article, I developed more questions as I diverted from the main thesis question. In the Arab world, the relationship among the three variables – middle class, further education and women's emancipation – was obvious. I thought that poor women had no time or energy to think about feminism. I reflected on the many women in my life and wondered if they ever thought about their rights as women. Perhaps after all the cooking, washing, ironing, cleaning and childcare are accomplished it is possible – for a few – to think about their rights, but I doubt it.

In examining feminist literature, I began to re-evaluate my life and the path on which I journeyed. The feminist sociology of knowledge had provided the framework for me to research my thesis. Furthermore, it encouraged me to rethink my femininity, my sexuality, my womanhood and the kind of person I desire to be. I arrived at a clearer understanding of the sexual experience as a normal component of a balanced life. For me, it represented an emotional act, a risky decision and a great personal responsibility. I was, however, now more certain that it is part of the whole noble human experience.

In a very important arena, I was free. At age thirty-one, I regarded my decision to practise celibacy as an independent choice. It disregarded the powerful societal sexual influences that shape the conditioned responses of those who do not examine their choices, or their lives. I was aware of my unconscious inhibitions. I had become more aware of the role and influences of family, society, education and media in how sexuality is translated and exploited in everyday life. Somehow, I had known that I was not ready. I also knew that when I was ready I would know.

I realised that I had struggled to avoid becoming the standard and accepted stereotypical image of a woman, an Arab woman, a Muslim woman. The cost of constant vigilance, on constant guard against being moulded into a stereotype is high. I had naively believed that I could become what I wanted. Clearly that was not the case in either Western or Eastern cultures. Yet I had no intention of giving up, although I had been continuously discouraged by the reality of women's lives. I had a simple request: to be treated as a human being worthy of respect regardless of my body, my gender, my religious affiliation or any other characteristic. Unknowingly, I had set myself up for disappointment. Wanting to be a person, "the woman I am", was not as simple as I had thought. My expectation of what I would be able to do for myself, as a woman in a Western society, would soon collide with reality.

I had wanted to avoid being an image, a copy of someone I might never recognise. In that situation, I would be imprisoned within myself. I had wanted to feel fully alive. I was prepared to continue the struggle to make a difference in a world deformed by greed and power. Was I too idealistic, too naive? It had been in the US that I had finally confronted the oppression of Eastern cultures. Now I realised that I would need to redirect that courage to fight and to challenge the manufacture of "womanhood" in Western society.

I imagined then that I had succeeded finally in finding my true voice. While the journey had been long and arduous, it had brought me to the confrontation with the manufacture of women's image. It seemed that I was locked in a vicious cycle of unworthiness in which both a voice and an image were judged inadequate, inferior. I found myself immersed in another battle.

I continued my visits to Lioness Books in Sacramento, a destination that became my ultimate outing retreat. I spent hours voraciously browsing through women's literature and feminist books.

By chance one day I entered the shop next door to Lioness Books. I wandered inside believing it to be a costume shop. Thus, I entered my first-ever adult, erotic sex store. I realised how naive I was with regard to the arts of eroticism.

I had avoided my own sexuality; I constructed impregnable boundaries around understanding my own sensuality, my sexual desires and my personal perception of eroticism. I had prioritised my life so that sexuality was always pushed to the bottom of the "to do" list. On the rare occasion that I entertained thought of it at all, I consigned it for consideration when in an intimate relationship. During this introspective period, I learned that I was emotionally inhibited. I had raised the bar of my own standards of illicit behaviours to block out, deflect any and all approaches to my sexuality. I was simply petrified of loving and of having sexual desires.

In my peaceful refuge, comforted by the sound of solitude, the sense of aloneness, I had accepted that the war ahead would be long and I had pledged to choose my battles. I savoured my success in rejecting the patriarchally manufactured cookie cutter womanly image that I "should" pursue. Therefore with the companionship of great women I found refuge, endured, lived and continued to grow emotionally and intellectually.

At university, I was welcomed into a circle of women friends where I found acceptance, support and solidarity. We were women of varying ethnicities, cultures, histories, experiences and religions with different goals and aspirations. We were all enrolled in the department of sociology at Sacramento's California State University, where we pursued further education and careers. Joining me in the study group were Janet, Mary Yu, April, JoAnn and Lesley.

Janet was an African-American woman who while approaching age seventy, appeared to be in her fifties. She wore her age and ethnicity beautifully. Her distinctive African features and beautiful dark skin revealed a few proud age-lines around her lips and eyes. She possessed a contagious smile that brightened the darkest of days, a smile that mirrored the spirit of her beautiful soul.

I was surrounded and supported by JoAnn's soothing spirited voice, Mary Yu's youthful outlook, April's pursuit of happiness and excellence as a future lecturer and Lesley's ironic sense of humour. In the company of those women, I felt blessed and privileged. In the end, I was overwhelmed in parting from them. Despite the distance that might separate us, I knew that I would always be linked to them through the spirit of the time, and the reason that brought us together.

I concluded my thesis with a pessimistic sentiment that was contrary to that spirit of the time. Despite women's achievements worldwide and the progress Arab women were making, I was not optimistic. As a member of the less-privileged sex, I saw a bleak future for feminism in the Arab world. I was not impressed by the boundaries that women were transcending or the change that was taking place. I was concerned about the nature of the changes that women were achieving. The absence of democracy and freedom of expression underlined my pessimism. A feminist discourse that contributes to a feminist theory of knowledge is non-existent in the Arab/Muslim world. The majority of feminist discourse in the Arab/Muslim world remains fictional. El Saadawi and Mernissi contributed hard-core feminist research yet remain peripheral, on the margins of "real" scholarship, i.e., masculine contributions. To my dismay, I realised that my thesis would remain an isolated monologue within a fragmented feminist sociology of knowledge.

I submitted my thesis on 18 May 1993. As I approached graduation, I succumbed to the hovering depression. I struggled to let go of my cherished, sheltered life of solitude and semi-independence, one in which I had a voice. I struggled to let go of my books and my privileged access to the university libraries at Sacramento State and the University of California at Davis. Returning the books to the library was more like a burial ceremony. Gradually, I was emptying my apartment of the spirits of countless books and the hundreds of photocopied articles that I had accumulated during the two years of study.

\*

Since 1990, I had been waiting for the award of my permanent residency permit for the US. Still there was no sign of it been granted. During the Gulf War, I had missed my chance to apply for an exemption to speed up the procedure, a process opened to nationals of Saudi Arabia and Kuwait. That missed opportunity meant that my options were strictly limited. If I left the US, I would not have been eligible to apply for US re-entry under a different visa. On the student visa I held, I could pursue a doctorate in Women's Studies, a genuine interest of mine. Alternatively, I could pursue employment, which would require securing a work permit on the back of my current student visa.

I had been clear about the type of work and career I wanted to pursue. With my master's degree, I could surely apply successfully for work with the United Nations, Human Rights Watch or one of the many women's development organisations. While finalising the editing and revision of my thesis, I had submitted numerous applications for graduate schools and jobs. The University of Wisconsin Madison had conditionally accepted me, a possibility that without a scholarship was not feasible. I had focused my job applications on research and research assistant positions, as I was soon to hold an MA in sociology with a focus on the feminist movement in the Arab world. However, it appeared that the doors of opportunity were shut until further notice.

I had been unrealistic in my assumption that my educational credentials, my commitment to human rights and women's development and my Saudi passport would open the door to my career path of choice. That apparently was wishful thinking. With my limited political activism and advocacy of women's rights, I was just another name with an interesting background. My mailbox was filled with letters of rejection, which did not alleviate my distress.

In that state of hopelessness, I considered surrender as I confronted yet another test of my will. It seemed as if the universe was pushing me to the edge of despair and demanding that I surrender my dreams. Endlessly, I examined the two credible options available to me.

First, I could return home to Saudi Arabia empty handed and wait for the US residence permit, not knowing when or if it would be granted. Alternatively, I could stay in the US until my student visa expired in the hope that I could avoid forced repatriation. Thus, I decided to remain in the US. As I was not financially self-sufficient, I moved to the Los Angeles home of my sister Saffiya and her family hoping that I could buy myself some time and perhaps create an opportunity.

Meanwhile, I joined the Middle East Studies Association and initiated contact with people, events, publications and research with a regional focus. With my limited financial resources, I registered for its 1993 autumn annual conference taking advantage of the student membership and attendance discount. The conference provided me with the once-in-a-lifetime opportunity to meet Nawal el Saadawi and Fatima Mernissi, expert panellists on women and gender in the Arab world. I was grateful for the opportunity, a gift from the universe, a reality check. I was destined to meet many of the women whose names had inhabited my small space and whose books had shared my bed and table during that year: Deniz Kandiyoti, Miriam Cooke, Margot Badran, Eleanor Abdalla Doumato and many others with distinctive voices.

In the presence of such an inspirational group of women, I refocused my determination and resolved to continue my quest to find my own voice. In the presence of those women writer/activists, I felt humbled vis-à-vis the limits of my own experience. The conference experience validated that study, research and writing on the feminist sociology of knowledge had been the correct path for me. As I surveyed the conference participants, I knew with perfect clarity that there was no one ideal for me. I recognised that the road ahead was open and that in humanity there is neither perfection nor just one model. Ultimately, I would always confront my true self. I had matured into the realisation that everyone is limited in some respect. Our horizons are circumscribed; we all have limitations.

As I progressed in my thinking, I clarified my notion of feminism and who is or is not a feminist. Feminism was no longer limited to women or men whose voices were heard, whose words were published and read and who had influenced the gender discourse. Feminism was accessible for women in everyday life and in everyday acts. It is about the difference that women make to nourishing and sustaining self-worth. My shifting perspective did not diminish my commitment to women. Women were and are underprivileged and

I am but one voice in the struggle for advancement. I have no doubt with regard to my commitment to women. The advancement of women cannot happen without the re-education of men; without that, the cause is lost. Therefore, another strand must be incorporated into the journey.

With the growing awareness of my voice came the realisation that I no longer spoke legitimately in any collective sense on behalf of Saudi Arabian women. Given my considerable expatriate experience, I was no longer a true representative of the reality of the Saudi woman's everyday life. I had journeyed too far to claim such a privilege.

Other women's experiences and how they define and redefine themselves and their lives fascinate me. After reading Dorothy Smith's works *The Conceptual Practices of Power: A Feminist Sociology of Knowledge* (1990), *The Every Day World as Problematic: A Feminist Sociology* (1987) and *Feminism and Marxism: A Place to Begin, A Way to Go* (1977), I experienced a paradigm shift in my thinking, a shift that rivalled my transformation on reading el Saadawi at age sixteen. At last, I could relate to sociology from my experience of everyday life as a Muslim Shia woman. I validate my everyday experience of the world. I do so with the realisation that I am participating in and engaging in social relations and organisations that are not fully visible to me.

With my new perspectives, I examine my own conception of reality as imposed by a male-dominant culture. Gradually, I have become more sensitive to the coercive language I encounter by both males and females. The very language itself imposes on me. Others – male and female – assume how I should feel, think, react and even experience my own life. While others may share the same or similar experiences to mine, that does not endow them with the right to assume automatically that we share the same feelings or interpretations about such events.

At that life stage, I experienced feelings of incompetence and vulnerability. To be considered a women's rights advocate requires more than one year and thirty days in a Saudi political prison and the publication of a thesis that collects dust on a library shelf. Nonetheless, I had no doubt about my serious hard-working research bona fides. I had nurtured myself to write and to pursue a career in research. I knew that there was much to be said. However, I found once again that my voice was trapped beneath my pen and my computer's keypad and silenced by my financial dependency. While I recognised my need for a scholarship, I was clear about not applying through the Saudi educational mission. I feared that I would be limited in my choice of subject matter and of dissertation topic. Therefore, I aborted – or deferred – my dream of pursuing postgraduate studies. For the present, I put aside the longer-term dream of designing my own women's issues lectures and of research and publication.

With the approaching expiration of my student visa I became tense, irritable and more pessimistic. With no guaranteed right of return, I was to depart the US. I had not heard from the immigration department since 1990 when I was informed that my residency permit application was pending.

Despair weighed heavily on me. Leaving the US was complicated by my keen sense of loss and my reluctance to surrender my dream of a better future through work and research on women's issues. Although exhausted from financial dependency, I had closed the door to compromise with the Saudi educational mission. In rejecting the compromise, I honoured myself, my voice. Nevertheless, the price of that choice was despair.

I noticed that an angry, resentful and aggressive tone had invaded my voice. I became easily irritated as male family members, friends and acquaintances made insensitive and unnecessary comments about feminism and my identification with feminism. It seemed that every political, economic and social discussion ended with the mocking of feminism. I felt as if my every thought and action was being measured against and or justified by some feminist standard, i.e., She thinks this way because she is a feminist or because she is not a feminist. In irritation, I experienced the impositions of others. Rather quickly, I saw that the debate was no longer for the sake of understanding, but for the sake of undermining the intellectual capacity of women. I felt that my approach to life and my ability to think independently were being questioned, even undermined. For me, being a feminist and having a commitment to women never translated into seeing the world according to a narrow feminist point of view as defined by males.

I observed also that I was becoming less patient and less content. It was time to move on, taking with me memories of accomplishment and of unaccomplished dreams. It was time to go forward and to embrace myself in another journey. I armoured myself with my lone distinctive possession, my true autonomous voice. I had been away from Saudi Arabia for four and one-half years. Given that so much had happened and changed over those years, I imagined that no one would expect me to remain the same as before I left.

In frustration, I had written a letter to my mother admitting my fear of giving up the fight. I was exhausted by my own hopes and dreams. I had seriously considered relinquishing my promise not to surrender my strength, my voice and my right to be truly me, not to compromise for financial gain.

As I repatriated to Saudi Arabia, death hovered, seemingly awaiting my arrival. It seemed that I was being abandoned by the whole world.

# Memoir: Fatema, a Woman of Influence

*Within the lingering resonance of my maternal grandmother's voice, I journeyed toward memory's gate. I was an innocent little girl following the hems of Fatema's veil chasing memories of the past, memories of what might have been and visions of what was never to be. Over the years, I had journeyed away from her gentle zone of influence. In due course, I returned to journey again towards her gate. While I had doubted my voice, I had never doubted Fatema's voice.*

*I view my life as if it had begun long before she was born. I knew that my life would extend beyond her passing; I anticipated that it would extend beyond my own passing. I was born into Fatema's lineage, but with a peculiar geography for my life. My comprehension of life extended far beyond the boundaries imposed by my parochial community.*

*Even in environments totally alienated from hers, I had – knowingly or unknowingly – always journeyed towards Fatema's voice. Eternally, I journeyed toward the small coastal town washed by sea salt on the shore of the Arabian Gulf. On that ultimate journey, I approached to find death hovering at Fatema's bedside.*

*As a child, I vowed to learn to read and to read well. I did so on discovering that my beloved Fatema could not read despite her ability to recite the Quran and the supplications flawlessly. My maternal grandmother introduced me to a life full of beautiful voices. In the sanctuary of her love I found my voice.*

# 8

# Shattered Lives, Shattered Dreams

After a self-imposed exile, I returned to that seaside town in 1994 and half-heartedly settled again in Saudi Arabia. I was more insecure financially than when I left. Emotionally, I was far more insecure as I had no clear idea of what I wanted to do. I had no clear career path. I had no passion to be there.

After my four and one-half year absence, I had returned to my society, to a post-Gulf War Saudi Arabia that was more restrictive and more rigidly fundamentalist than when I departed. The disparity between the rich and the poor had widened into an unbridgeable chasm. The distinctive middle class had become even more alienated. In its isolation, it was not motivated to pursue any substantial, or indeed any, changes.

During that time, I viewed myself as a transient, a casual visitor to my homeland. I sought to be true to myself and to do things in my own way, not as determined by external forces. I focused intensively on the friendships and the family relations that I wanted to maintain. Intentionally, I ignored all else.

I consciously decided to enjoy that transitional period as much as possible. I considered re-applying to Aramco only to face certain rejection. As a Shia woman, a political activist and a dismissed former employee, I was unlikely to be re-employed, regardless of my qualifications or the company's shortage of capable Saudi females.

Ultimately, I had to search outside of Aramco, outside of the Eastern Province. One of the many vacancies for which I applied was at the King Faisal Specialist Hospital in Riyadh. In September 1994 after four restless months at home, I was assessed, accepted and assigned to the hospital's social service department. My initial assignment was as a rotating social worker filling in for well-established social workers while they were on leave.

## Fatema's passing

My new employment coincided with the deterioration of Fatema's health. She was standing at her gateway to death. She became extremely ill and was taken to hospital. Very soon, she would leave it for her new home, her final resting place, but briefly, she enveloped me in the grace of her heart. It was a fleeting moment as she paused at the portal of her sanctuary. It was a treasured moment that would sustain me for a lifetime of love and of bereavement. Into my heart Um Hameed whispered, "You have returned to walk alongside me the last few steps." Into my heart Immy Um Hameed faintly raised her voice in supplication and whispered into my ear *almoaawthat*, an invocation from two surahs in the Quran. Her last words were a benediction for my protection from envy and from Satan and for the lonely years to come.

For the last fourteen years of her life, Fatema had suffered Parkinson's disease with sharply progressive deterioration in her final four years. She discontinued her doctor's appointments. My uncle continued to obtain her prescriptions without her being seen by or examined by a doctor. I was present on the day that, motivated by her obvious pain, my uncle called the doctor to Fatema's bedside. Immediately, he ordered her to hospital on finding a large tumour in her womb. Fatema was diagnosed with an advanced stage of cervical cancer.

Motionless, I listened as the doctor delivered Fatema's death sentence: "She has cancer. It must have been there for some time now. She is too weak to be operated on and the only thing we can do is to make her comfortable." She was exceedingly frail and in agonising pain.

Helplessly, I stood beside her hospital bed wishing that I could divide the remaining years in my account between us in order to have Fatema live longer. If I could have suspended that moment in life and remained beside her bedside, I would have done so. I knew that the world was going to be harsher without her.

Devastated, I approached Fatema and whispered, "Do not leave me stranded at the door of your sanctuary. You asked me to return and I came back unwillingly, but I came back. Now, you are leaving me. Please Immy Um Hameed, please Fatema stay with me." There was only a faint smile and warm glances of love. As I knelt beside her bedside, I felt the world kneel with the imminent departure of she who had given me my voice.

In those final days, Fatema rarely spoke to any of us. There were only faint tears and smiles. I wished to be in her heart, to feel what it must be like waiting to die, waiting to take the last breath, waiting to hear the last sound. By her bedside, I clung to her selfishly. She was ready to leave, perhaps to a much nicer place, one as serene and as beautiful as Fatema herself. I did not want to grieve. I was not ready to let go.

I returned every weekend from Riyadh to Dhahran to visit Fatema, as she lay sedated. In those days, she was even more beautiful, more serene, more at peace. I was not. I was there beside her bed on 30 September 1994 before returning to Riyadh. After work the following day – 1 October 1994 – I returned home to receive the news of her passing. Immediately, I flew back to the Eastern Province to be with my mother and younger sister during the prayers and remembrance observances.

Swiftly, Immy Um Hameed, Fatema, had passed away. In the shadow of her voice, I journeyed toward my voice. It was during Fatema's *fatha*, a few days of Quran readings, prayers and remembrance that I felt death's presence. In that epiphany, I realised that I had embarked upon another life stage, one of living with death as an integral part of life's journey. For the first time, I realised that loss and grieving are not about letting go of someone. For me, they are about the celebration of Fatema's life and of experiencing her spirit, her presence in my life.

During the prayer ceremony, I looked – really looked – at the women around me. For the first time, I embraced them with my heart rather than measuring them with my head. I was overwhelmed by my prejudiced perception of these traditional women, largely without formal education, as the living dead. What gave me the right to impose my prejudices, my Western feminism on these familiar and unfamiliar women? I questioned the legitimacy of my quest for a better world for women and men. My vision was far removed from the reality of their everyday lives. During that observance for Fatema, I decided that if I could make a difference in any woman's life, if I could lead one woman to realise and appreciate her self worth, I would contribute toward a better world for all humanity.

Turning a new page, I returned to Riyadh's King Faisal Specialist Hospital to resume work. Reluctantly, I settled into my repatriation to Saudi Arabia. Anxiously, I prayed for the arrival of my US residency permit before I totally surrendered to the new reality. I did not want to become enthralled within a luxurious, suffocating cocoon.

I need not have worried. Things never fell into place in Riyadh and I never felt settled. In my determination to live with integrity, I continued to believe that transparency and truth are the best way to people's hearts and minds. While most people tolerated the changes they found in me, they persisted largely in selectively hearing what they wanted to hear rather than listening and accepting my honest views.

During this mourning period for Fatema, I realised more than ever before that while I can live in Saudi Arabia, I do not want to do so. In my mind I was clear about my love for family and friends. However, I knew that staying in the Kingdom would slowly inhibit and stifle me. It was not about the inequality, the lack of freedom or even dismal quality of life. It was more profound, as it was about the simple and basic respect for all humanity, women and men. I was a changed person returning to a country trapped and confused within its own identity.

Soon, the honeymoon period ended. There was no fulfilment, no satisfaction, no joy in being in and living in my own country. Even the love and warmth of old friendships and familial relationships could not thaw the ice encasing my heart and my soul. I had become more cautious about forming new relationships and friendships. The friendships and the relationships that I had prior to my self-imposed US exile sustained me. During this transitional period, I recognised that I did not whole-heartedly engage with others. Gradually, I resisted the temptations and intrigues of others. I knew that relationships and friendships do not necessarily ask permission to invade one's life.

\*

As a social worker at King Faisal Specialist Hospital, I had to engage with people, specifically women. Reluctantly, I undertook my first assignment in the nephrology department. As the substitute for the social worker on annual leave, I was to follow clients in the dialysis unit and transplant units. Quickly, my resistance melted as these women's voices started to flow into my life. On those daily rounds of unit and surgical wards, I confronted birth and death as part of my daily life. Hospital work is about the fight for life and my rounds were defined by stories of the ordinary, everyday lives of those women.

As I sought to come to terms with the loss of Fatema, death took on a new, different meaning. In coming to terms with it, I realised that death does not end the relationship and the presence of those we love in our life. I was shocked to realise how selfish I had been. How could I have been willing to make the choice to prolong her life just because I did not want to deal with life without her? In reconciliation, I felt Fatema's presence. I realised that she was and always will be part of me, part of my days and of my nights.

In my work, I had to confront death as I conveyed the news of the passing of loved ones. I had to be there to console family members and friends; people I did not know and will never meet again. I searched for a language that is worthy of death, one worthy of life. In equal measure, I was confronted by and lived with both life and death every day.

As my temporary assignment with the nephrology unit was drawing to a close, to my surprise, I was invited by the nephrology department head to continue as the permanent social worker. Although I realised that my acceptance might create challenging issues within the social services department, I answered "yes". It did create some discontent; however, I chose to ignore it and to get on with the job and with my life.

In addition to my permanent social worker position with the nephrology division, I was also assigned to the liver transplant unit. For the next eleven months, my days began and ended at the dialysis unit. During the day, I divided my time among the wards, the transplant patients and the dialysis unit. I spent most of my time in the unit where women, men and children were connected to dialysis machines. Not every client required social services support or requested to see the social worker; however, each needed to be seen and heard.

Quickly, I found the flaw in the academic concept of social services and social work: services are not delivered to clients. Rather, the practice was a reciprocal engagement in which the clients supported me as much as I supported them. They taught me how to appreciate life and to count my blessings. They taught me that life is not about what I do not have, but about what I have.

I had observed the courage required to give a part of one's body for another to live a better life. I had learned to accept both the generosity and the selfishness of people. I came to understand how fragile we humans are. Living with the realisation that everything could change and everything could end in a split second made life more precious. The King Faisal Specialist Hospital's patients taught me to be humble. There, my defences collapsed as women's voices and the narratives of their lives triumphed over my self-defence. I was lured into listening to different voices. Eventually, I became engaged with, often enthralled by, those voices.

Stories of family neglect and/or sacrifice circulated within the dialysis unit. Typically, those told were related partially in barely audible whispers. There were countless stories of life journeys with eternal illness. There were stories of the will to live, narrated in the powerful voices of those who suffered. There remained many untold stories.

I was partial in that I naturally gravitated toward women's voices. To them, illness was seen as part of their journey, as their destiny. Repeatedly, I stood speechless before the courage and the generosity of simple, mostly illiterate women. None of the patients commanded the sophisticated language to cope with the complexities of their illness. They knew only the simple language of love that informed them as to their duty with regard to kidney failure and dialysis.

The patients, the families and the medical teams were obsessed – consciously and unconsciously – with the search for a matching donor, for healthy kidneys. People were willing to and did take the substantial risk of organ rejection, of further complications and of the aggressive side effects that often accompany the treatment to safeguard the new organ. Each journey was a quest for a normal life.

## Other women's voices

Every day at the hospital, there was a powerful reason to kneel before the extraordinary human sacrifice and unconditional love on display. Regrettably, there were too many occasions on which the cruelty of humans was on exhibit also. There were no simple ordinary ailments. Every case was critical; every simple act of courage, selflessness and selfishness was an act of love.

As women connected to a dialysis machine told their stories, I would draw nearer. As I listened to their stories, my voice faded. Just as the women did not have a language with which to articulate their sense of self as an ill person, I did not have a language to express myself without reference to women's rights and liberty.

Without the language of feminism, I did not know how to express myself. It defined my persona. Feminism became at once relevantly irrelevant. Concepts of liberty and rights were far removed from those women's voices, their realities in the dialysis and the transplant units. With each entrance into a treatment session, women needed closure to the stage in the journey from which they had exited.

There were many patients, many women and many voices. In their suffering and in their illness, women were equal regardless of their privilege or lack thereof, regardless of their level of education or family background. Illness was the common denominator of their lives. They all shared dialysis; they were all connected to the familiar machines. Some also had their share of failed transplants, as their bodies had rejected donated kidneys. Still, their voices expressed hope for normality through transplantation, despite its complexity.

The women I served had no language with which to articulate the new relationship between the self and the body, the loss of control, the loss of health and the loss of choice. We explored questions of self-worth, of esteem, of feelings and what it means to be normal. These common grounds were the starting point for the narratives of these extraordinary women. Within them, there was also a keen desire for acceptance, the acceptance of a dysfunctional body. Psychologically, the women alternated between the acceptance of sickness as punishment and sickness as a test of their faith in Allah.

The narratives of women's lives with illness were different from those of men equally afflicted. The voices of women were broken.

Men with a similar illness, although suffering, were comparatively untouched in their masculinity, their sense of self worth.

Echoes of past voices, of other hospital units from another life were resurrected and shared. I witnessed a different kind of courage, love and an imprisonment quite different from my own incarceration. Imprisoned in their dysfunctional bodies, these women dismissed neglect, emotional abuse and social injustice as they searched for a donor, a matching healthy functioning kidney, or at least for someone, anyone, kind enough to drive them to their next dialysis appointment.

Eternally, I will remember the voices as they narrated their lives while connected to the only lifeline – the dialysis machines – the only choice. I remember particularly the voice of the thirty-eight year old college lecturer who branded herself a rebel, a selfish woman and one who loved and enjoyed life, perhaps to excess. Since puberty, she had been aware of her femininity and beauty. At thirty years of age, she was diagnosed with Lupus. Despite her education and her role as an educator, she had dismissed the medical diagnosis. She simply could not imagine being vulnerable to such illness. Tragically, she had ignored it far too long. Now approaching kidney failure, she rationalised that her illness was Allah's punishment for her pleasure-seeking and selfish ways. Guilt was the product of her pursuit of desire.

Silently, I listened as she expressed her conviction that her suffering was due to her pursuit of happiness in religiously and socially forbidden realms. She rejected her knowledge and intelligence, attributing to them her pain and suffering. I listened as she diagnosed herself with multiple personality disorder, as she spoke of the numerous voices in her head. Some voices urged her to socially and religiously forbidden behaviour while other more subtle voices urged obedience to Allah. Some voices urged her to attempt suicide. She resisted, saying, "People like me do not commit suicide. I love life too much." In the end, the desire to live and to enjoy life to its utmost surpassed her desire to end it. Suicide requires extreme courage, which she admitted she did not have.

I puzzled over how she had never connected her unreasonably anxious mother, alcoholic father and a tyrannical alcoholic brother to the multiple voices in her soul. Meekly, she had accepted her brother's violent behaviour, as he had assumed their father's responsibility for the discipline of women in the house. Clearly, she feared life in a household headed by her brother. The alternative life with a husband she had never desired in the first place was attractive.

When I last saw her she was still searching for peace of mind and a way to escape the relentless voices in her head. Her love and zest for life, her illness and her sense of abandonment by Allah coalesced to create inner turmoil. As she searched for a path out of chronic illness, the lecturer was stymied, as she had no idea of how to reinvent her life. Although not divorced (which she desired), she did not live with her husband. While she realised the need to be heard and acknowledged by others, she was reticent to reveal her story. She contemplated seeing a psychiatrist, but desisted, as she knew that she would never express the voices of desire and pleasure that defined her. Instead, she settled for a protective healing charm blessed by a well-known religious man. In her view, it was the only acceptable cure. She believed that for a medical cure or a healing charm to work, she had to regain her soul.

Rebellious tones often defined the voices of these women as they recounted their experiences of illness. Typically, there was always another woman, another voice and another narrative.

Vividly, I recall one especially memorable voice. It was that of a woman fully surrendered to fate and to the will of Allah. That voice belonged to the school clerk who sought and succeeded in finding purpose and meaning in life beyond her illness. In honouring her paternal grandmother's wishes, she had married at the age of sixteen and had become a mother soon after. She managed her relationship with her husband and his first wife by avoiding domestic disputes and conflicts. She sustained her pride and self esteem by completing high school at the age of twenty-four. Shortly thereafter, she found a job.

Quietly, I listened as she told of her illness.

> During my first pregnancy at age seventeen, I began my journey with illness. At that time, I was diagnosed with high blood pressure and a kidney infection. Now, it has been four years since I was diagnosed with kidney failure. I did not mind kidney failure as much as I felt the

pain of my siblings' rejection. None of them exhibited any willingness to even test for a possible match. My husband spared no time in departing in search of a new wife freeing me of my wifely duties and obligations and leaving me alone with illness.

Her greatest loss was of her paternal grandmother and her father. Since their deaths, she felt that her voice had ceased to be heard. Endlessly, she worried about her daughter's future. Her greatest fear was that her husband would marry their daughter to someone of his choosing without consulting either of them as he had repeatedly threatened; that would have consigned the daughter to a life like that of her mother.

A third memorable voice was that of a shrewd poet. As I listened, I studied her nomadic facial tattoos, although she was not of nomadic lineage. Her voice issued sorrowful, effortlessly flowing poetry that wove together the narrative of her life. In poetry, she revealed her life story. Without consultation, she was married at the age of seventeen to one of her mother's relatives. That event led to a life of humiliation.

Her poetry spoke of being buried to life with a spiteful man who lived to humiliate others, especially his wife. He had no compassion whatsoever and was miserly with kindness and love, but not with his lust for her body. The poet took in sewing, managing a meagre income to support their ten children. Meanwhile, the husband went travelling to experience other women free of commitments.

Her poetry revealed an abused life and the course she chose in order to retain custody of her children. She was haunted by childhood memories of neighbourhood children who were confiscated and taken away from their mothers by vengeful fathers. Helpless, the poet's voice was trapped in that memory.

Yet, the poet's heart and life were filled with forgiveness. Her life, her poetry were sustained by her dreams of a loving, compassionate and respectful husband and good natured children living a simple harmonious desert life. Her dreams, however, were carried by the winds and scattered over the dry earth of reality. For the poet, the blossoms – the rewards – of life are in the children nurtured in the unconditional love of the mother's heart. Despite her best efforts, she was not rewarded with blossoms. Helplessly, she watched as her daughters contracted marriages as miserable as her own. Similarly, she has sons who were equally as cruel as their father had been. The poet's voice never blossomed as her dreams died, unrealised.

In the background, I heard another distinctive voice, a gentle voice of love and devotion. It was the narrative of a woman who had been blessed with the ultimate expression of a sibling's love and devotion. She told of how her husband ostracised her during her first pregnancy. Subsequently, he proceeded to marry another woman during her fourth and died during her fifth pregnancy. Then as if not having suffered enough, she was given an ultimatum: marry her deceased husband's brother or lose custody of her five children. That experience broke her will. Her marriage to her brother-in-law was legalised rape. Each day of life with him, she was violated and broken. As if being violated, broken and raped were inadequate, she became pregnant. During her pregnancy, she suffered a sudden surge of high blood pressure that led to kidney failure.

It was her youngest brother who devoted his life to a search for a cure, a transplant option. He travelled with her to the United Kingdom and the United States. She experienced two failed kidney transplant operations. Her body rejected the matching donor kidneys. The doctors had no explanation, no answer. When she returned to dialysis, she knew that with her broken soul, her body could not be healed.

As single women narrated their stories, their voices changed. I listened as a twenty-five-year old woman spoke in her thirteen-year-old voice, narrating the story of the kidney failure she sustained at that young age. Her childhood had been stolen as she endured ten years of kidney failure, recurrent hepatitis and a failed transplant. When her transplant failed six months after the surgery, her whole attitude to life and self had changed. At age twenty-five, her name was crossed off the list of kidney transplant candidates. With that loss of hope, her only option was life connected to the dialysis machine. Like her life, her voice became even more marginalised. She had lost interest in living and had become more sensitive as people took pity on her. For her, any hope of returning to school and finishing her education also evaporated.

In her experience, illness was torture and punishment. Hers had the sound and contours of a voice that had lost hope, a sound distinctive from all others. In her, hope had expired. She had no hope of leading a normal life like other young women or of being eligible to marry or have children. She found no hope in life with dialysis and no purpose in speaking of her illness. Even reading and reciting the Quran, which had been of benefit in the past, ceased to provide any comfort.

The voice of the thirteen-year-old accepted the illness as punishment, for it could not be a blessing by Allah nor a test of faith. Simultaneously, the voice of the twenty-five-year-old was more inclined to accept a life with dialysis gracefully in the hope of being rewarded by Allah's mercy and compassion.

In this culture, the single woman has no value. A woman must marry. It does not matter if the man is sick, old, illiterate or dysfunctional. Her value is totally dependent upon the perceptions of society. For the single woman to be deemed normal, she must be desired, sought after and married.

Certainly, that was the case of the young woman who was afflicted by Lupus at the age of sixteen. In her view, her self-worth could only be restored by marriage. She had no doubt that in order to be perceived as worthy, she must be desired by a man, any man.

The voice of denial and rejection became clearer as she spoke of her illness. Instead of planning for an ordinary, fulfilling life ahead, she was watching her dreams being narrowed to the hospital corridors and dialysis unit. To her, the tour of the unit seemed a warning. Surely that was not life ahead? Lupus and the possibility of kidney failure eroded her self-worth. As her life and dreams had been readjusted with the thought of dialysis, the young woman's voice had surrendered into helplessness. In her illness, university had remained the only option available to her to lead an ordinary life. She had been fighting hard to succeed, trying hard to be in control of success.

The bargaining options of chronically ill women are reduced to zero. The young woman's life had changed irrevocably due to illness. Before her parents' silence, her voice was defeated. They possessed no language to express how they had failed her. Confronted with her illness, they too were powerless.

Her voice strengthened only when she spoke of her love for a man with whom she became involved in a telephone relationship. They had never met. The man was brutally honest in admitting that he would never marry her; he simply would never marry a woman willing to have a pre-marital telephone relationship even if it was with him. Nevertheless, she viewed the telephone relationship as preferable to the absence of any relationship.

Bitterly, she spoke of the injustice of society's negative view of the chronically ill, the handicapped and of women who even in the prime of their health were deemed unworthy. In these expressions, her voice would veer between denial and sorrow. The voices of those in the dialysis and transplant units continually sought some sense of self-worth through normal physical abilities. They were courageous voices. Women, single or married, were equal in their sense of worthlessness and defeat; they were simply unable to see themselves as persons of worth. I left the hospital with fragmented memories of those broken voices of courageous women. Those narratives and voices lingered between the hospital corridors and a stranger's memory.

## Flirtations

Twice during my Riyadh transitional period, fate flirted with me. Distracted by the shattered voices within the hospital and Fatema's death, I was insensitive to the potential of both opportunities.

The first flirtation was with Seif – my second love – whom I had not seen since that September day in 1985 when his sister Husna placed his blue farewell envelope in my hand. In November 1994, Seif's sister, Norah was rushed into the emergency room at Riyadh's King Faisal Specialist Hospital.

There, he and I sat facing one another. After nine years apart, my heart did not skip a beat. I knew instantly that I could never hate him, no matter how brutal he had seemed in ending our relationship. How could one hate someone as gentle as Seif? I was incapable of hating, certainly not a man I had loved so deeply.

He spoke first, asking what brought me home. He thought that I had become a US citizen and had settled in California. I explained that my Green Card was pending.

I asked how he was. Gently, he replied: "Trapped and chained." I expressed regret on hearing that, while thinking that it was a choice he had made. I asked about his children. He smiled and said, "They come naturally."

Unconsciously, the lyrics of Fairuz's *"keefak inta"* ("how are you?") filled my head. She sings of someone who left her and then she sees him again years later; her lyrics mirrored our responses. As we said our farewells, I recalled the words that he wrote to me in that long-ago September: *"I hope that one day we will be able to meet for coffee and talk."* He did not ask if I had loved anyone else after him. If he had, I would have answered him truthfully: "No."

The second fateful flirtation was in London, England, in March 1995, when by coincidence Suhail – my first love – and I met alone for the first time. This was almost fifteen years after we were last together and at that time we lived in different parts of Saudi Arabia. We had the occasional communication and sometimes met in the Eastern Province among friends. On that March holiday, I flew from Riyadh to visit my sister Saffiya who had moved to England the summer before. Suhail flew there from Dhahran for his annual heart check-up.

As Suhail had tickets for *Miss Saigon*, we went to the theatre. Later, we concluded the evening at a café over coffee and ice cream on that cold winter day.

During the play, Suhail cried. His mother Batool had died. He felt that he had been abandoned, that he was alone in the world. With her death, he realised that he had lost the two women who had truly loved him.

What were the chances of meeting in London in 1995? It was pure coincidence. We did not talk much about ourselves. We made small talk, about nothing of importance. I was aware of my vulnerability and my status as a single woman. Although I was aware that I did not attract men, I had not examined why this seemed true. Nevertheless, I was not going to let Suhail feel sorry for me. I was not going to allow him to think, "You could have been married to me with children." In those days, I was constantly on guard. I was aware of what might go on inside a man's head, even a man who truly loved me.

Suhail had always given me ammunition with which to fight him. Often, we had invested many hours in blaming one another, blaming the world and in discussing politics. In all those hours, we never blamed men who in the name of freedom violated women's freedom to choose.

We had invested far fewer hours in marvelling at the gift of love and respect that we shared. I tired of arguing about the strength of our mutual love. While Suhail loved me, he did not wait for me to be released from jail. He was the only man who could have understood, the only man who could have waited. He chose otherwise, thereby dooming for ever any chance that we could be together.

Clearly, I had misjudged him. Subsequently, I realised that Suhail did not take risks. Conveniently, he fell in love with another woman. He did not choose to wait for me. Indeed, when I was released from jail, Suhail was engaged. Clearly, he loved me in his own way. It did not include waiting without a promise, without any assurance of hope.

Too late on that cold March 1995 day, I realised that fate was flirting with me. Stubbornly, I never acknowledged the opportunity. We talked about everything except ourselves. Again we parted, as if being together was as taboo as our love twenty years earlier had been. I realised that I had missed him, his friendship and companionship. I did not reveal those feelings to him.

There had been invitations to love; there had been the possibility of love. In the end, they were but flirtations.

However, while working at the hospital in Riyadh I tripped, taking a misstep that turned my world upside down and inside out. Disobedient to my usual strict moral code, I pushed the boundaries and flaunted my sensuality as I flirted on the brink of losing control. I navigated the delicate line between morality and immorality. Love is a noble emotion, but in this situation I felt cursed. There is no better description to being in love with a married man than that of being cursed.

Momentarily, I resisted the confrontation with my heart. I questioned if it was love, chemistry or pure sensual attraction? I questioned my desire to feel wanted, loved and worthy of a man. In this respect, I behaved just like other women who sought recognition in the only socially acceptable manner, i.e. being loved by a man. However, I was not behaving in a socially acceptable manner for I had fallen for a married man with four children. Clearly this was dangerous ground morally and ethically. To reclaim the high ground, I had to deny my heart, my sensual self and this fatal attraction.

I was not prepared for defeat. My heart had defied my rational core. It had rebelled against the moral base to which I had until then adhered so staunchly. In the distance, my mother's face peered at me through shuttered windows and closed curtains of thirty years ago. Firmly, her face was planted between my heart and my voice.

I confronted the resolute boundaries that I had created for myself. I summoned my strength and kept my distance. With each encounter, I had to face the battle anew.

Then, all my defences collapsed. I did nothing to stop the collapse as the inevitable happened, as if my heart had been waiting for the gate of love to open. It had been exactly nine years since my heart experienced a skipped beat. It must have skipped thousands. Mentally, I repeatedly rejected rationality. In crossing that red line, my morality was redefined. Briefly, I lived in a zone without any rational or moral boundaries. In this unknown territory, I was inventing myself with a new social consciousness.

In that space, I was on trial for being in love with a married man, an officially accepted social norm of immorality. Did I have the right to love, the right to choose or the right to defy society's norms? If I had such a right, was it moral or immoral? Endlessly, I examined these questions and my heart.

In doing so, I recalled a 1985 experience when I was in love with Seif. At that time, a single woman fell in love with him. She was determined and vowed to win Seif despite our relationship. As we three were all single at that time, I was told that I did not have any legitimate cause to resist. Apparently, a single heart does not have the same rights, does not have the same claim as that of a married heart. This was the morality with which I lived. I recognised that love is complicated as a moral issue; indeed it seemed that love could be at once morally immoral.

As my world had continued to spin, I needed to listen to others. My struggle was brief for instinctively I knew who might help me make sense of what was happening. Thus, I turned to the only person who could listen without judgment, without imposing guilt on me.

Across thousands of miles, I dialled and spoke to my father. His initial cheerful voice went silent as I greeted him. My voice gave me away. I sought to smooth the way, "Baba, I do not know how you will feel about me and what I am going to tell you." My father responded, "I am listening." Trembling, I confessed, "I am in love with a married man."

He was silent and there was no interruption. I heard my own voice as if it spoke to me from the other end of the line. I was listening to my own voice speak of my emotional struggle, confusion, weakness and the breached boundaries. My voice changed tone as I related how it felt to experience skipped heartbeats after so many years alone. Then, I realised that I was crying. I told my father that my heart was still capable of falling in love despite the hurt and pain of betrayal. I explained that something had changed within me; I felt that something was alive that I thought had died. I became aware of my own betrayal.

My father assured me, "It is your choice and your decision. Ask yourself if you can live knowing that you have broken up a family and taken a father away from his children." My father was struggling, "I am not saying this is not true love or that this man does not truly love you. If you pursue and marry him, it will always be you who destroyed his family life. For that, you will bear the burden. He may never forget that you were the reason, no matter how great his love for you."

My father and I were worlds apart. As I listened quietly, I forgot about my heart and listened to my father. I became more confused as I tried to make sense of what he was trying to say to me. In this revelation, he had lost track of my voice.

Was this a belated confession, an apology? It would have been thirty years ago when my father had left my mother and three little girls to follow his heart with another woman. I had called him for consolation, not for more confusion. Was this a typical way for men to confess, to apologise and re-evaluate decisions?

Nothing further was required, as I knew what I had to do. Without my conscious awareness of it, the decision had been made before I made the call. From my mother whose experience will always inspire my voice and heart, I had learned – the hard way – that the only way to mend a broken heart is through mourning.

As I struggled with the temptations of an impossible love and while nursing a broken heart, I walked – a last time – through the hospital corridors. There, I bore witness to the many voices from the transplant and dialysis units. While the names and faces faded, the voices and the narratives drummed themselves into me to remain in my memory, in my life as I voluntarily chose another journey of self-exile.

# 9

# A New Chapter

In August 1995, I resigned from Riyadh's King Faisal Specialist Hospital and relocated southeast to Dubai in the United Arab Emirates [UAE]. This was to be the next station in my journey. There, I was hired on a three-year contract as a student counsellor at a college for women.

With my world still spinning, my broken heart and my questionable morality, I believed that whatever the future held must surely be better than that which I had left behind. For the first time, I considered my misfortune, as I counted my blessings. Although I believed in destiny, I did not choose to believe in bad luck or envy. Despite my misfortune in love, I was fortunate in life.

As I summoned all my strength to celebrate my new beginning, I nursed my wounded heart and soul. Everything that I had believed about my life was in question. How could my heart long for a married man? How could I betray my mother by being the other woman situated between the heart of a man and his wife? How could that happen to me? When and how did my heart learn to love without the express permission of my rationality? My own heart and head had betrayed me.

In January 1996, six months into the Dubai contract, I was charged with treason. Speaking on behalf of his sisters and brothers and their husbands and wives (except of course my parents and siblings), my uncle Najeeb delivered the charge. I was summoned to trial without a warrant. My only witness was my paternal grandfather Mula Ali who was to judge between his children and me. This beloved, respected paternal grandfather, who was renowned for his wisdom and fair judgment, was compliant in listening. All evidence against me was based on incidents reported by family members when solicited by my uncle. There was no investigation and no attempt to settle accounts. The accusations were delivered and just as in prison many years ago, I was expected to confirm them without question. Like the secret service investigators who did not believe I had the right to defend myself, my uncle presented the allegations as the only truth.

As I listened, my mind raced back many years. Over time, I had become at peace with my own voice, with expressing my ideas and thoughts without feeling the need to justify or explain myself to the listener. I had been oblivious to what was being plotted against me since my return from the US in 1994.

Apparently, there had been confidential meetings with uncles and aunts as he gathered evidence. I had failed to see it coming. The meetings and evidence gathering must have taken years, as the documentation presented to my grandfather was an accumulation of incidents and depositions since the 1980s. My every interaction, decision, conversation and idea was submitted for scrutiny. Perhaps there was a board or a committee that reviewed the allegations before they were presented to my paternal grandfather. I will never know.

For the occasion, my uncle had worked himself into a fury. I viewed his rage as unwarranted given that there was no evidence to support the accusations. My heinous crime was that I was attempting to shatter the unity of our family. That was the only coherent statement my uncle expressed. He openly warned that I had no choice but to adhere to the family's code. If I defied him, he would see to it that the entire family shamed or shunned me into submission. Apparently, he forgot that I have sisters and parents who know my character.

While my uncle Najeeb was presenting the list of allegations to my paternal grandfather – who at that moment was speechless – I made the decision to save my voice. In disbelief, I sat silently, listening to each individual accusation. I was blindsided; I had not anticipated this trial.

The only words uttered were those of my uncle. He ensured that there was no opportunity for me to refute the allegations. Incredulously, I stared at this man, the man who had once been the primary source of inspiration during my early political activism. On hearing his charges, the doubt and confusion I experienced were similar to those that bewildered me during the first political debate I had ever heard; at that time, I was age fourteen and the debate was about the existence of Allah. The chasm between his lies and the truth was like the difference between the theory of evolution and the belief in divine creation. Through his eyes, my innocent behaviour took on a quite different, even sinister meaning.

This was the ultimate test of my courage. I sat before my paternal grandfather to be condemned by the man I had once revered idealistically. Before them, I was confronted with the family's charges. It was also a test of my own substance, resilience and strength before my family. I realised that I had to choose my battles. Taken completely by surprise, I could not rely upon my lone voice to refute the vast litany of allegations.

In analysing the situation, I sensed that a veil had been lifted. This was not about my truth in opposition to that of the others. It was not about moving my voice from the margin to the forefront. It was not even about being heard. Far more importantly, it was about having the courage to refuse victimisation.

I was not on trial, for that suggests an opportunity to respond to charges. Instead, I was berated by an evasive patriarchal discourse that demanded that I accept and agree without question. For me, the exercise was about my conscious presence in which I sustained determined concentration on the real issues. The bottom line issues were rank, power and control.

I had strayed from the grip of my uncle Najeeb's reins and I had to be brought back into the fold. I had become too critical and no longer revered him as my point of reference. I had an independent mind and soul. I no longer needed his or my family's approval for my thinking, feeling and actions. I was able to be who I wanted to be. While growing up, my critical insight and independence were admired attributes as long as they were viewed within the limits imposed by my uncle.

Now, as those once-admired attributes had matured, they had become threats, as they were no longer kept within limits established by others. I had become a threat to the structure my uncle had established almost twenty-three years earlier. I had become a threat to his personal power and control. I had challenged the status quo as I dared to ask when others did not; questioned family members' choices, words and actions and expressed disapproval of what I deemed to be racist and sexist jokes when everyone else laughed.

To defend his power and control, my uncle Najeeb had no alternative except to use his male privilege to intimidate and threaten me with isolation from the family if I refused to submit and repent. It had become clear in my mind that I owed no one an apology or explanation for the way that I think, the way that I perceive the world in which I live. I refused to submit to accusations based on taking my beliefs, ideas and stances out of context. The trial stage ended with me feeling that I was standing outside time and space. The startled judge, my paternal grandfather, had managed to mumble a few words, none significant. This was my first conscious experience of emotional and psychological assault. In it, my uncle sought to totally humiliate, destroy me before the family patriarch.

Before returning to Dubai, I stopped at my sister Saffiya's home taking with me the long list of old and recent allegations. This was not the time to choose silence. By the end of the day, I had called every member of the family who had filed an allegation against me. I repeated to each what my uncle Najeeb had represented as their words before my grandfather Mula Ali.

While my expectations were minimal, I was interested to observe and record the responses from people directly regarding their so-called accusations. As I asked about the allegations and the appointment of uncle Najeeb as their representative, not a single one – including his wife – confirmed that what he charged were exactly their words. Each explained that their comments and criticism of the way I think and behave were taken out of context. I had spent my last vacation day in Saudi Arabia on the telephone asking questions. I wanted one family member to explain to me what was going on. Not a single relative was able to pinpoint my uncle's motive.

Unbowed, I returned to Dubai knowing that I was able and ready to let go of the relationships with my father's siblings. There was no looking back and I have never looked back since. The family trial had revealed the unwritten code of relationships that had ruled our family. Since I was released from prison, I had observed and experienced

## A New Chapter

illogical incidents and inconsistencies between what was said and what was done. I had obscured my own intuition as I convinced myself that I was too serious. In rationalising every word and deed, I was branded by others as a spoilsport, as no fun at all.

Upon returning to Dubai, I replayed all that had happened during the family trial over and over again. I had to go back many years as the allegations were backdated to 1983, the year I was released from prison. All the allegations were related to me having an independent mind and the courage to express it. I had moved away from the stage of idealising my uncle and other leaders, all males, of course. As I became more open to the exploration of different possibilities and groups, I had stopped idealising men and ideas.

I had developed a new affinity for "questioning" actions, people, ideas including my own assumptions and actions, my own language and voice. I had become aware of my own use of language when I spoke or addressed different groups, cultures and people. I had become clearer and more forceful when evaluating or judging an issue or a conflict. I no longer necessarily sided with my family, but rather I supported what I saw to be just and fair. In my development, I had become a threat to my uncle Najeeb's personal agenda, a fact that I had yet to discover. His real agenda was unknown to any of the family, including me initially.

Beyond all the accusations, there must have been something, another truth to be protected. I had not realised that the more independent I became, the closer I was to unveiling an unwelcome truth behind the façade of my uncle's commitment to freedom and justice.

I proceeded to live my life leaving my uncle and other family members with their machinations against me. In his view, his public charge was necessary to protect the family's integrity, to keep it united. He believed, apparently, that only the united family's force could bring me back into the circle.

I had been far away from the controlling grip that had kept me in check for many years. From a distance, I had gained new insight. I was able to observe and to learn without his guidance; these capabilities were the greatest threats to him. I was able to differentiate myself from his views and those of the family. I had become more consistent in examining life objectively, regardless of my relationship with the person involved. I was no longer eager to judge and criticise simply because family members did so and sought encouragement. I was castigated for disagreeing with family criticism, as if I did not have the right to my own judgements.

I reviewed the allegations one by one trying to make sense of them and to connect together the incidents leading to the trial. With my independence and at a greater distance from my uncle's controlling grip, I perceived family dynamics differently.

For years, there had been one controlling family member and we were all willing captives. I had parted the veil and stepped out of the circle to observe how we behaved as his captives, his puppets. I was able to see and I was willing to speak truth to his power; therefore, I had become a threat, one that had to be neutralised. The generosity and kindness I had received were not acts of love; rather they were favours granted. What I had not recognised was that for each of those acts, a quid pro quo was attached, i.e., I was expected to repay my uncle through unquestioning obedience, silence and compliance.

For me, this was the ultimate test of my allegiance to ancient tribal conventions. Indeed, this trial marked the fall of the last façade, the final veil. My political beliefs and ideological commitment did not guarantee obedience to the teacher, my uncle. My political education had the unintended consequence – from his perspective – of transforming my conduct and attitudes. I had become disciplined in my thinking but not in the discipline he required – unquestioning submission to him. While he taught that self-criticism is essential to change, he did not practise the precept.

In a powerful epiphany, I realised that it was time to let go. I was free of a relationship that was morally inconsistent. I was free of his double-standard relationship rules that changed according to the parties involved.

Thus, I settled into a new life stage that excluded my uncles and aunts. I transformed my life to distance myself from them. It was much easier to do than I could ever have imagined.

Given his ultimatum, I chose my authentic voice, my dignity. I had clarified my position with my parents and my siblings. This was my issue and it was my choice to distance myself from my father's siblings.

## A New Chapter

I was determined to remain true to my beliefs. I made it clear that I did not want people to choose sides. Exclusion from family events did not trouble me; indeed, it suited me. I exited the experience more self-aware and more conscious of my expectations of others. I began to relearn and to practise giving of myself for its sake and not as a trade-off. From that point forward, I progressed in liberating myself further to the stage where I now give with no expectation of reciprocity. This unexpected consequence of that challenging experience was a much-needed blessing.

While I was adjusting to the family's new dynamic, my paternal grandmother passed away at the end of the summer of 1996 in Mecca where she performed her *Omra* – a voluntary religious ritual that is similar to but different from *Hajj* (pilgrimage). Of course, I returned from Dubai.

On realising that she was dying, she had asked my mother to be near her when she drew her last breath. She met her death on the Holy ground of Mecca blessed and in peace. She was a devout Muslim and was fortunate in her faith. During her last years, she devoted most of her time to praying and reading the Quran. An indelible lifetime image of her wrapped in her white prayer garment lingers: in it, she is kneeling before Allah on her prayer mat or reading the Quran.

My paternal grandmother had a distinctive presence and unique scent, a whisper of Dove soap, rose water and Arabic *Ooud*. She was meticulous and fastidious. Her skin was that of a newborn babe, soft and fragile. Her uniquely strong presence naturally enveloped the space around her, emanating from her poised demeanour. Before she sat, she would gently move her hands over the intended seat, as if sweeping away impurities. She demanded and received respect for the person she was. She was funny and appreciated good humour. She had a beautiful smile and when she laughed from her heart, her eyes were filled with laughter's tears.

Her kindness and love were not to be taken for granted; they were earned. From childhood, I understood that our relationship had boundaries. It was a different relationship from the one I had with Um Hameed, my maternal grandmother. Between us, there was an understanding of the love and respect that bound us.

I was not known for cutting any slack with anyone, including my grandparents. She was not known for granting forgiveness easily. She would address me differently depending on the state of our relationship or the particular request. She would call me *"Bintie"* – daughter – or *"bet waladi"* my son's daughter. I knew that when she addressed me as *"Bintie"*, she was relaxed and the informal boundaries applied. When she used *"bet waladi"*, although it too is a term of endearment, it creates a space where formal boundaries ruled. At times, she would ask me to cook something that she could give to her neighbours or ask me to help her fix something that had defeated her repair attempts. We would share a pomegranate, a few scoops of vanilla ice cream or a cherry Popsicle. When she finally trusted my cooking, she requested her favourite dishes. As she suffered high blood pressure, she dictated the amounts of salt and oil to be used.

In less than two years, another part of my lineage, my history was severed. Growing up, I had always felt special as I had grandparents and even great grandparents. Now I had lost both grandmothers, my two Fatemas.

I had seen her last a few weeks before they left to perform *Omra*. She was in a joyous mood as she always was before such religious journeys. During my short trip, I had a terrible toothache. Before the noon prayer, we sat in the living room near the wall cabinet where she kept her daintily flowered white porcelain pot filled with rose water. In that same cabinet, my grandmother kept her dried oregano leaves and other herbs for home remedies, *henna* powder to dye her grey hair and numerous small bags of treats. I rested my head on the cushion next to where she sat in perfect serenity and joyousness. It had been many years since I had seen my paternal grandmother so content.

I forgot about that toothache until after her death. I had struggled with the pain during the last few days in my paternal grandmother's presence. Subsequently, it occurred to me that the toothache was a sign. The commonly held dream interpretation of losing a tooth is as a signal to a loved one's passing. My toothache was for real, not a dream. Was it a coincidence, or was it really a signal that I had missed totally?

While grieving over my loss during the prayers and condolence service, I was conscious of family pressure to forget the recent trial, to mend the relationship and to move on. They did not realise that I had moved on.

In my heart, I had no desire for revenge. I was content and at peace with myself. I was free of the restraints of such a dysfunctional, unhealthy relationship. I had no desire to rejoin the herd, to surrender my independence and objectivity. I wanted to be able to disagree and to love and be loved. I wanted to be in open relationships where my disagreement would not be viewed as a rejection of the other person. I wanted us all to be capable of saying, "I do not like what you said," without doubting the love and commitment to the relationship and to one another. We create our lives around assumptions that we create about others and the way they relate to us. Typically, we never confirm our assumptions with the others. On the rare occasion that we ask, we persist in believing our initial assumptions only to end with disappointment. We misjudge true responses because we doubt our own truthfulness.

During the days of mourning, my paternal grandfather hinted that this might be a good time to mend, to restore the family circle. At the time, I realised that no one within it understood that this was not a simple rift in relationships. For me, it was a critical life-defining issue. Now free of it, I was not going to surrender to that circle of power and control. My paternal grandmother had died; patching up the relationship would not bring her back. I had been assaulted emotionally by the trial; I was not about to be manipulated further .

*Soon after my paternal grandmother's death, I dreamed of her walking with my grandfather in a lush garden overflowing with fruit. In my dream, she had called for me to see what she had brought me from her journey. She asked me to sit down in her bedroom in the old house as she had when I was a child. There, she unwrapped a beautiful length of cloth like the ones she used to wrap our gifts from Mecca or Najaf. Within them, she had secreted precious beaded necklaces. She handed me an emerald necklace, "I have selected this for you. Look, there is nothing else like it. It is different from all the others I brought your aunts and sisters."*

*In my dream I had asked her to keep it until I returned from picking some fruit. On return, I found that my necklace had been taken by one of my aunts. I went back to my grandmother seeking her consolation. She smiled and said, "The emerald green necklace was my gift to you and no one can take it or wear it except you."* With that dream, I knew she had accepted my decision to distance myself from the family.

While nursing a broken heart and grieving my grandmother's death, I experienced the shattering of trust with a man who almost convinced me that he genuinely loved me. More importantly, I experienced the shattering trust within my family. Thereafter, I proceeded on my journey recognising the nature of the excess baggage that defined me.

## Transition: toward sanity

Although rejected and sexually molested as a child and emotionally raped as an adult, I neither perceive myself as a victim or a survivor. As I retrace my steps in life, I cannot once remember feeling sorry for myself. I live with who I am, a woman with a voice that once failed her but who now commands it.

My life had never been about why and how I was rejected, molested and emotionally raped. Those experiences were excess baggage; the perpetrators were miscreants. What was I to do with those shattering experiences: Confront? Tackle? Or be victimised? Clearly, denial was not an option.

In an effort to free myself, I consciously chose confrontation, i.e. to salvage those horrible, repressed memories and to give them a voice. For as long as I can remember, nightmares had plagued me. Miraculously, since I stunningly confronted my father, my nightmares vanished. I had confronted him with charges of rejection and my perception that he had left us to pursue his education. I had also confessed to him my experience with molestation and emotional rape.

From childhood, I leapfrogged into adulthood, skipping adolescence, skipping countries. Meanwhile, my life was replayed in my dreams.

### Dubai 1995

I have a clear memory of that fine November day in 1995 as I walked toward the Hyatt Regency's Galleria in Dubai. As I approached my first therapy session, I was aware of taking one step forward and a hundred doubtful steps backward. My psychotherapist was a Canadian Lebanese male, as I had failed to find a bilingual female therapist. I felt as if I was walking naked with exposed wounds and unveiled memories in the middle of a staring crowd. I realised that my dreams would be recorded in a stranger's journal.

By that time, I had recalled everything that I had repressed about a sordid experience when I was eight years old. In detail, I had confronted molestation, the "who, what, when and where" about it. The process of unblocking the memories began in 1987. In essence, I had rescued my memories. Although I had faced them, I hesitated at the clinic door. I was hesitant to share my memories with a man, fearing he would try to influence my voice. While observing myself from a distance, I hesitated for a long time.

In his office, I sat on one of the floral wicker armchairs. Softly, he asked me to speak when I wanted and to say whatever I wanted, beginning from any point in my life. "I don't know if I want to be here or even to talk. I almost went back home, as I doubted that this would do me any good," I said. For an eternity, I hesitated, secure in the silence between us. I thought to begin with my nightmares and dreams and to share my interpretation of them. For nine months, I went twice a month. Quietly, he sat and listened.

### *Memoir: Dreams of Snakes and Other Nightmares*

I traced my life through nightmares. As I lived my nightmares, I no longer associated them with sleep. The recollection of them released my memories of the life I lived and the one I feared. In the end, my life and my nightmares became one and the same.

On unlocking the one previously sealed nightmare, long inaccessible to me, the puzzle was solved. After confronting that memory, everything made sense. At last, I understood the enigma that had haunted me.

In my quest for understanding, I began from the premise that for many years I observed much that I could not understand. *In my earliest recollected nightmare, I was eternally swimming in a large pool with three other girls. Typically, I was swimming at top speed. The other three would laugh at me as I gasped for air. It seemed that I was racing, as if in a competition.*

*There on the opposite side of the pool, my demon waited for me. The snake would enter the water and chase me. It terrified me, tormenting my whole being. Persistently, the snake chased me, always failing to catch me. As I reached the other side of the pool, I sweated and experienced suffocation. That exertion woke me fully.*

Awake, I lay rigidly in bed, nearly suffocated by the strong, noxious odour of dirty, sweaty underwear smeared with baby powder. Fearful of vomiting, I could not go back to sleep.

This nightmare started invading me more frequently, coinciding with intimacy. The price of that intimacy was sleepless nights. I would lie next to my body and pretend to be asleep. To sleep meant to lose myself in the sordidness of my imagination. As I slept, another body emerged to seek pleasure. As those images emerged, I could not tell if the body had a head or eyes. I only knew that the body touched me and filled me with disgust. Although I never looked, I knew that the image was not that of the man I loved.

In time, the image shifted to visit me during the day. It seemed dissatisfied to enter only through the window of darkness, to be captive to the nights. It intruded, violating my existence. I wanted the lightness of my sensuality and pleasure without the terrifying image. However, the lone option was to accept or reject both, a package deal.

One night the images were transferred into the dark room of my soul where they were developed as snapshots. They had colour, smell and sound and were accompanied by terror and filth.

When the intimacy ended, the images remained. The snake continued to chase me in the swimming pool, never to catch me. Too, the odour lingered as I cried myself to sleep.

Then, two years passed before the images re-emerged. With the recurrence, I could not control my visceral reaction. The images were so revolting that I vomited endlessly.

I saw a young man sitting next to a window, guarding against an interloper. A little girl sat on his legs, horrified by the moistness between her thighs. She too watched the window and prayed for rescue. She experienced pain as the fingers penetrated and revulsion at the filth of her own moistness. She screamed, but her scream was trapped between her thighs and her throat. I saw her, the eight-year old girl who sat in silence waiting for rescue. No one interrupted to stop the pain.

The little girl had nowhere to go, no choice but to stay there on his legs.

## A New Chapter

There was nowhere to go. One day, she left him sitting there with the eight-year-old immersed in her filthy moistness. Only she knew how long he continued to place her on his legs and to force his fingers into her moisture.

Then, at age twenty-seven, traumatised by that image, I connected the face with those fingers. I searched for the eight-year-old girl. I found her in the darkness of my soul, clutching her own memories. Fiercely, she was clinging to my heart. With the remnants of my timid strength, I found her. Each time she called me to utter the words that would save her, my voice betrayed both of us.

Six years passed with that hushed voice and those little girl's eyes fixed on mine. Then, one night she decided to stay until I woke. I found her waiting for me, refusing to leave. I did not want her there. She belonged to the nights. But there was no escape. I knew that if I wanted her to leave I had to share the images with someone; I had to summon someone to her rescue. Yet I was terrified that if I tried, no one would want to listen to her and that I would be left alone with her. I knew that if I wanted the little girl to leave, I had to free her from the darkness.

I summoned all my courage and sought my sister Saffiya. Leaning against her car window, I trembled, overwhelmed by the odour of sweat mixed with baby powder and dirty underwear. I was nauseated and I sobbed. I wept. Struggling for control, I sobbed: "I think ... I am not sure ... But would you promise to still love me?" My sister's eyes were filled with terror and tears. They were fixed on mine. I continued, "I see an eight-year-old girl sitting next to a window. She is seated on the legs of her caretaker and his fingers are between her thighs. She feels filthy, horrified, and ashamed. She sobs and swallows her tears. The girl and I keep sobbing. The girl now has a face." I reach out to my sister, both of us trembling. "The little girl has a face identical to mine." Then, I heard my own sobbing voice, as the words escaped.

Now, the other nightmares made sense. When I was eight years old in the late 1960s, I spent most of my free time at Immy Um Hameed's house. Nearby, a mute young woman, Zainab, lived in the neighbourhood. She terrified me both awake, and asleep. She would chase me, catch me and shake me. Each time I went to sleep, she waited for me. In my nightmare, I tried to scream to call for help only to discover that I had no voice. Although my voice reverberated inside my head, people around could not hear me nor notice my struggles to scream. Daily, I would wake up with a sore throat.

Eventually, the disturbing Zainab experience was replaced with another nightmare. In it, I was endlessly falling. Again, I would call for help and still no one responded. As my voice was trapped, no one noticed. I continued to wake with a sore throat.

*In the early 80s, I endured recurring nightmares in which I saw myself naked. As I walked around town with relatives and friends, I was keenly aware of my nudity. My companions were not; they seemed not to notice. At other times, I saw myself in a transparent shower enclosure centred amidst a large residential area; through their open windows, people peered out at me. I was naked and I realised that many eyes watched me, but I did not seek to conceal my nudity as I showered.* I examined my life and my nightmares in search of the life I had lived, one with which I was unfamiliar.

Zainab, the mute, terrified me most because I suffered a similar speech impairment; although I could speak, I never had a voice that was my own. Her invasions of my dreams never ceased. Even when I discovered that I could raise my voice, she remained in my dreams. She served as a reminder that I would never have a voice of my own until I had the strength to unveil my life, to give voice to my life.

In the end, I was freed for ever by the fear of inheriting the destiny of my maternal grandmother, my mother and the countless other women who will live and die without discovering their voices in this man's world. I believe that I was twenty-one years old when I first said *no* to my mother. In doing so, I said *no* to many things, most importantly to not having my own voice. Years were required for my mother to confront and understand the limitations on her voice.

I was thirty-two years old before I finally protested to my father his assumption that "You and your sisters were well taken care of." "No," my voice thundered, revealing all at once the raw wounds from my childhood experiences of rejection, molestation and emotional rape. In my memory, I will always retain the image of my father's face at that moment. It appeared as if life had stopped, frozen at the sound of my voice.

I watched, as he sought the nearest chair in the kitchen. Momentarily, he too became mute. I heard my voice; I fought to control it. I sobbed as the words rushed out.

Then, silence prevailed. I was determined to claim my own voice, to claim my own life with all its memories, good, bad and indifferent. I was determined to live my life.

As a mature adult, I now understand the fear of being labelled and rejected. In this patriarchal world, to be labelled as an outspoken woman with her own mind means being rejected as a woman. Now that I knew the truth, I recognised my own nudity in my dreams. That recognition paved the way to unlocking the painful suppressed memories and allowed me to acknowledge my pain. It took me over a decade to speak all the truth without falling, without the fear of my nudity and without a trapped voice.

After I had freed the eight-year-old girl trapped inside me, I dreamed only of me swimming in beautiful blue waters. In my dreams, I gave birth without labour to many children, although I was a single woman. I took these new dreams to my paternal grandmother who embraced them with a smile. Whenever I told her of my dreams of childbirth, she would say, "*It is a good omen, you are fortunate.*" I see myself giving birth while swimming. And with the good omen and the fortune of my voice, I dream of a chorus of free, unharnessed harmonious voices.

In my dreams, I listened to the echo of the silence that lingered between us for an eternity. I woke in silence, watching myself as I pushed a beautiful baby through a spacious lobby. *As I approached the lift, the lobby began flooding with water. Frightened for the baby, I hurried to the roof. As I entered the lift I stepped over a black bug. Then it multiplied into thousands of little black ones. They followed me onto the roof where I confronted a sea of water. I was overjoyed as I watched the magic transformation of the black bugs into beautiful dolphins. For me, dolphins and women speak for all the greatness of compassion and tender strength.*

No more nightmares. At my therapist's office, I sat on the floral wicker chair for the last time. In silence, we sought the word or statement that would mark the first step in a conversation. Gently, he asked me about the nightmares I had reclaimed.

With me, I had a letter I had written to my molester – he, who had defiled my childhood. I placed it into the hands of my therapist; he opened it and asked me to read it. This time, there was no hesitation. As I serenely and securely unfolded the letter, I read, allowing my tears to flow, my heart to ache and my voice to choke. I permitted myself to taste my tears and the pain that accompanied every word that I had written. As I finished reading, the therapist asked, "What do you want to do now? What do you want to do with your letter?"

On that day, I had arrived with the letter that I wanted to send. As I began speaking, I was no longer overwhelmed by my own emotions. My voice was free, no longer inhabited by nightmares or other voices. Something profound had changed; there were no more nightmares. My voice and I were free.

Again, he asked about the letter. I replied more certain than ever, "I do not wish to send it. I know the truth. I know what happened to me when I was eight years old and I know how long it lasted. The perpetrator will never admit to what happened, but I know."

I folded the letter, sliding it back into the white envelope. I no longer felt the need to send it. The act of writing the letter in itself was my closure. It would make no difference whether or not I sent the letter, whether or not I received an apology for the wrong that had been done to me. I believed that one day my tormenter would admit his guilt and that would be adequate. At this pivotal point in my life, it was not necessary. I had moved on.

As I walked away from my therapist's office for the last time, warm tears streamed down my cheeks. I was certain that my life was not and never would be wasted on revenge. Despite the pain and violation of molestation, I chose to overcome the experience. To live my life holding on to pain was not an option. I had been betrayed and in retrospect, I was thankful for the betrayal.

While it may seem curious to the observer, the reality is that I would not have tasted betrayal if I had not been able to trust completely. Only with that ultimate trust was betrayal possible.

I began a new journey to discover my own voice free of the legacy of past negative experiences. I was poised on the brink of blending the many voices into an anthem of one voice – one that is solely mine.

It was time to face new challenges in the journey ahead. I was ready to trust completely, to experience joy and indeed new pain and betrayal. I was fortunate to be ready to trust, to love and to experience hurt again. This time the pain would be different. The pain I would deal with would be mine alone. It would not be shared with that eight-year-old girl. She was now safe; content that she had finally been heard, that I had finally listened. She would no longer intrude between my voice and my pain.

As if I had replayed my life hundreds of times, I returned home exhausted, but uninhibited. I was at the beginning of a turning point in my life.

## Rethinking student counselling

That day, I decided to rethink my role as a student counsellor in Dubai. Theoretically, the position was honourable, as the stated purpose of the post was to support local female students in their pursuit of higher education. It was to coach, mentor and inspire female students to achieve their highest potential, acquiring critical minds and professional skills needed for the job market and the future of their country.

Early on, I found that the reality of my role was to support the institution's philosophy and the vision of senior management, a patriarchal one that did not resonate with me. I did not see that it served the students or the long-term development goal in the Emirates [UAE]. There were too many contradictions between goals and discipline. There was no consideration for the student's transition from government-run schools to the Western educational system.

Two years earlier, I had been extremely excited as I sat for my interview. In accepting my role, I had high hopes as a student counsellor among young women. The institute seemed on the right track, the way forward toward progress and development. The idea of establishing such an educational institute to develop local talents among females (and a separate one for males) was what the region needed. The UAE was developing local capabilities, adapting different educational philosophies and strategies while maintaining its cultural identity. I was enthused by being part of this inspirational project.

The contract, the pay and benefits were excellent; however, there was something disconcerting about my role. As the end of the first semester was approaching, I had begun to feel a sore lump in my soul that swelled each time I had to force myself to act against my own convictions.

I had not envisioned my role as a spy, tasked to watch

over student conduct inside and outside of college boundaries. Some of the college rules and regulations were unrealistic given its philosophy and long-term strategies. Cheating regulations did not take into account the standards of conduct within the public school sector – standards that were cooperative, not competitive. In certain scenarios, it felt as if I were merely a secret investigator – a spy – working in a detention centre. Despite the new social, academic and professional skills the college offered its female students, there were contradictions and inconsistencies between the rules and the development of future capabilities. The concepts of trust, independence, freedom of choice and responsibilities toward the consequences of one's own actions required gradually re-educating young women to adapt old behaviours and learn new ones for a global workplace.

I could not incorporate the personal relationships and issues of the young women unless they had taken place inside the college and had involved or had impacted other students. As for personal relationships beyond the college gates, I felt they were out of limits, despite parental and administration permission to interfere.

Gradually, my aspiration to serve and inspire young Arab female students faded away as my role seemed more at the service of the dominant patriarchy. I found myself in a struggle to enforce rules that would not produce what the college was established to achieve. I was working with young women who held the key to future progress in their hands, only to realise that I was working against my belief that women are able to make their own decisions about their future. Women know best about their aspirations and what they want to do with their lives. I knew that I had not invested my life in order to police the conduct of young women.

The more I engaged with students and staff, the more I was confronted by the reality of the traditionally conservative society in which the college is a part. My hope for change was challenged. The strictly conservative part of the society believed that the college must reinforce the expectations of parents and guardians for young women and that we should simply ensure those results.

I had struggled against this idea, as I perceived that these college women were being trained to enter the professional world. Here in the college under moderate supervision, women could receive workforce training. I believed that both the traditionally conserva-

# A New Chapter

tive and more progressive students should have the right to achieve their potential. The fact that the college was highly regulated should not have limited these students in the achievement of their potential.

Increasingly, my role was becoming more administrative with little to do with inspiring young women. I had become hostage to my own ideal and perception of the aspirations of young women. In fact, the mainstream of the student body appreciated the outlet that the college offered them. Very few aspired to more.

As I was approaching my second mid-year, I thought to resign my post. I continued to be committed to the students and their families but I felt that I was working against the voices of young women; that I was going against the voice of the future generation. I felt that I had become a tool to reinforce the dominant male culture's perception of what women should be and could be. At that point, what was left of my motivation was dissipated due to the college's Western professional management which seemed devoured by a hunger for power and control. In Dubai, I watched as contempt and inflated egos drove highly professional people to manipulate their power to serve themselves rather than the best interests of students and the college.

It was painful to watch the injustice as a colleague was dismissed and to be unable to intervene. In that staunchly patriarchal world, male decisions are not subject to the comment or review of women subordinates. Had the colleague not been so threatening to the director, she could have made a difference in the lives of women students. As a threat, she had *no* effect and had to be eliminated.

Change – with respect to existing traditions and values – and the training of women to qualify and compete in the UAE's job market were not incompatible goals in my view. I struggled to understand the college's Western management approach as patriarchal representatives on behalf of the local traditions. I questioned management's failure to listen to the real needs of the nation and to become true consultants and agents of positive change.

I struggled as I observed how Western senior management men adopted tribal codes without truly understanding or respecting them; they did so for the sake of power, privilege and wealth. I struggled as I observed their inability to integrate their skills and capabilities with local codes and customs to bring change that could have benefited the students and the community.

I realised that I could not function within such an unjust system. I went to sleep that evening knowing that I had resigned myself to leave my job and to leave Dubai. The next day, I submitted my resignation letter terminating my contract a year earlier than my original intention. Empty handed and without financial security or prospects, I relocated to my parents' California home in June 1997. Another journey began.

# 10

# Living in Transitions

Optimistic and determined, I returned to El Cerrito, California in July 1997. Until the fifth of October 1998 – fifteen months – when I moved to England, I ricocheted through a series of transitions. I became more aware of how my life and future were in the hands of fate.

Initially, I was optimistic and hopeful, as I believed that I was a step closer to settling permanently in California, a place that I could call home. I had returned to Berkeley and its famous Telegraph Avenue and equally famous Moss and other beloved bookstores. There I devoured books, discussions and lectures. I returned determined to create a future into which I could settle comfortably.

Immediately I launched the search for a permanent full-time job. To that end, I invested my savings from the sale of my car and furniture on hiring a recruitment consultant to expedite the job search. Nevertheless, I spent all of my time actively searching for work as well.

The recruitment consultancy went bankrupt six months after I signed on with them. Thus my financial investment produced only impressive return letterheads with one paragraph: *"Unfortunately your application has not been successful. We wish you success in your job search."*

Daily, I received these constant irritating reminders of how under- or over-qualified I appeared on paper. Thus, it seemed that finding a job would be harder than encountering water in the desert. Clearly, without a job, life in the US would be near impossible. Hence, the letters were a good exercise in managing rejection and in coming to terms with the decision that I had to make eventually.

They aided me in mastering self-management over old complex, lingering residues of inadequacy.

With the help of friends and acquaintances, I found a part-time managerial position at the Arab Cultural Center in San Francisco and freelance consultant work with Chevron in nearby San Ramon. Emotionally, I barely managed to keep my head above water as I coped with the hundreds of rejection letters. The wait for the mailman was the highlight of daily events, as it was the link to dreams and hopes of finding a job and starting a career.

With agreeable employment, the Bay Area would have been a highly desirable home. In that transitional period, I felt trapped, frozen in time and place. My options were severely limited, as returning to Saudi Arabia or the United Arab Emirates was not agreeable; indeed, such options were positively undesirable.

Despite its form or shape, rejection leaves an unmistakably bitter, almost metallic after-taste, even in the presence of a generally positive attitude to life. I was exquisitely conscious of my pain, my low periods and my discomfort and irritability. Subsequently, I felt the pain in my uterus and had no idea what to do with that discovery. I became intensely aware of the locus of my emotional pain. For comfort, I located the physical source from which the discomfort radiated. There, I placed my hand and drew my breath, conscious of living the experience.

Continuously, I reminded myself that I had not been in therapy for nine months merely for a "quick fix". I had invested in therapy to work not with my feelings of rejection, but with the source of that rejection. Through therapy, I had come to understand the source of my pain, my anger and many years of dysfunctional relationships. Despite my political and social awareness and commitment, I had permitted those unhealthy relationships to limit me.

In therapy, I had traced the eruption of my pain to early childhood. It arose and cascaded in the wake of my father's abandonment of my mother and their daughters for another woman. In my immature five-year-old mind, that had been translated into rejection. Subsequently, that bitter rejection was compounded by my physical violation as an eight-year-old child. In real life there are no magic wands or elixirs with which to wave away, dismiss the pain. The only elixir required is time. Sometimes a lifetime is needed to overcome rejection and its residues that accrue over the years.

While I could not halt the onslaught of the rejection letters, I could control my reaction to them. I had a life to live. I had a life that I wanted to enjoy with parents, sisters, children and friends whom I loved. I had more battles to win. Consciously, I fought the negative emotions produced by every rejection letter, however elegantly dressed. I had moved well beyond the despair felt by the eight-year-old girl.

Thus, I took charge of my life outside of the job search. I accepted that it was in the hands of fate. I was eligible to work in the US and I possessed a set of valuable, transferable skills from my previous employment; thus I reasoned that it must be my fate. I refused to entertain the possibility that I might have been discriminated against as an Arab Muslim woman.

I enjoyed my work at the Arab Cultural Center and the freelance consulting sessions at Chevron. I was determined to savour life each day in that beautiful part of the world. In making my peace, I forged contentment into my lot in life.

While working for the Arab Cultural Center in San Francisco, I became acquainted with the collective "San Francisco Women Against Rape" [SFWAR] through its brochures. One sexual assault flyer featured prevention, education, empowerment and change on its cover. Another shouted, *"Did you know that women can be raped by other women?"*

That second brochure threw me off balance. The idea of women raping other women was totally foreign to me. Until then, I had blindly believed that rape is an atrocity inflicted by men on women. As I continued reading, I felt as if the leaflets were there for a reason. They assaulted my blind prejudice and challenged me to unlearn and to grow. The SFWAR initiative beckoned me to investigate.

The next morning, I dialled the coalition number and enquired about SFWAR's principles. Subsequently, I attended a screening interview and was selected for training, a welcome validation of my professional bona fides. The fates had led me to SFWAR's intensive training to become a certified volunteer Rape Crisis Counsellor. It proved a turning point in my personal development and my life.

In that training, the ground beneath me quaked as I confronted my prejudices, examined my values, embraced feminism anew and acquired the skills essential to advancing my dreams of making the world a better place. The complexity of human violence that I encountered during that experience irretrievably and indelibly altered my perspective on life.

The training strengthened my commitment to the search for truth and to the necessity of confronting reality directly. The truth that whether the perpetrators of violence or any form of tyranny were women or men was irrelevant. What matters is that I struggle against, take a stand against violence in all its various manifestations from the subtly emotional to the overtly physical and sexual.

I realised that the struggle is not about feminism; it is about and for humanity. It is about the nature and the quality of life that we live. It demands confronting the abuse of power to control and humiliate another human being. It compels the prevention of the unsolicited, unwarranted destruction of the core of a human being by an individual with the power and the opportunity to do so.

While I had studied and researched social issues, control, power and privileged versus unprivileged status, I had much to learn. Although I had been violated physically, I was unprepared to learn about the extent of rape, sexual abuse and other forms of domestic and public violence.

While the ground beneath me shifted, I realised that the discomfort was essential for me to learn and to grow. The opportunity for growth in my own humanity arrived when I was open to seize it. In that redefined realm, I incorporated commitments to zero-tolerance of violence and claims of elitist privilege.

As I approached the initial training session, I believed that there was no pain or revulsion that would ever rival that which I had experienced during my therapy sessions. Given that I had experienced imprisonment, molestation and gut wrenching, excruciating pain in my stomach and uterus, I imagined that the training would not emotionally challenge me.

As the certification course commenced, I opened the manual to a quote by Toni Cade Bambara, an African-American activist, "*I am well aware we are under siege … But death is not a truth that inspires.*" As we progressed through the training, that quote became exceptionally relevant.

In the initial session, the lead trainer asked us to be kind to ourselves; she encouraged us to exit the sessions should we become uncomfortable with the raw narratives of rape victims and the visual evidence of violence. To give myself permission to leave the room was empowering, as it allowed me space to deal with my emotions. Rather than weakness, I had learned that strength is required to say "I cannot handle this."

As I listened to the horrific narratives of violation and of the victims' courage to live, I learned the value of that permission to exit. Women, the victims, the survivors were inspired by "*I am life despite violence and atrocities.*" Daily, I returned home revolted. I took with me only strength for one thing: to vomit. I learned about women and men who had the courage to live, to endure through the inhumane brutality of rape, sexual assaults and domestic violence because death did not inspire them.

The sessions were intense. Simultaneously, I was unlearning and relearning. Every aspect of the training demanded rigorous discipline. I had to identify and be conscious of my own perceptions, biases and assumptions about others. I had to confront my own prejudices toward prostitution and drug abuse.

Rape has no justification in my view. How has humanity simplified violence, sexual assault and rape and succeeded in normalizing them as common occurrences? How can women live through multiple rapes? How can humanity accommodate such obscene crimes?

Stripping away my biases meant that I had to learn a new language. I had to adopt language that would enable me to motivate change in others. Such language skills are essential to effectively advocate for the cessation of all violence along with other abuses of power. The commitment and discipline that were essential in the unlearning process enabled my relearning and growth. I was there to acknowledge when women turned against themselves the blame for their fault, their complicity in their rape. I was there to acknowledge their pain, to be there for them regardless of what action or inaction they chose.

For me, the work was the essence of giving. That work influenced my life well beyond those twenty-four weekly counselling hours. During those exchanges, I was both a giver of and the recipient of support. We do not intrude into other lives without evolving, without incorporating the experience into our own journey. The journey is continuous and mine is always a struggle to improve myself. To train myself to be non-judgemental and to confront prejudiced ideas directly was an incredibly valuable part of my journey. With satisfaction, I observed my language and my immediate reactions change through those counselling sessions. Numerous anonymous women on the other end of the hotline helped me to become a better person.

The nine months of therapy in Dubai proved to be worth far more than I had imagined. It enabled me to understand my own feelings and to separate my life from the lives of the anonymous women I served. I no longer felt the need to retaliate, to be resentful or to be aggressive when engaged in conversation or when debating gender issues. Violence is far too complex for a simplistic analysis of brutality's effects in our everyday lives. I sought a better understanding of power and control. The training enabled me to abandon the cultural lens that had blinded me to the absence of East–West distinctions with regard to these issues.

I saw that both Western and Eastern men exercise power and control because of an assumed, socially constructed gender ranking. While cultures and societies may package male dominance differently, the underlining biases that govern female/male sexuality and relationships remain identical. I was fascinated to learn of and to observe the similarities in which Western and Eastern women respond to violence. Although some Western cultures provide women with judiciary systems with which to combat violence, such systems often do not deliver justice; indeed, many are further victimised in the legal process. Both Western and Eastern cultures are predicated on the assumption that when a woman is raped or violated, it must be the woman's fault, i.e. *she was asking for it*. This is the universal automatic default assumption.

While some women in the West have access to the justice system, those violated often opt out in fear of further victimisation. Women in the East rarely have such access. In both situations, women typically choose not to report being raped. This does not differ across ethnicities, languages, cultures or religions. The deterrents to the pursuit of justice are fears of further victimisation and of being labelled and even targeted again. The risk of jeopardising their precarious, fragile social status dampens the desire for justice.

The identity of the anonymous, faceless voices proved irrelevant. In the rape crisis counselling work, I developed empathy, a way to stop feeling sorry for the surviving victims and to find ways to empower them. I quickly learned how to respect women's choices to report or to remain silent. My experience of their suffering was secondary. I was there to work with them to gain or to regain the power they needed to continue life. In that role, I had begun to learn to be detached from the results. My role was to be there for women in pain, women I did not know.

Working for victims of domestic violence and rape provoked me to examine issues not only of civil violence but also the ethical standards and international conventions of war. I am no longer naive about the effects of violence within revolutions and the involvement of revolutionaries in war crimes. Regardless of principles and conventions, violations occur.

In reviewing my own past beliefs, I now found it hard to justify any atrocity regardless of the cause. For the freedom fighter, the resister, it is a humanitarian question, a challenge to be disciplined and to respect all humans regardless of the position of the opposition. Violence, rape and assault are crimes like any others with no excuse and no justification. I thought of the many cases of soldiers honoured as war heroes who had raped women despite the essence of humanity, and that of the Geneva War Conventions prohibitions. With my new perspective, I saw that rape and other forms of violence have become embedded in societies everywhere and have become normalised.

While I was immersed in offering support to anonymous women whom I did not know and never will, images of faces and voices visited me. Women from my previous life and work were walking this journey with me. They did not inhabit my voice; they were silent witnesses of numerous painful life journeys. They were not my life, but they formed part of my life. I wondered if I had missed part of their stories. Now, I was listening with a difference; there was no anger or resentment, only sorrow for lives so victimised by violence.

More consciously, I observed women and children in public, paying attention to bruises and scars, noticing and being careful not to readily assume violence. I had grown less tolerant of aggressive attitudes and language while learning not to intervene on behalf of someone unless I was asked for support. I recognised how such support had helped me transcend my own self-imposed boundaries. More importantly, I noticed that my language had begun to change profoundly. I noticed that I was better able to separate what had happened in my past life from what was happening now. The relearning process and language change had altered the level of control I was able to achieve within myself. My sense of serenity, contentment and control had deepened.

In the midst of this engagement with learning and dealing with victims of rape and domestic violence, I was engulfed by an overwhelming desire for motherhood. I began to fantasise about the possibility of getting pregnant and giving birth to a child. There was no rational explanation for such an overwhelming desire while concurrently witnessing the brutality of rape and domestic violence.

Yet, as I listened to those survivors of violence and learned the extent of the cruelty of human nature, this persistent maternal desire surged. I did not consider the logistics, the justification or the legality of having a baby. Was I perhaps unconsciously listening to my biological clock as it ticked away my life? Was I responding to some physical uterine urge desirous of bearing and nurturing a child? It was pointless to search for reasons, as they were secondary to the overwhelming desire of wanting to be a mother and believing that I could do it. I was emotionally and physically ready and therefore it was possible. I was age thirty-seven; it was still possible for me to become a mother, despite a recent finding of uterine fibroid lesions.

The overwhelming desire to bear a child invited back the memory of my old dream of watching myself as I gave birth to a child. I have never forgotten the dream and the way it made me feel.

Now, I was not dreaming. I could imagine the horror on my paternal grandmother's face if she was still alive, and I were to tell her about the reality of my desire as a single woman and at age thirty-seven. Many years had elapsed since I had last experienced that overwhelming maternal desire, before the birth of my second nephew in 1984.

As I was a single woman with no prospect of love, the only

possible solution was to think artificial insemination. Hypothetically, considering artificial insemination was less shocking to me than the sudden overwhelming desire to become a mother had been, as I had considered myself a mother since the birth of my first nephew. Thus far however, I had only played a part-time maternal role with my niece and five nephews.

The desire for motherhood was intense and real. Where this desire would lead me was the question that I had not yet fully considered. I had to share this desire of mine; I sought acknowledgment, validation.

Naturally, I chose to test the impact of my hypothetical idea on my father, as there was a good chance he would not think that I had lost my sense of reality. The expression on his face conveyed his rejection. His initial response was, "How could you consider having a child without a father? It is not the way it works."

I responded with the artificial insemination scenario that I had prepared. I had to rethink my immediate response to my father as I thought to myself, my mother raised three girls without a father's presence. Despite it being a fact, it was irrelevant. I thought to myself that a child does not need a father, a child needs a fatherly role model.

Silence settled between us before we resumed discussion about single parenthood. I wanted to exhaustively discuss the possibility of artificial insemination. I wanted to explore the support I could anticipate from my father, as it would make a difference.

Living in the US, I had not considered the religious implications of my desire, i.e., the religious views vis-à-vis the legitimacy of a child conceived and born through artificial insemination. Nor had I had yet considered the numerous other potentially complex issues surrounding pregnancy, such as breaking the news to my sisters and explaining my justification. To myself, I justified the desire as an opportunity to give my body one last chance to experience the use of organs that had thus far remained idle. The adequacy of this justification for such a life-changing experience was at this point irrelevant and therefore unexamined.

Of course, I was only testing an idea. While securing family support was essential, I first needed my father's blessing. Further exploration of how far I would go in pursuit of having a child awaited his signal. I often smiled as I replayed his question, *"How could you possibly entertain such an idea?"* I just did.

With the passage of time, the desire to bear a child faded. The discussion with my father got lost in other topics. I believe the discussion had created a space for him to speak about himself as a forward-looking young man with bold dreams and ambitions. This was the first time my father spoke explicitly about his unrealistic expectations of my mother and of their relationship.

In retrospect, my father was finally acknowledging how he had undermined the power of the traditionally conservative society and culture in which he and my mother lived. He acknowledged how much harder it was for women to transcend those cultural barriers. With heartfelt appreciation, he said, "Although I so often claim that you girls take after me, deep down I know I cannot claim any credit for the way you are. Your mother is the one who is to be credited for the way she brought you up and for that I am grateful and proud. It was your mother's due diligence and disciplined principles that had the greatest influence in shaping your personalities. Alone, she brought you up."

My heart leaped as I listened to what my father had said and what he did not say. In his explicit acknowledgment and tribute to my mother, I received his apology for not being there for us when we were growing up. At that moment, I accepted that I had long ago reconciled with my father.

I thought how hard it must have been for him to watch us, engage with us infrequently and acknowledge that he was not there to influence and shape our personalities. I had begun to realise my father's indirect influence. It was because of my mother's love and commitment to him and in honour of his vision that she consciously instilled in us both her discipline and his vision.

My father has always been the ever-absent presence in our lives. As I matured, I closely watched him and no longer wondered whether we would have been better off if he had stayed with my mother. In the end, I knew that it did not matter, as I have stepped into a new space with my parents. It is a space where I no longer perceive that my mother was a victim of my father's circumstances or that my father is solely responsible for the circumstances in which he found himself. I had learned that it was easy to make a victim of my mother given the circumstances of women in our culture.

Over the years, my mother's perception of her life if my father had remained with us shifts according to her circumstances. At one time she might say, "I wish he had stayed, but then perhaps if he had stayed we would not be happy." It is the possibility of losing happiness that suspends her certainty.

From this new place, my relationship with my parents was shifting onto new ground. As my friendship and love of my father strengthened, the more I appreciated and connected with my mother. My mother is simply a remarkable woman whose assets are common sense, a remarkable sense of humour, a strong will to live and faith that helped her to be and to do her best. It is to my mother that I owe the strong bond I have with my father today even when he granted me no support for what was my last chance to have a child.

Disagreement and discouragement were no longer translated emotionally into rejection. I persist in order to grow. That is only possible by pushing myself to the next edge, to a new domain, a higher plane in search of my own humanity, my own limits.

If souls were made of substance, I wonder about the composition of mine. Now and again, I reflect on how and in what way I am going to surprise myself next. Certainly, I have encountered numerous surprises during this brief journey.

During those months in search for a homeland, in search of a city to house my heart, in search of a place that I could call home, my spirituality flourished. I had very intense discussions with myself about meditation. During this period, I made a conscious decision to resume praying and to be disciplined about observing prayer. Now, sixteen years after imprisonment, I remembered being told to pray as if Allah was going to award me credit. I had finally realised how spirituality and religious commitment are such personal aspects of human life. Although they may be exhibited publicly, at the end of the day spirituality is a relationship between the individual and God.

This was not an easy transition into this new discipline of spirituality. It launched my search for a meaningful spiritual interpretation of my religious commitment and my relation with Allah. I was familiar with the Islamic heritage and I found it is easier to access my spirituality through something that had played an important role in shaping the person I am.

I returned to reading the Quran with new lenses and perspectives. There is no mediator – no priest, pastor or other intermediary – in Islam. I was determined to access its teaching following its contextual themes and logic. I had not forgotten my position, as stated in my dissertation, with regard to the Quran's statements on women. Those statements accord greater rights to men than to women. I argued with its positions in the areas of witnessing, status, marriage and inheritance. I disagreed as these statements gave legitimacy to greater inequalities in Islam between women and men.

Nevertheless, I no longer took issue with personal statements and interpretations. I no longer wished to deprive myself of a whole body of knowledge just because I did not agree or accept its interpretations and implications. I disagreed knowing that I opened myself to contradictions. In my view, the believer is always entitled to doubt, question and disagree.

Although unsettled by the absence of any prospect of a permanent job, I had resumed living and enjoyed each day. I spent time with my father discussing everything from spirituality to religion, politics, poetry, the economy, my most recent failed love relationships and more challenging ideas. I had reconnected with my California friends, allowing the relationships to evolve as they rediscovered the new me. I had changed, yet my friendships had strengthened as I became more comfortable in my being and in sharing myself.

I had expanded my job search beyond the state of California. I refocused my search on specific jobs and with specific organisations that serve women and children. During that period, I had learned about the numerous organisations that provide services to women. Working with and for women had always seemed a natural fit for me if such a fit exists. The search beyond California resulted in me hitting the same brick wall. Again, my schooling and previous paid work experience with women did not qualify me. Concurrently, the Arab Cultural Center's effort to obtain grants to keep me as a fulltime permanent employee and to develop programmes had failed.

Thus, I continued to seek a silver lining while I continued my volunteer work as a rape crisis counsellor. I kept busy working three days a week at the Arab Cultural Center and delivering the occasional cross-cultural training session for Chevron.

# 11

# Transition – on to – Transition

In September 1998, I received a hint of hope in an interesting proposal from my sister Saffiya. She proposed that I move to the UK. As my brother-in-law's business project had terminated, he would return to Saudi Arabia. My sister was to remain in the UK with the children in order to complete her PhD. She reasoned that as I had not found a permanent job in the US and had always wanted to pursue a further postgraduate degree, this might be the time to follow that dream.

The invitation presented a promising alternative to remaining in the US; it proved too attractive to turn down. Thus, I determined to exercise the option before yielding to a return to the Arab world. Although concerned about financial dependence on my sister, I quickly accepted the offer despite my apprehension about continued transitional living arrangements. At the time, financial dependency was the major negative aspect of the move. No matter how meagre the income, I had a need to earn my way.

Soon I began to sort out my personal and professional commitments in the Bay Area. There was not much to sort out as I had barely completed a year's residence; in reality, I was still in a transitional period. There was no need to sort out personal belongings, as my Dubai household shipment remained largely unopened, stored in the basement of my parents' El Cerrito home. With the exception of a couple of boxes that I had opened in search of personal items, all the other boxes had remained sealed. I only needed to place them aside so they would not be mixed with my parents' storage.

On packing my personal items for the UK move, I entertained little hope of return to the US. In my heart there was a bitter taste of failure, of loss. It arose from the failure of my qualifications in the US job market and from the surrender of hope. The sense of loss accelerated as I severed friendships and relationships I had briefly reforged. My hopes and dreams of life in the US were shattered. I questioned the meaning of equal opportunity in a market where I received not one single positive response to the hundreds of applications I had submitted. Contemplating this state of affairs would only lead me to despair. Thus, I bandaged my soul and gratefully made the transition.

On moving to the UK, I decided to embrace whatever life handed me. I needed to establish realistic expectations with regard to my future career. I was desperate for a chance to prove myself. I decided that if this transition did not work, I would consider returning to the Arab world. I was open to where the road might lead.

For sanity and self-preservation, I researched possible courses of action before landing in the UK. Recognising the importance of doing something meaningful to keep me anchored during this transition, I had begun to research universities. I initiated the information gathering process necessary to make a decision on the focus of my postgraduate degree and where I wanted to do it.

On the fifth of October 1998, I landed in the UK. On the sixth of October – somewhat jet-lagged – I attended my first women's creative writing course. One of the first things I had to sort out on arrival was registering at the University of London's library. There, I immediately started to work on my postgraduate proposal on women's training and development in the Arab world with a focus on the Arab Gulf region.

Happily, London was a familiar destination. I had visited the UK several times since 1977, and had been coming to London on a yearly basis since 1995 to visit my sister and her family. In fact, I often visited several times a year.

The contrast between the Bay Area and London was sharp. The landscape, the demography and the spirit of the place and people seemed more than oceans apart. I left the US eagerly anticipating new cultural challenges. I was fortunate in having intimate British friends. The major adjustments were to the overcast days and the formal feel of the city.

How precious the British smile! My immediate observation was of the rarity of it. I decided that the Brits would not smile even if their government paid them to do so. That was a major difference between the overstated and the understated cheerfulness of American and British nationals. I quickly modified my expectations regarding a response to my polite, cheerful greetings or apologies.

It proved easy to adapt to the quiet underground tube commute compared to the comparatively loud BART subway ride in the Bay Area. On the tube, there were no unsolicited comments about the books I read or my dress. Each individual resident behaved as an independent island as if surrounded by an ocean. There was an invisible line that was not to be crossed even visually. It was interesting to observe the discomfort displayed when someone dared to look at a neighbour's newspaper. I had begun to hear words such as please, sorry and excuse me quite differently. I found that being left alone was helpful during this transitional period.

Between October and December 1998, I developed and submitted my proposal to the University of London. Although it was accepted, the university asked me to defer entry until September 1999, as at the time, there was only one available adviser; two were required to form a committee to supervise my dissertation. If I persisted along that path I would have to idly wait for a year. As I was on a visitor's visa, this was not an option; I needed student status to remain in the country.

Therefore, I opted to study for a second master's degree with a major in business administration reasoning that it would advance my career progress. I submitted my application to begin in February 1999. Luckily, I was accepted into the MBA programme, which was made possible due to the generosity of my sisters and brother who funded my degree.

Through my sister and her family, I met a few new people. Concurrently, Husna, Seif's sister, was living in the UK with her husband and daughter. We had reconnected the previous summer holiday. I decided to get settled at university first before contacting her.

## In memory of love

For Seif: November 1998–December 2002

That October of 1998 in London, Saffiya beamed at me: "Guess who is working in London?"

After thirteen years since we broke up, and four years since we last met, I wouldn't have guessed it was Seif under any circumstances. Saffiya obtained Seif's telephone number from his sister Husna who was living in Reading, just outside of London. Saffiya telephoned and left a message for him. The following evening, Seif returned the call while I was in the other room. As Saffiya talked to him, she waved to summon me to the telephone. I declined.

I am convinced that there is no luck or coincidence in life. Life is a gift and at times it presents us with opportunities wrapped in luck or coincidence. Then it is left to us to recognise the gift extended to us through a stroke of luck, a coincidence. I admit that I did not recognise the gift that life presented to me that October 1998 day until a couple of years later.

Seif's phone call woke me the next morning. *"You were not asleep last night. You did not want to talk to me,"* was his accurate opening remark. I did not respond, as both knew that was the truth. I laughed as this brought back memories of his morning calls many years ago. In a loving, healthy relationship, the partners know that you cannot lie, as the face and voice will betray. This was true for us.

From the end of 1998 until Seif's health deteriorated in September 2002, we resumed our friendship. During that period, I did not know that cancer was claiming his life as we teased out what remained of our love and passion for one another. As friends rediscovering one another after a long separation, we filled in the gaps. We shared our dreams and the new lives that we had created. This time we did not leave our meetings to fate.

Over many cups of coffee, we shared our thoughts and filled in the history gaps. Seif did not need to tell me why he had left me for another woman. I was well beyond that and the "why" did not matter any more.

The first time Seif and I met was for dinner at Pasha, a Turkish restaurant in Islington, London. As we walked from High Street Kensington to Knightsbridge, Seif pretended to hurl me into the street. "Are you trying to stage an accident and get me killed?" I bantered. "I would be doing your family a favour," he replied. "You mean that you would be doing yourself a favour. Is my presence so hard to accommodate or ignore?" I enquired.

As we got into a cab, it was enough that he said, "When you left, happiness traced your footsteps; when you left, you took away happiness." It was Seif's atonement. I did not need to ask; I knew perfectly what he meant. Being the woman I am, I replied, "I didn't leave; it was you who left happiness."

During dinner, Seif asked, "Would it not have been better for you to meet me with your partner rather than alone?" I smiled, silently thinking, *Am I making it harder to resist the temptation of revisiting an old romance?* Perhaps I had wished to think of myself as irresistible in Seif's eyes. Being so familiar with Seif's eloquence, I smiled and accepted the question as a figure of speech. I had accepted Seif's invitation with no intention of reopening the wounds of the past. The wounds had healed. Now the only thing that remained was an affinity that was deeper than the wounds. As always, we carried on playing with words. However, the conversations would not be about who did what and why.

Despite the long separation, we were both able to profoundly and intimately reconnect in a friendship that was a lasting gift of true love. We talked as if it was yesterday that I had received Seif's last letter. He asked about the letter. "I burned it when I moved to the US in 1989," I said.

"Shame! What a loss! It would have been interesting to read and revisit what I wrote you then," he responded. "I never thought that we would meet and have the promised cup of coffee together," was my reply.

We laughed as we remembered Seif's first gift to me in 1984. He bought me three rabbits from a pet shop in Riyadh. As I could not have a cat in my uncle Adnan's house, Seif thought rabbits would be a good compromise. They must have been sick when Seif bought them for they started dying, one after another. I suggested to Seif that we should have taken that as a signal for the future of our relationship.

There was no malice, no grudge, and only two old friends meeting at a turning point in their lives. After dinner, we strolled down the street ending at the Moon under Water pub. As we said our goodbyes, we knew that our bond had never broken.

Seif asked me before parting if I had read *The Unbearable Lightness of Being* by Milan Kundera. He suggested that I do so. A few weeks later, he left me a voicemail message that he had left something for my collection at The Royal Garden Hotel in Kensington where he was staying. The concierge there had a package for me; it was the film, *The Unbearable Lightness of Being*, starring Daniel Day-Lewis and Juliette Binoche. Then, I knew that it was possible for us to meet again. The film was Seif's token expression of what no longer needed to be said.

Again, I left with no trophies, only keepsakes of Seif. Long ago, Seif gifted me with a simple dedication that he wrote in one of al-Harbi's poetry collections. In addition, he gave me a pearl necklace. Later, in April 1999, at a Gloucester Road café, Seif gave me his copy of Ahlam Mosteghanemi's novel, *Thakirat al Jasad (Memory in the Flesh)*, published in Beirut in 1993. In it, Seif traced some of the story lines noting, "That is for me" and "how I feel exactly." I had read the book in 1995, and now I found myself re-reading it again.

On page 14 Seif left a mark next to *"I question after all these years where to place your love now. To list it under the ordinary stuff like that of sickness, tripping off or momentary madness? Or to place it where it had begun that day?"* On page 27 Seif left another mark next to *"I was an orphan and I was profoundly conscious of it. It is painfully terrifying to hunger for tenderness as this hunger taunts you in the core until it finishes you off."* On page 60 of the novel, Seif underlined a passage that reads, *"I was a man rejected by death, rejected by life".* On page 73, he underlined *"you live in a country that respects your talent and rejects your wound. You belong to a country that respects your wound and rejects you. What would you choose? You are both the man and the wound. Your dysfunctional body is merely a façade for your dysfunctional memory."* The entire novel was annotated with Seif's notes.

We shared a love for reading and writing. He was the creative gifted journalist and I was the inexperienced writer. In those days, I typically burned or threw away what I had written. Regrettably, this included a chronicle of my time in prison, along with Seif's comments and notes, which I fed into the fire.

Alone, Seif's dedication in the poetry collection documents that once in our lives we were in love. On Friday 3 February 1984, Seif wrote: *"My Darling Muna; It may be that the Palm trees have perceived you a perilous cultivation; here on the Arabian Gulf's shores; as you untie your hair inundated in its water, scented by a glowing emergence; wonderful morning every morning."*

The last time that Seif and I met was briefly in June 2000 before he repatriated to Saudi Arabia. We met for coffee in Richmond upon Thames at a café next to the tube station. We did not speak of keeping in touch or meeting again. When it was time to part, we did not embrace or say goodbye. There was but a small wave of the hand and a smile. We parted as friends who would meet again for a cup of coffee the next day. If I could have seen into the future, I might have exchanged the wave and the smile for a lasting, lingering embrace.

Unexpectedly a few months later, I received a call from Seif who was then in Dubai on business. He asked if I could do something for him. I said, "Yes" without asking the nature of the request. I had never imagined that one day Seif would entrust me with the translation of one of his short stories, *"Zagzagah"* (Chirping). It was published in the journal *Banipal*, issue no 8, summer 2000.

Accidentally, I learned that a cancerous brain tumour had struck Seif. The news arrived in a reply to an email in which I was copied but not included directly. Despite my indirect receipt of the shocking news, I did not feel estranged. As I felt so close and so well connected, I patiently waited until Seif was over the initial critical stage. I spoke with Husna, his sister, his doctor, Philip Salem, and his treatment programme's coordinator, Saher el-Baba, whose life was claimed by cancer a few years later.

I did not know what to feel. I knew only that Seif was in his prime with life ahead of him and a young family that needed him. Believing in the gift of fate brings a sense of comfort in perceiving life as a journey. In that journey, there will come a time when we transcend into another stage. I was filled with sorrow for a life about to be cut short.

*I had a dream of Seif before he left the UK to repatriate to Saudi Arabia. In my dream, I saw myself in a car with Saffiya and Seif. We were driving at dawn in the English countryside. It was a gorgeous day with the sun breaking through the morning sky. Wild horses roamed freely. We stopped the car for Seif to get out and take pictures.*

*Saffiya and I continued driving until we came upon a narrow lane where the car could go no further. We waited for Seif, but he did not appear. I returned to look for him only to find him precisely where he left the car. He was standing beside a woman who was helping a horse give birth. Seif asked me to sit down and he placed the horse's head on my lap as she was nursing her newborn colt. I woke up with an uplifted feeling about life and a sense that despite misfortunes life is worth living. I regretted that none of my grandmothers were alive to interpret my dream. I closed my eyes and heard their voices at the birth of a new day saying,* "Khair, inshallah khair."

I recalled the dream when I learned of Seif's illness. I sought meaning from the cancerous brain tumour and a beautiful horse's head in my lap with the newborn happily nursing. When Seif successfully emerged from the initial stages of treatment, I began to follow his health progress directly with him by telephone. It was not possible always to get through and at times I would speak with Saher el-Baba, his medical coordinator or Dr Salem. I formed a deep affinity with Dr Salem, especially after Seif shared with him letters I had written in November 2001 and for the 2002 New Year.

One of the letters included a poem entitled "First Fig" by Edna St Vincent Millay (1892–1950), which was published at the London Underground's initiative. The poem reads:

> My candle burns at both ends;
> It will not last the night;
> But ah! my foes, and oh, my friends –
> It gives a lovely light!

The poem spoke to Seif. He was fascinated by such open literary access. I remembered his question about the publication of poetry by the London Underground; before moving to London, he had wondered if it published poetry as the Paris Metro did. I had copied the poem during one of many journeys on the tube.

It is fascinating to observe the way in which human bonds develop. I did not personally know any of Seif's caregivers, yet I was made to feel welcome, a member of an intimate circle of friends. Despite Seif's denial of my wish to visit him in Houston, I did not feel rejected; rather I felt a profound respect for his rights and wishes. Seif and I had continued to work together on translating some of his selected writings and interviews into English in order that he could share them with the medical team at the treatment centre.

Seif's last request was that I translate his eulogy to Mnirah, his paternal grandmother. This was while he was under Dr Philip Salem's care in Houston and shortly before he passed away. He wanted to share it with his caregivers. Mnirah was Seif's first and only true love and this act was his second atonement. He had predicted that he would follow her fate and he was indeed the first to follow her in death. The last time Seif and I spoke, he recognised me, but sounded disoriented. I kept in touch with the coordinator who I believed had recognised the gift of Seif's life; she kept me informed.

Seif died on the fifteenth of December 2002. I learned of his death through an email, one that was intended for me. One never knows how to feel and react upon facing the altar of death, especially that of a loved one. I was not ready to receive the two-line email, despite the fact that I had known of Seif's prognosis. His repatriation home to Riyadh's King Faisal Specialist Hospital honoured his wish to die and to be buried in the land of his birth.

I realised the coincidence-wrapped gift that life had offered me. It is painful enough to lose a loved one once; to lose a loved one twice is devastating. I closed my eyes and as my warm, salty tears flowed, I recited *Surat al-Fatiha* for Seif's soul. In reality, I did not lose Seif twice; I had found him twice.

Several years earlier, I had written "Untitled", which depicts images of my own death. I had written it for my women's creative writing class on 7 February 1999. Seif's death altered what I had imagined. How could I assume that death can be designed?

Twice, Seif had asked me to read "Untitled" to him. The first time was early spring of 1999 after having brunch at Saffiya's house. The second time was early spring of 2002; I read it to him on the telephone while he was receiving his chemotherapy treatment at the Houston clinic.

I read:

Softly she whispered into my ear, "Welcome to the world, here you are greeted by the Arabian Gulf and blessed by its palms." Twenty-four years later you emerged into my life, a vision that I claimed as my own. Or you might have been an illusion? Before you left me you wrote, "It may be that the palm trees have perceived you a perilous cultivation; here on the Arabian Gulf's shores; as you untie your hair inundated in its water, scented by a glowing emergence; wonderful morning every morning."

Now from another world as my ashes were set afloat in the Arabian Gulf, I was in awe of her whisper and your words. Had I requested cremation because of your dedication, which strengthened my bond to the Arabian Gulf? Had I gone against what my inherited religion teaches to become closer to a reality drawn by your word, to the blueness that eternally meets the desert?

As I look to the future beyond life, my ashes will float freely over the Arabian Gulf. Here I am today – ashes afloat from sea to ocean – carried by one wave after another until one day some of my ashes will land upon a beach on which you are taking a stroll. My ashes rush to embrace your feet just as I embraced them so many times. You felt the sensation of your feet spreading upward through your heart just so that momentarily you remembered me. It has been many years. You were filled with wonder about what might have happened.

You dialled a number you obtained from your sister only to be greeted by a distant familiar voice. You asked the woman on the line if you could speak to me. Choking with her tears, she told you that I had died a year ago. You asked her where I was buried only to learn that my ashes floated, that you could greet me at any time you are near a sea or an ocean.

For you see, I was born a marginal number in a census somewhere where things like me were not supposed to happen. I gathered that I had either arrived in life too early or too late. Most importantly, I believed that I had arrived at the wrong place. I never bothered to ask why it seemed that always I had to go against the current.

I was a simple woman, defeated in my own victories. I had learned to accept the irony of my life, but never learned to accept life's wickedness. I was not looking when I found life. I found life on the tips of a man's fingers, between his lips, in his eyes, embraced in his arms. Only then my life came into a complete existence.

I lived inhabited by a man without realising his presence. He was merely a vision and he became my emancipation. Finding and losing him were illusions, and I was all that happened in between.

It had begun where I was deserted. I had walked through life invisible. The commitment and the words did not liberate me. It was simple human pleasures that freed me. I began a journey of self-discovery into discovering others.

I knew that he had loved me for a fraction of time, a lost moment. It was with him and through him that I had transcended. He had taught me how to read body maps for the first time. He had illustrated how the body exists and extends beyond one's own. He took my hands and navigated the way into a world that before him I had not known. Through him I learned to listen to my body, to listen to the world beyond.

Naturally, when people we love die we mourn. I mourned Seif in silence, as it is culturally inappropriate for an unrelated woman to publicly mourn a man. Only three people other than my sisters and cousin Wafyah called to comfort me: my best friend Eynas, Dr Salem and Suhail.

Suhail was the lone surprise. Suhail, my first and only other true love, was the last person I expected to call. And yet, on reflection, I did not expect less of him. For Suhail, Batool and I share bonds not of blood or marriage, but only of devotion. I still ask if I loved Suhail for Batool, or loved Batool for Suhail.

The two men in my life, Suhail and Seif, never met. I was the remote link they had, falling in love with Suhail before I was imprisoned and with Seif after I was released. Long before Seif, Suhail had written: "I will never have true happiness, since Muna left with my true happiness." Men have a talent for modifying the storyline; they have a peculiar way of evoking reality. Perhaps we all do.

# 12

# A Monologue: Shattered Silence/Shattered Soul

In April 2000, I was assaulted by conflicting realities. One was an idealised reality of a liberal, open, loving and democratic family. The other reality was a family scandal that erupted, forcing me to revisit my past and re-validate my memories. In that difficult re-examination, I searched for signs, voices and shadows of that which I have lost.

Painfully, I recalled memories of voices speaking *"I am helpless, my hands are tied. I cannot support you."* I found myself at the crossroads of numerous irreconcilable lives and muted voices, all defined by a conspiratorial silence and domestic violence that I had never known of, and therefore had never challenged.

Uncovering the truth about my own family's share of domestic violence and sexual violations would unveil the disgraceful scandal with the resulting hurtful consequences visited solely upon women. The truth and facts as presented by women would become irrelevant to the scandal. The voice of women had to speak the truth or be silenced for ever.

In that bleak hour, I despaired as I contemplated molestation and rape, old and new cases. How can the sin of rape be shared? Who would choose to share the sins of rape and molestation? How would those sins be allocated? Beyond the violation, muteness prevailed.

Women, what is it with us? Have we a love/hate relationship with silence? We live our lives without finding and using our own voices. We fall in love with and succumb to safe, secure internal silence. Terrified, we live in the comfort of silence, while repressing the

## A Monologue: Shattered Silence/Shattered Soul

desire to speak, to shout the truth to those powers that mute our voices.

Indeed, we desire to exercise the robust voices that we reject as too strident. We desire our strong voices, but we fear to endorse them. That reluctance yields silenced voices that do not challenge, that are respectful of the masculine, patriarchal prerogative.

What is the effect of a lifetime of self-imposed, suppressed silence for a woman who desires the truth? My subdued voice possessed an unmistakable muted quality defined by that lifetime of suppression. From birth, it had been edited, dismissed and expelled by the chorus of masculine voices. Initially, my voice had blossomed before the transmission between it and my fingers ruptured. The resulting numbness proved shattering. How can one edit one's own memories? How can one rewrite one's own history?

From my nightmares, I had awakened to confront my silenced vocal cords and what remained of my severed fingers. The nightmares dissolved my pen and writing pads. Questions streamed through my consciousness challenging the lives and voices of others. The paths before me have been poorly defined and those I have walked have been muddied, contaminated by the belated revelation of rape and molestation.

In dismay, I studied my options. I refused to see myself as merely a shadow and my life but a mirror image of another. The "other" would not be just anyone, some anonymous entity. If I did not reclaim my life completely, it would be subsumed into that of someone whose life is intimately connected to mine in an unbreakable timeline of history. In my anger, my rage, I vaulted into a place from which I could not return. There, I balanced on the edge of my own contempt. That voice, my own voice, was my only salvation.

At age forty, it seemed as if I was eternally drifting into or out of a dream. At forty, I had rejected one reality and entered another in search of the core essence of my life. It was a reality that I had failed to notice or one that I chose to ignore earlier.

I am not the story. I am only the voice, the narrator of a story that I can neither claim nor deny. It seemed that everything for which I had struggled was slipping through my fingers. At once, I became the persecuted and the persecutor.

Shuttling back and forth between England and Saudi Arabia

between the summer of 2000 and 2001, I had been assaulted by the magnitude of domestic violence, rape and sexual assault incidents that were belatedly revealed. Confessions from long silenced sources were more revolting than shocking. Vile violence and atrocities against women are as common in both geographies as they are everywhere else in the world. No woman is immune, no child is immune and no family is immune. It is shattering when it is one's own family.

In silence, I had wondered if my countrymen are also raped in order to be humiliated, to be silenced and to be controlled. My questions about how men deal with rape and sexual assaults had been unspoken, as I had never worked with males who are violated in such ways. Do men remain silent? How do they conceal their humiliation? I believe that victims in most, if not all, cases choose not to speak of the attack. They choose silence in order to protect themselves from society's retribution and a legal system that punishes them for provoking the attack. You may be sure that society will retaliate. Women and men alike will penalise the victim and create an excuse for the aggressor.

As a woman, a violated woman, I naturally think more about women. Repeatedly, violations are perpetuated, as the only choice for women when violated is to remain silent. With the absence of any appropriate punishment, the perpetrator repeats the violation.

The woman's silence is transformed into internalised self-incrimination, guilt and shame. Women are predisposed to, socialised to fear exposure and persecution. Society prefers women to remain silent, compliant. Such women are deemed virtuous

In that silence, intervention support becomes redundant, superfluous. Without survivors' voices, my voice alone would not suffice. I sensed that my own voice had become subdued.

I feared this normalising of violence. I was terrified of its implications. My pen had collapsed and my voice was constricted as silence prevailed.

The violations were not mine. The stories belonged to other women whose fear of social stigma is greater than their pain. Being violated, broken and manipulated were of less concern than the retribution of the local community and society at large.

Through my training, I had learned to respect women's choices. I believed that women knew their circumstances and their

## A Monologue: Shattered Silence/Shattered Soul

community best. I knew from experience how difficult and how painful it is for women to choose silence. The option for women to seek help is non-existent, as neither the patriarchy nor the legal system is capable of delivering justice.

Deep inside, I longed to hold on to hopes for change. Deep inside, I believed that I needed to act to mobilise change. Change requires courage. For it to happen, women must demonstrate the courage to tell their stories in their own voices.

Blind submission would have shattered me. With the skills developed earlier in that California rape crisis counselling programme, I could intervene. Now qualified, I possessed the language and the skills to listen. I had the language to speak with other women about rape, sexual assaults and domestic violence.

Thus, I started anonymous counselling work with Arab and Muslim women who had been raped, sexually assaulted and/or who were living with domestic violence. I had learned that anonymous work does not necessarily grant women the confidence or the trust to use their voices. Often, anonymity does not create safety and security, as women remain inhibited by fear of exposure. I thought of their ambivalent desires: to seek help and yet to remain silent, mute. In my training, I had questioned if women genuinely desire help. If a woman seeks help and is not exposed, does she feel grateful? Should she? I shy away from such an assumption.

I worry that women excoriate, blame themselves for their own violation. I worry in silence. I know that in seeking help, women subject themselves to accusations. Rarely do they obtain justice and the perpetrators are rarely convicted. Therefore, life becomes even more challenging, more terrifying for women to navigate in their search for voices that do not blame the victim.

As my awareness of victims of violence with their preference for silence grew, I felt increasingly powerless. How can I help victims who prefer to edit their memories rather than confront them? How can I help women who do not have the language to talk about such atrocities? How could I help a woman who exchanges her mental health and sanity for silence because of her fear of exposure? How could I convince women to pursue justice when I know too well that for women in my world it is not obtainable, and if it was obtainable, it wouldn't be granted? Justice was never meant for women!

Within this culture, violence against women is a taboo topic. Mere references to a woman's conduct can stigmatise her for life. Sexual assaults and rape are massive liabilities for the reputation of women whose voices are secondary to those of men. Proper sexual conduct is the sole asset on which a woman's reputation is judged. Therefore, women live with silenced voices and self-censored memories. Rape, sexual assaults and domestic violence remain taboo subjects as long as societies penalise and silence women.

As in many other cultures, my society, my community, is a harsh place for women. Extraordinary courage would be required to take a stand against rape, sexual assault or domestic violence. Empathy has no place in such a society where women betray their voices in exchange for conditional and typically temporary endorsement by men. As women choose not to confront and prosecute, they reveal their powerlessness before violence. I cannot accept that objection to aggression and violence is inappropriate. I cannot stand by idly as women suffer and yet I know deep down that I do not have the right to speak on behalf of women, to tell their stories.

I remember reading Ntozake Shange's *"With No Immediate Cause"*:

every 3 minutes a woman is beaten
every five minutes
a woman is raped/ every ten minutes
a lil girl is molested
*************************
"there is some concern
that alleged battered women
might start to murder their
husbands & lovers with no
immediate cause"
i spit up i vomit i am screaming
we all have immediate cause
every 3 minutes
every 5 minutes
every 10 minutes
every day
women's bodies are found
in alleys & bedrooms/ at the top of the stairs (1–4, 50–63)
    (Ntozake Shange, *Nappy Edges*, New York, 1972, pp 114–16)

## A Monologue: Shattered Silence/Shattered Soul

In my home country of Saudi Arabia, there are no reports of or about domestic violence, just silence. Within the patriarchal world, women's presence is taboo and women's lives are less valued than men's lives. The concept of women's wellbeing is foreign.

Apart from my career, I had my own personal challenges. I wanted to put aside, to relinquish my anger and resentment of men, women or circumstances that have been shaped and influenced by history, culture and religion.

I examined my own feelings and perceptions of violence. I recalled an expression often referenced in feminist literature, "The personal is political". In *The Whole Woman*, Germaine Greer wrote, "The personal is still political. The millennial feminist has to be aware that oppression exerts itself in and through her most intimate relationships, beginning with the most intimate, her relationship with her body" (*The Whole Woman*, Anchor Books, New York, 1999).

In silence, women shroud themselves in the face of societally condoned violence. That shrouding is not a personal problem but a reflection of a wider political oppression. Women share a hidden history of violence. It is a history that connects the past to the future and it perpetuates sexual oppression. It has the unfortunate outcome of making women unwillingly complicit agents in the perpetuation of violence against themselves.

I am now convinced that without men taking responsibility for the violence, without men challenging their own privileges over women, that progress toward a safer and more humane environment for women and society at large is impossible. I confess that I am haunted by images of men praying at the mosque, who came there after they might have just raped a woman, assaulted a child or inflicted violence on a loved one. I am unable to escape images of respectable men of social and professional status speaking on the topic of violence who may have just violated a woman. I am unable to erase memories of the lustful glances of the religious police as they scrutinised fully robed and veiled women while herding them like sheep from public spaces.

How could men hiding behind their social and professional status speak with confidence and without shame against what they themselves inflict on women? How could someone pray to Allah when he had transgressed? How do Muslim societies justify penalising women when Allah opposes violence of any kind, enjoining man: "Do not transgress" The accounts of violence are common among conservative, traditional, religious and liberal men alike, as if these acts are an inherent right of manhood.

So how could I live quietly, silent before such violence? Although I had learned to accept and respect people's choices, I struggled mightily against standing idle. I awakened to the realisation that I had lived parallel to violence and the violated unable to recognise either. I realised that I needed the solitude to think silently and that I needed to act freely, even though realistically I could only achieve the first. I wished for the ability to screen my life as in editing a film. With regret, I realised that reality does not come with a drop down menu with editing options. Reality does not offer us possibilities of revision and resubmission of life events.

Despite pain and despair, I felt exceptionally fortunate to know the truth behind the scandal. The ethical questions the truth implies are secondary: what or whom the truth serves and who is entitled to know the truth. For me, knowing the truth was a gift, despite its consequences. I was no stranger to rape, sexual assault and domestic violence. However, knowing personally – whether closely or casually – the individual involved had complicated my reality. I did not need the details to determine who was violated and who perpetuated the violence.

As I examined the issues surrounding the molestation and rape scandal, I reviewed the experiences within a small circle of intimates. Among we five women – *same family members and companions* – two had been molested, two were raped, and one remained physically safe. Three out of the four perpetrators had been trusted relatives. Each of us was subjugated by fear; each was violated, including the one who had not been physically violated. Yet not one of us was able to speak the name of the aggressor or the aggression; not one of us was able to confront the patriarchy. Not one of us had sought to expose the violence. While we prayed for the courage to expose the aggressors, our fear of the social repercussions and persecution had confounded us, silenced our voices.

From within a survivor's perspective, the world seemed to revolve around violence. I observed that as narratives of violations were shared among women, more experiences of violation emerged.

Among those violated, there is an involuntary and unconsciously shared body language that signals trust. In an exclusive trusting environment, only the voice of one woman with the courage to say, *"I was molested"*, is required to unblock the repression. Other voices would cry out, *"my cousin was sexually assaulted", "my niece was violated", "my sister was attacked", "my mother was repeatedly assaulted"*. The voices of pain rained down unabated.

Women reported incidents of incest packaged and presented as "forbidden love", spontaneous, unpremeditated acts that were masked by emotional manipulation. The manipulation made speaking about it even more difficult. There were neighbours, distant relatives, and gardeners who took advantage of unsupervised little girls. They would return to repeatedly abuse the children and terrify them with threats that they would not be believed; thus they had better keep silent. Each incident was different; yet manipulation was the common denominator among all the experiences.

Women asked: *"Why would I want to talk about it? Who would I tell? Who would believe me?"* These were some of the concerns and worries, a few of the questions that women had contemplated but were too terrified to address directly. There were the other terrifying questions of whether their larger families, communities and societies would believe them. They lived within constricted boundaries, behind countless barriers and with no escape route from the social stigma that would follow revelation of the abuse. That stigma would hound them as long as they lived. As experiences of violence unfolded, more victims shared similar violations. Such is the reality of sexual abuse that families entrusted their children to the care of relatives and friends without realising that their children were violated by the caregivers.

Now, there was a veritable flood of stories of violations. The stories, the revelations and the many women's voices had hovered like djinns locked inside an enchanted lamp for someone to rub the lamp and release them. Rubbing the lamp unleashed the voices and narratives of victims. With those revelations, the victims were freed to speak of long-suppressed pain, of shame and of survival.

Emboldened by the voices of other survivors, more victims shared their experiences. As the experiences multiplied, I was challenged to grasp the totality of the violations and to comprehend the years of suppressed silence. Women recognised their own voices resonating in the experiences of other women. There was a subtle, unspoken bond between women who unknowingly had shared similar experiences.

For the vast majority of women, it is excruciatingly painful to disclose incidents of rape, sexual assault and/or domestic violence. And yet many people assume that such accounts are exaggerated when in reality such abuse is underreported. The voices of others – women and men – criticise the revelation and minimise its importance. Many strive to normalise such incidents or simply deny their occurrence. Often, I encountered the typical male rationale, *"the woman wanted it"*, or *"they enjoyed it"*, or *"it happens all the time ... what's the big deal?"* Aggression against women is often blamed on other cultures, i.e., it was imported from the West, the product of liberal ideas. The brilliance of the human's capacity for self-deception fascinates.

No matter the reasons, the justifications or the excuses, they do not change the realities of the women and children who are targets, the objects of such violence. Is it in the nature of society to avoid pain, or is it just too uncomfortable to recognise and discuss such taboo topics? Is society too weak to face the truth and take a stand? Perhaps it seems easier to assume the virtue of humanity. Perhaps such violence is too painful to imagine. Perhaps it is taboo to question patriarchy's role in such violence?

From women's narratives, I had learned that in violence there were no differences between the literate and the illiterate, the traditional and the modern, the conservative and the liberal. Universally, aggression and violence against women is a reality of women's everyday life everywhere. While they may be packaged differently, under different labels, they are violations against women. Segregation and sexual deprivation do not justify or excuse sexual assault. While reported incidents of violence vary between East and West, aggression against women is equally common.

Violence is a complicated phenomenon. It is not so simple as pointing out that it is fuelled by a patriarchal structure with its male supremacy core anchored in privilege, power and control. It can be understood partially as the mindset of male supremacy; partially the grossly unequal division of power and control; partially the disparity between privileged and unprivileged; and in some measure by the culture, socialisation patterns, the economy and lastly by complicated human nature.

We are challenged to create a different world, one that guarantees the protection of women, children and men. It is a daunting challenge given the ignorance and superstition of uneducated women and men who have internalised the perpetuation and normalisation of such violence for centuries.

I had learned that speaking out against violence was less challenging than confronting the emotional and psychological manipulation that dominated and controlled the lives of surviving victims. Victims have a right to confidentiality and protection. Can that right be exercised if they expose the perpetrator and thereby subject themselves to further violation?

This ethical question haunted me. For self-preservation, the male perpetrators would likely retaliate by accusing women of misconduct. The patriarchal society would side with men, as it places a higher value on men's voices over those of women. In many of the cases I encountered, women were socially coerced to choose not to expose their assailants in order to avoid community censure or retribution.

I restrained my powerful desire to speak the truth in favour of protecting the victims from further damage through exposure. From a difficult lesson, I had learned that revealing the truth might not protect the victims from the dreaded exposure and further victimisation by the community. It is one of the many ironies of my community that even when perpetrators are exposed, society tends to forgive and forget. *Boys will be boys* is as true in the East as in the West. It will matter only to women, with profound impacts on their lives.

I struggled against societal rationalisation of violence. How can humanity not only accept it, but even deny its pervasiveness in our everyday lives? As a child, I had experienced violation. As an adult, I came to understand my terror of speaking the truth about the perpetrator. I had internalised the social code of silence.

I could not seek help and refuge in my mother. How could I explain in my childish language, in my childish voice what had happened? My mother would have either ignored me or blocked it out just as my father did when I recounted the experience many years later. She might even have slapped me in the face to further silence my voice. Had she sought advice from her women friends, they might have comforted her with the rationale that children are imaginative, or that it could have been a bad dream. Women do not want to doubt or mistrust other adults in the family, particularly those who are viewed as protectors.

For years, I had lived in silence, my voice muted. I knew intimately how it feels to have one's voice trapped between the heart and throat. I had known the bitter taste of the suppression of violence. I had known the taste of suppressing all the memories surrounding violence.

As a child, I had sensed it; subsequently, I learned that decisions are not in the hands of a child, a minor or a woman. The world has changed little since then, as women still have no power. In the rare event of a woman exercising power, men influence it.

In relation to violence, women are divided into those who have experienced it, those who know that it happens and those who accept such as reality as long as it does not involve any of their male family members. Yet, they are all united in silence. Thus, the support that violated women receive from others remains conditional upon their relation to the parties involved, not by the nature of the violation itself.

Until this time (summer 2000), my life had been stretched across various boundaries. Although the future course of my life was about to be altered profoundly, it was not because of my learning of the magnitude of violence against women. Rather, it was prompted by my realisation that I might unconsciously contribute to the further victimisation of women.

Sensing discouragement from family and friends, I debated: could I use my training to take a stand against violence? Who would be served by exposing the truth? As I believed that there is no true justice for women, I vacillated in the decision-making process.

Confronting the truth about a family molestation and rape scandal comes with a high price tag. I believed it my inherent right to know the truth and then to choose my own actions and positions accordingly. It seemed to me that knowing about the violations and being able to take a stand against them were both equally valid.

In my traditional Arab-Muslim culture, there is an assumption that one should disregard incidents of violence. To expose the family reputation publicly is to risk the collapse of the family network. In that silence, violence becomes acceptable.

I had anguished over my right to choose according to my own principles. I felt trapped between the choice to do nothing or to take action, as if caught between a rock and a hard place. My concern was with the sensitivity of the victim's position within that narrow, traditional society. It was equally as intimidating and distressing for me as it was for the victims with whom I worked. Navigating a course against the perpetrators that would also ensure protection of the victims proved challenging.

Does the truth matter to witnesses of unfolding violent events? I understood that people compartmentalise their experiences and their memories of events. Thus, they shield themselves from the truth that violence is not a passing incident, particularly when the same person in many different guises premeditates it. As long as no one knows, the truth about violence did not seem to matter to people, irrespective of the degree to which it may have scarred their lives.

I doubted that those in my close circle noticed as I journeyed through this peculiar turning point in my life and my relationships. I suspected that if they had noticed some would have judged my severance of certain relationships as an impulsive reaction, a temporary aberration.

In the end, I had needlessly overwhelmed myself with worry and doubts. In reality, it did not matter at all, as people paid no attention whatsoever. While I had consumed myself with worry, people went on with their lives as usual. They simply did not care as long as they were themselves not required to live up to their stated principles by taking a stand.

People follow their own principles in dividing the world into many compartments, depending upon the degree of involvement, their proximity and their interrelationships. Time neither changes the reality of violence nor its consequences. Similarly, personal knowledge of violence does not motivate people to reconsider their principles and behaviours.

My decision to sever certain relationships within the family had complicated outcomes with relatives and acquaintances. It made familial negotiation difficult, as it required delicate understanding of and sensitive skills in dealing with human emotions and relationships. I was aware that knowledge of the truth had the potential to devastate all involved.

In the end, I made my decision to confront the face of violence, not simply because the violations were close to the home front; I was driven more by the arrogant denial of the violence and the smothering coercive silence demanded. I made the decision because silence gives consent, i.e., not standing up to it is accepting and giving violence my blessing.

Sooner or later the perpetrators would strike again to violate women physically, psychologically and emotionally. The perpetrators and witnesses alike would view my silence as acceptance. I could hear them whispering, "You kept silent which means you did not mind it then, so why would you mind it now?" It would make it more difficult to confront any form of future violence. For me, silence in the face of violence is to submit my voice and myself. It places me at the service of the patriarch, the tribe and a code that is dictated by men for the protection of, and in the service of men.

My voice and position were non-negotiable, now more than ever. In standing up against domestic violence, I accepted the consequences of my own decision. I was ready and well equipped emotionally and psychologically to live with the consequences.

Truth seems contagious as the revelation of one truth leads to other truths. Theoretically, people have the power and the will to face adversity. However, the real test of character, of principle, is when people are forced to re-examine their behaviour and their relationships.

In my case, the truth about violence revealed the genuine character, principles and values of family and friends. It had become evident that every act of love and kindness I had received from certain family members had been conditioned upon my personal submission and silence.

Mysteriously, life works like a sieve, sifting and sorting character as people experience difficult periods in their lives. In this period, I recalled the events of 1996 during which the same members of my family tested me. Then I was accused of trying to destroy family unity because of my refusal to submit to the status quo and the patriarchal tribal code. Now, that previous accusation made more sense within the context of the new revelations of violations. In the past when I distanced myself from the family, I had posed an intolerable threat. Beyond tribal control, I had been able to observe clearly. With that clarity of vision, I posed a mortal threat to family unity: I might unveil an ugly family secret.

Endlessly, I rewound and replayed every memory, every life event; endlessly, I searched for what I had missed, what I had failed to notice and how I had been deceived. I desired to reclaim my life in its entirety. I did not want to rewrite or edit my life. I did not wish to rewrite my history or to recreate my memories.

I have the right to all my life's wholeness, to all its sorrow, to all its anguish, to all its goodness, to all its disappointments and to all its joyous and happy memories. Denial of the totality of my life would have been both abnormal and soul destroying. I realised that I can change the future, but I cannot change the past. I can appreciate the past differently, count my blessings and be grateful for life's goodness. I had to relearn how to live with the past while changing the course of my future.

This was a life-transforming experience. I had let go completely to trust myself and to trust in the goodness of the world in which I live. I had chosen to break my silence and stand up against violence: I rejected submissive silence in favour of severing all relationships with the perpetrators and their allies. In doing so, I rejected a life of submission and chose to pursue life defined by assertive sovereignty. With that choice, I claimed ownership of my memories of deceit and pain. I had chosen to live and act based on my knowledge of the truth. I was completely at peace with all of the memories of my life.

Immersed in my own thoughts and actions, I had forgotten that under the tribal code a woman is not allowed to have her say. She is not permitted a final word, a final act. To think independently and critically is not permitted. Only on very rare occasions is it permitted within strict, male-circumscribed boundaries.

Loathing the code, I had rejected it and refused to heed it. I rejected any justifications of the violent act, along with the following years of manipulation and emotional violence. In the midst of dealing with my feelings, my loss and my pain, I lost the will to write. It seemed that I am destined to be mute in one way or another; the pain had paralysed my fingers and my pen.

Distracted, I was rudely awakened by a new act of violence, one initially difficult to fathom or explain. Contempt! That is how the new act of violence was expressed. The contempt was packaged in three long letters delivered in three stages. My uncle Najeeb wrote all of them. The letters were subsequently sent to four different friend and family groups with a covert command intended to discredit my position, my principles, along with those of my immediate family: my sisters and my father.

The three letters reminded me of others written and distributed by the then newly emerging Shia fundamentalist groups in the late 1970s and early 1980s. Those letters accused women viewed as progressive of everything from atheism to prostitution. Those letters bore a long list of women's names. In the view of the male and female letter writers, the women were not adhering to established codes that were validated by religious groups.

Now, I was reliving the same experience. On the current occasion, the letters had documented the most intimate details of my life experiences and were intended to compel my silence. Three different letters of accusations were sent to coerce and control. My intimate life, my struggles, my wounds had never been secrets. I was beyond being silenced, although keenly aware of the importance of protecting one's reputation.

It was clear that such an act of desperation was motivated by fear of exposure; the letter writer feared losing control through exposure that would threaten his reputation and status. I sought to understand the complexity of that fear and the desire to protect self-image. However, there was no understanding of the desperate terror of someone who proclaimed lifelong devotion to the pursuit of liberation, freedom, justice and respect. The dissonance was too great.

I marvelled at life's full circle. The very person, my uncle Najeeb, who had railed against the Shia fundamentalist letters, had resorted to the same tactic two decades later. No contemplation of the event or of the contempt conveyed altered in any way the powerless nature of the letters: they had no power over someone who was free. I was for ever free of his contempt.

On reflection, I realised that my conceptualisation of contempt as the language, the behaviour and the solution had evolved over time.

## A Monologue: Shattered Silence/Shattered Soul

In view of the current contemptible behaviour and retaliation, my experience and struggle with the conflict between the stated principles and the behaviour of others were making sense. Although encouraged to read and to think, to develop a liberal, critical mind and to be knowledgeable about world affairs and politics, I was required to be in check and under control at all times. When I dared to defy the tribal code of the ruling liberal patriarchy, my voice, my decisions and my actions threatened that control.

Manipulating the truth is an act of self-defence. The exposure of old wounds to coerce submission is emotional and mental blackmail. In retrospect, it felt like I suffered shock in a massive traffic accident. Only much later did I realise the damage, notice the limp and determine how much blood I had lost.

Beyond my pain and my disappointment, my life was unfolding with an introduction to new realities and new truths. I felt that I had become more grounded and more understanding of how difficult it is to make life-transforming decisions. I was reminded of my time in prison when I felt that I had aged ten years within 365 days.

Like an old woman who surveys her life, I realise that I had matured, developed new insights, sensibilities and a little wisdom. Suddenly, what was important in my life became clear. I had greater clarity about my priorities and those for whom I cared about the most. The longer I lived the more complex my life became. There were no simple answers.

It was time to abandon the contemplation of humanity and human nature. It was time to stop trying to understand what drives us to be cruel, to alter the truth, to harm and inflict pain on others. I had to stop asking how we can go to sleep knowing we had not served justice. The boundaries between what is moral and what is immoral had become blurred.

I understand that the world is arranged around the privileged and the unprivileged. Our world and our humanity justify violence and excuse violators. Even personal freedoms and the right to self-defence have become pretexts to permit violation.

Humanity is disturbingly contradictory, enthralling in its complexity and humbling in its compassion. The observation that in every act of violence, humanity delivers an ultimate act of gentleness confounds me. I am ignorant and limited in my acquaintance with the depths of humanity. Mine is but a limited exposure to people and life. What fascinates me about humanity is our ignorance of human potential, that is, of what we, you, I, and the next person are capable of being, doing and becoming. Through living, we reveal our capacity to ourselves and to the world. We assume knowledge of others without ever fully realising or knowing the other. Humanity has become a minefield. At the time that I thought I was re-balancing my life, I was experiencing an eventful, life-changing year quite unlike any other.

# Memoir: Struck Mute by Persecution

*At age forty, I jousted with self-censorship and suspense, both of which petrified me. I was tormented by questions about the right to speak on behalf of others. I was suspended between the fear of abandonment and the fear of being trapped.*

*Meanwhile, I silently observed women sentenced to lives of shame, guilt and fear. I worked with women who deemed themselves worthless; their flat, lifeless voices were forever trapped between shame and guilt. Deceptively, they believed that their silence protected those whom they loved the most.*

*In my work, I was blindingly aware of my own perceptions, my own judgements of them. When I challenged myself with the question of who has the right to speak on behalf of women's protection and preservation of self-respect, I recognised and reasserted that the violated have the right to their own suffering.*

*It is my belief that women who are violated have the right to choose silence. Nevertheless, I cling to the possibility for change in the discourse of victims' rights, i.e., the choice to speak out or to choose silence. I continue to dream of a future free from fear of the truth and free from retribution for being truthful. Along with other women, I too struggle against the restraints imposed by societal violence. Perhaps I am most challenged in the struggle with the issue of women's choice to be silent.*

*Is life just as it is? The person who opened a window introducing me to a life beyond the boundaries of my own narrow world – to humanity, philosophy, ideology and politics – became a predatory perpetrator. Now, I only have to confront the rapist and the last fortress of fear.*

*At last, my dreams made sense. In those nightmares, I had consistently dreamed of being pursued by a water snake, of nakedness and of muteness. I came of age with my dreams and they followed me as I moved in between lives, boundaries and countries.*

*Consistently, my grandmothers were always beside me with their benediction: "Inshallah khair" (Good omen, God willing). Both interpreted water as the symbol of wealth and abundance. Then, I never talked about nakedness and muteness. I did not have a voice for them.*

*Dreams of muteness terrified me, as it was my voice that was silenced. Inevitably, I woke drenched in sweat with the realisation that I have a voice that no one heard.*

*Thus in my fortieth year, I continued to force myself out of sleep to confront my fears. More than ever before in my life, I was keenly aware of the strength of vulnerability. I know the pain of exposing and touching one's own raw wounds. I know the terror of standing powerless before women with silenced voices.*

*Water was and is my own life. It flows constantly within and I flow with life. Nakedness and muteness defined me. Nakedness is exposure. It revealed my rawness, my wounds. Muteness is however what petrified me most. I was terrified that I would wake one day and not recognise my own voice. I did not want to confront the possibility that I was not worth the gift of voice.*

*Daily, I encountered voiceless, faceless and sterile, impotent lives. I live in terror of waking to find that I am mute. Those dreams of muteness, nakedness and water snakes haunted me. Finally, my dream of muteness ended and my voice was freed. At last, I heard my own strong, true voice. Nevertheless, my raw wounds exposed my vulnerability and fragility.*

# 13

# Terror's Real Victory: The Surrender of Rationality

Perhaps coping with the monstrousness of rape had shielded me from the virulence of persecution and the atrocity of terrorism. Eternally, I will associate the taste of persecution with Tuesday 11 September 2001 and with the numerous atrocities that followed. Those atrocities have overwhelmed humanity's voice; they have claimed as casualties those innocent citizens who have been denied a voice, denied a future.

On that day, I was returning from Derbyshire after delivering an intercultural training programme for employees bound for Canada. On arrival at King's Cross Station en route home to Richmond, I observed that everyone was reading the *Evening Standard* newspaper. On its cover was the iconic photograph of the 747 aeroplane hitting the Twin Towers. Was this reality or fantasy? I searched everywhere for a copy of the paper, new or abandoned. Not one was available. A conspiratorial silence prevailed, as if the world had lost its voice.

At last, I reached home where silence also prevailed. The family was frozen before the TV set. There, the footage of the collapsing Twin Towers was played and replayed and replayed endlessly on every channel. Clearly, I remember overhearing my nephew's comment; his prophetic words are indelibly imprinted in my memory, "I hope it is not true that Muslims are behind the attack. It won't be good for Islam or Muslims." His young voice faded. Unable to grasp what I saw, I succumbed to stunned confusion. Was this a macabre Hollywood re-creation or a present-day, real-time event?

Nineteen Muslim men, fourteen of whom were from my homeland, inflicted an act of violence, an atrocity, against a country that hosted them. Those men are as alien to me as they are to the country they violated. They are men who are equally capable of inflicting atrocities on Muslim Sunni and Shia women, men and communities indiscriminately. Although we share the same native land, I have no bond with such men or their ideology of hatred. The language they speak and the religion they claim are not mine.

That day, I became aware of persecution not only for being a Shia and a woman but also for being a Muslim. My religion had been hijacked by men whose beliefs are as alien to my Islam as they are to the country they violated. The simplicity and moderation of the Islam I know were ignored and rejected as inconsequential, quaint and not front-page news. A new mercilessly fanatical Islam emerged after a makeover, with a new face and a new identity card.

Assaulted, outraged by the false image projected, I found myself searching for the Islam I know, the one in which I was nurtured as a child. My voice was overshadowed, silenced by the voice of their atrocity and the ensuing eternal war on terror launched in the aftermath of that horrific day. Now, the public voice that prevails is the voice of extremism.

For the first time in my life, I am keenly aware of being a Muslim, a Shia woman at all times. Before 9/11, I had always identified myself as an Arab woman, with Islam as a given, integral part of my identity. Now I have a heightened awareness of the essence of the true Islam. It stands in stark contrast to the newly created identity and reality of the extreme and deformed pseudo-religion practised by fanatics. I felt persecuted by everyone: Muslims and non-Muslims. I felt that I was being persecuted for being a Muslim, a Shia, a woman, as if I had determined my religion and my gender.

When I ask if Allah defies people or if people defy Allah, I question in silence. I choose to live with the bittersweet consequences of my rebellious nature. Allah granted me the right to develop and use critical thinking, to question and to doubt. These rights and numerous others are all now denied by some fanatics in the name of the same religion that granted them to me.

The new order of the day is persecution by Muslims and non-Muslims alike. Islam and Allah have become part of a worldwide commodity under a fragmented banner. For those ignorant of the essence of the true message, the only legitimate face of Islam is that of the ultra-conservatives who are mistakenly associated with the niqab and the headscarf for women and the beard and cropped trousers for men. Thus, the persecution is waged against the apparel, rather than being directed against the mindless power that feeds the ideology of a war on terror.

Senselessly, Muslims are judged according to their attire. The Muslim who does not adhere to the prevailing "hijab-niqab" or the "cropped trousers and beard" stereotype, does not qualify as a true Muslim by those who adopt the dress code. The Muslim who adheres to this dress code is viewed by some as a fanatic, a fundamentalist conservative Muslim who is probably associated with terrorism.

In some circumstances unintentionally and in others intentionally, Islam and Muslims endorsed and funded an Islamic extremism that defies Allah's teaching of a moderate and balanced approach to life.

> Thus, have We made of you an Umat justly balanced, that ye might be witnesses over the nations, and the Messenger a witness over yourselves; and We appointed the Qibla to which thou wast used, only to test those who followed the Messenger from those who would turn on their heels (From the Faith). Indeed it was (A change) momentous, except to those guided by Allah. And never would Allah Make your faith of no effect. For Allah is to all people Most surely full of kindness, Most Merciful. (*Surah Al-Baqara* 2:143)

The 9/11 atrocity inflicted by a handful of men who call themselves Muslims was grossly inconsistent with the essence of Islam: peace, love, compassion, respect, justice and kindness. The claim of waging war in Allah's service served the interests only of the ruling classes in their quest to retain power and control over the masses. To advance their interests, many verses such as, *"Fight in the cause of Allah those who fight you, but do not transgress limits; for Allah loveth not transgressors"* (Surah Al-Baqara 2:190) are distorted by concentrating on the first part and omitting the second part. Instead, verses such as *"Let there arise out of you a band of people inviting to all that is good, enjoining what is right, and forbidding what is wrong: They are the ones to attain felicity."* (Al-Imran

3:104) have been interpreted beyond their context and beyond their meaning. Positive, inspirational verses such as *"Invite (all) to the Way of thy Lord with wisdom and beautiful preaching; and argue with them in ways that are best and most gracious: for thy Lord knoweth best, who have strayed from His Path, and who receive guidance" (Al-Nahl* 16:125) have been excised from the everyday life of ordinary Muslims.

Such positive, uplifting messages were replaced with the language of the day: abuse, humiliation, threats and terror. Those using such language in their invitations to join the fellowship of Allah defied the quintessence of Islam, the call to: *"Let there be no compulsion in religion: Truth stands out clear from error: whoever rejects evil and believes in Allah hath grasped the most trustworthy hand-hold, that never breaks. And Allah heareth and knoweth all things" (Surah Al-Baqara* 2:256). Accusations of infidelity and atheism were hurled against fellow non-conforming Muslims and people of other religions, especially against those who dared to challenge and to differ.

Despite the incompatibility of the 9/11 acts with the essence of Islam, the atrocity was far from an isolated incident. Viewed within historical and current affairs and regional conditions, the resurgence of the Islamic fundamentalists was predictable. The continuing political power struggle within the Muslim world was not news.

Nevertheless, the 9/11 atrocity was irrational, insane. Momentarily, I viewed it as a case of temporary insanity. In more rational moments, I was equally certain that it could not be shrugged off as a case of momentary insanity; indeed, it must have been many years in its complex design. The reality is that we may never get to the root of its origins.

The days following 11 September 2001 brought more chaos, confusion and violence. Anticipation, fear, emotional confusion and intellectual blunders were feeding off one another. As the casualty numbers rose, I recalled my father's comment on return from his routine gym session in Riyadh, *"I bet you these men who I see training in the gym are being deployed to Afghanistan."*

In the 1980s, Afghanistan became a priority on the international affairs agenda. The country was to be rescued from the grip of communism in the name of democracy. The goal was to overthrow

## Terror's Real Victory: The Surrender of Rationality

the government formed by the People's Democratic Party of Afghanistan (PDPA) and the army in favour of installing the Mujahideen and Taliban "freedom fighters". Massive funds poured in from East and West to back that brave war against the government. In the view of the Western-backed coalition, no one has the right to choose to be a communist or to forge a relationship with communism; however, everyone is free to choose capitalism.

Equally, East and West had funded the atrocity of 9/11 and will, no doubt, fund many more to come. Long before 2001, money was indiscriminately dispensed to mosques and fundamentalist groups worldwide. The funds poured into the hands of Imams who benefited in the name of religion and on the presumption of being religious.

Religious trafficking continued, no longer contained within the local Muslim communities, no longer impacting those communities alone. Similarly to drug and other trafficking operations, it spun out of the control of their creators long before the 1980s Afghan War. Freely and abundantly, money was dispensed into the hands of people who cared less about religion, Islam or Muslims and cared more about the gift of power that the money granted them.

With that power and those dollars, the corrupt recruited and indoctrinated soldiers for Allah. The Islamic way of moderation and the balanced view of life were shunned in favour of more extreme views and positions. The latter attracted more dollars and were a more attractive commodity with which to easily influence ill-educated or illiterate "soldiers for Allah". The joint promise of more money than those soldiers had ever seen together with salvation proved irresistible. In addition to Muslims being victimised by the events of 9/11, Muslims continued to be victimised by their own governments, by clergymen and imams of mosques who served as government agents to reinforce control.

When the only language is that of money and power, there is no place for rationality, there is no place for justice. In the face of violence, rationality is surrendered, as if humanity had obliterated it from its repertoire.

I clearly recollect the religious books I was offered when imprisoned so many years ago. Continually, I questioned how ordinary Muslims could accept those "so-called" religious books. How could such books be cleared for publication and distribution when they deny rational and critical thinking?

How can people read with no desire for critically examining and rationalising what they read? Silence and apathy become our response in the face of irrationality. We are responsible for our passive acceptance of wild irrationality. With prolonged oppression and coerced silence, Muslim cultures and communities have passively adapted.

To differ is to sin; to object is to be labelled an infidel. Religion remains taboo; an oppressive tool used by the few against the masses rather than being employed in service of the people. Religion remains the most effective, coercive silencing device of the ruling class against the majority. Access to accurate religious instruction has been denied to the majority and limited to the few. As no enquiry, no questioning, no doubts are permitted, we Muslims have stopped learning.

Governments, in their own interests, employ the religious voice. That voice has ceased to address legitimate issues and challenges. Today, the religious voice ignores the demands and needs of the social, economic and political domains in favour of expanding its list of negative commandments on behalf of advancing the government's agenda. Controlled, it is rewarded for its compliance.

Despite my knowledge of and understanding of the basic message of Islam, I returned repeatedly to the Quran. I understood that Islam like any other religion has been employed to control the rationally minded and to keep the masses in a state of submission. I returned to the Quran, not in search of answers or justifications, but in search of confirmation of my understanding of its essence. *"Say: 'O ye men! Now Truth hath reached you from your Lord! those who receive guidance, do so for the good of their own souls; those who stray, do so to their own loss: and I am not (set) over you to arrange your affairs'"* (*Yunus* 10:108). If prophets and messengers were not assigned to arrange people's religious affairs, then what qualifies ordinary Muslim men and women today to determine for the rest of us the right way and the not so right way?

Allah's revelation to the Prophet was clear in requesting the messengers to kindly invite people to follow the right way and basic humanitarian teachings. Then, if people do not adhere to the teaching, it is for Allah to judge. Messengers have no role to play in judgement.

The new version of Islam, what I call postcolonial Islam, requires censorship of the Quran's true, original message. In the mosques, the imams deny people the right to choose to practise their religious duty towards Allah, a right clearly articulated in the following:

> It is not required of thee (O Messenger), to set them on the right path, but Allah sets on the right path whom He pleaseth. Whatever of good ye give benefits your own souls, and ye shall only do so seeking the "Face" of Allah. Whatever good ye give, shall be rendered back to you, and ye shall not be dealt with unjustly. (*Al-Baqarah* 2:272)

People are actively discouraged from seeking the moderate way of Allah; rather, they are forced to accept a narrow, rigidly prescribed Islam that is based on the fear of punishment – sticks, humiliation and persecution.

Postcolonial Islam is no longer about faith and worship; it has little time for justice, compassion and kindness. Islam is no longer defined in terms of the individual's direct relationship with Allah. Today, Islam is adhered to out of fear of retribution or in order to obtain privileges. Powerful intermediaries subvert the direct relationship and interpret the words of Allah to serve the interests of the ruling classes and the powerful. Today, the ruling classes and those with money, power and prestige are served by and sustained by religious forces that provoke local rifts and regional conflicts. More importantly, those religious forces control the masses through fear.

In those post 9/11 days, I was challenged to be an ordinary human without a label. While uncomfortable with the desire to disguise an identity of which I have always been quietly proud, I wanted to be an ordinary person. I did not want to have to justify my identity or my religion. We are born into communities, cultures and religions. We do not choose our community, culture or religion and we should not be victimised because of them.

At times in those days, it had become hard to breathe. The minute I spoke, questions and accusations about Islam would overshadow, disrupt the conversation. As a human being, I was reduced and shrunk to fit within the boundaries of my newly redefined religion.

For some, the only thing of importance or of interest about me was my religion; my humanity was reduced exclusively to my religious identity. For some, that religious label justified my exclusion and victimisation.

Within this resurgence of extremism, moderate and critical Muslims have been devalued, ridiculed and in some cases, ostracised. The hardline extremists accuse moderate Muslims of defying religion as defined by the fundamentalists.

In this internecine struggle, moderate Muslims have a responsibility toward Allah. While the terrorist acts are claimed by a small group of people, they are encouraged by the silence and passivity of moderate Muslims. That silence gives the appearance of approval, suggests that extremism and terrorism are condoned. The fanatical fringe has been strengthened by the refusal of moderate Muslims to employ its teaching to contradict and counter extremism. As moderate Islam adopts self-censorship and chooses silence in fear of retribution, it contributes to the cycle of terror. The parallel with the silence of rape victims is powerful.

Thus, in my view, every Muslim bears equal responsibility for the terror inflicted in the name of our religion. As long as we remain silent, we equally share the blame with those who incorrectly define the Quran in opposition to its core values: moderation, balance and justice.

Religion has become our justification for passivity and our refusal to question authority. Those educated in the authentic moderate faith know that Islam encourages us to be critical thinkers. We must ask ourselves how we are to stop this vicious cycle of atrocities ignited by injustice and terror inflicted by religious and secular governments. Those same forces have inflamed the Muslim world, saturating it with anger and hatred. How to break the cycle? I wonder.

Whether we are committed, practising or non-practising Muslims, we have all been equally demonised. We have been demoralised and compelled to surrender our humanity. Collectively, we are responsible for failing to serve humanity, which is the ultimate way to serve Allah.

As I reflect on humanity, I observe that it is easy to forego mercy, compassion and critical thinking. The pursuit of knowledge, justice and the maintenance of a balanced view require endless energy, patience, vigilance and sacrifice. I observe that casually many claim to be Muslims, to be religious and to know Allah. Although it was our destiny to be born into Muslim families, we rarely ask if that automatically qualifies us as true followers of Allah. In fact, we only become Muslims when we acquire the knowledge, and practise our faith according to the essence of Islam. That essence prompts Muslims to do the right thing, the human thing, with kindness and compassion.

Contrary to the right granted by Allah to Muslims to directly access the Quran and Islamic heritage, the pseudo *postcolonial Islam* has manipulated Muslims into false beliefs, i.e., in this misinterpretation, only the elite few are gifted with the understanding of Islam and the masses must follow their guidance. Today, Muslims are brought up accustomed to reciting the Quran without thinking of the words, the messages, the lessons, the themes and the contexts. Many Muslims are unable to read and understand the Quran in its authentic Arabic language, the language of revelations.

My nephew's words on 9/11, *"I hope they are wrong and that Muslims have nothing to do with the atrocity,"* reverberate as I continue my quest to understand how we as Muslims may have contributed not only to the demise of Islam, but to the demise of humanity, irrespective of religion. I have been and I believe I will always be challenged by the gross subversion of my religion in my lifetime: the dissonance is beyond comprehension.

To reiterate, one of the distinctive features of our religion is that Muslims have direct access to the Quran. *"And to rehearse the Quran: and if any accept guidance, they do it for the good of their own souls, and if any stray, say: 'I am only a Warner'"* (Al-Naml 27:92). However, we have happily surrendered our right to direct access.

The Quran is clear about repentance, clear about Allah's forgiveness and mercy. *"To Allah belongeth all that is in the heavens and on earth. He forgiveth whom He pleaseth and punisheth whom He pleaseth; but Allah is Oft-Forgiving, Most Merciful"* (*Surah AAl-Imran* 3:129). Even when we are rationally certain about our interpretation of such obvious, clear language, we seek advice from those self-anointed experts, thereby surrendering our sovereignty.

*"O ye who believe! stand out firmly for Allah, as witnesses to fair dealing, and let not the hatred of others to you make you swerve to*

*wrong and depart from justice. Be just: that is next to piety: and fear Allah. For Allah is well-acquainted with all that ye do"* (Al-Maeda 5:8). Within moderate Islam, justice and balance, and those who are just and balanced are preferred. However, under *postcolonial Islam*, Muslims who deviate from justice and balance are not challenged and are free from sanction for such behaviour. While significant deviations from the moral lessons are ignored within fundamentalism, moderate Muslims are challenged and chastised when they fail to observe minor, less significant teachings, i.e., not covering the face for women.

In the greatest irony, so-called Muslims, the extreme fringe, became the persecutors of Islam. Guided by the definitions of a self-selected elite, extremists co-opted Islam and condemned moderate Muslims who were denied the religion they knew. Those extremists chose to ignore that the correct Islamic path is the moderate position; it is a course that favours compassion, kindness, and pardon.

The pseudo Islam of today is an ideology, not a way of life. It has been co-opted and is employed by an extremist Islamic identity that thrives on power, and control. Muslims who live with Islam as a way of life, who are committed to Islam in its simplicity and moderation are persecuted and silenced. Muslim extremists deny the ordinary worshipper the direct relationship with Allah. They have assigned themselves as Allah's representatives on earth. In this heresy, these demagogues renounce Allah as the sole judge, although He alone has the knowledge of the worshipper's heart and intent. In the name of Islam, they have assassinated the true spirit of Islam. Thus, I remain fascinated with humanity's capacity and willingness to surrender critical thought and rationality.

Eventually, I rose above the waves of persecution following 9/11 and re-emerged with a stronger voice. As I reclaimed my voice, extremism re-emerged and with it the media's infatuation was redirected toward Muslim women.

In the eyes of the media, only Muslim women of a certain profile qualified for attention. The world clamoured for news of Muslim women who measured up, covered up and fit the mould. The world had no interest in voices inconsistent with that media-constructed stereotype.

As a matter of course, Islam had readily accommodated diverse cultures and traditions. After 9/11, the race to "appear" Islamically correct began with no consultation of the Quran, or the history of Islamic thought and most certainly not with women.

As the stories poured forth to suggest that Muslim women are the only women who are subjected to abuse and violence, that Islam is the only religion interpreted to accord men more privileges than those of women, I reflected on the manipulation and abuse of women. This was the time for ambitious Muslim women who were frustrated with their social status to capitalise on their stories as the media and numerous institutions sought to link the status of Muslim women to terrorism.

The stories seldom provided any intelligent analysis of what the Quran says about women or the egalitarianism that the Prophet (pbuh) exemplified through his life. Such shallow articles had no space for a discussion of how diverse cultures and traditions influence the interpretation and the reinterpretation of Islam today.

Muslim women were re-victimised by both local and international media, by Muslim extremists and by the new world order. Instead of standing up in the face of the coercive powers that monopolise religion, Muslim women disparaged Islam. The religion was blamed instead of the patriarchal institutions that decide for women which version of Islam they ought to follow for the day. It is far less challenging to blame religion rather than to fight to reclaim its true essence.

Persistently, I returned to re-read the Quran. I am equally as qualified as any religious clergyman to understand Islam through direct access to the Holy Book. As I studied, it became clear that any Islamic statements and interpretations that contradict Allah's words and basic message should be rejected. The Quran follows a pattern, a certain logic. In my quest for understanding, I read extensively and intensively.

Through re-reading and study of the Quran, I sought relief from the insanity of a world gone mad. I escaped to the heavenly sanctuary of my beloved maternal grandmother, Fatema Bint Abdallah. In her earthly sanctuary, I had developed my love for an unassuming simple and humble Islam. In her memory, I sought refuge from violence, from atrocities. In my view, the 9/11 atrocities were directed against Muslims, challenging them to both doubt and justify themselves and their religion.

I chose to read the holy book in accordance with my understanding of the essence of all religions, not only Islam, and to situate it within the context of Islamic history. As I studied, I observed that Allah's messages clearly distinguished the transactional – human-to-human – from that of the duty and obligation of the worshipper toward Allah. The transactional is another form of worship that we Muslims fail to observe and obey.

*At age forty-one, I was questioning and challenging religion as I had done at age sixteen.* What is religion? What is it that Allah intends for the world and what is the true intent of his message? Did Allah intend terror, injustice and extremism for his creation, for humanity? What had become of the critical thinking and the inquisitive mind that Allah endorsed?

Islam! Isn't its essence still that of justice, compassion, humility, kindness, pardon, honour and respect for all living things? Does it not yet command us to eschew transgression and compulsion?

This revision exercise was not necessary for me to determine that the crimes committed in the name of Islam are *"haram"*, illicit/forbidden. There is no way that can they be justified in the name of Islam. Historically, Islam has been identified as the religion of mercy and compassion. Yet Muslims who know the truth stood by silently, allowing it to be grossly redefined as a religion of condemnation and retribution.

In rethinking religion, I believe that it was not created to convert the immoral into becoming moral or to deter those driven to violence by their hunger for wealth and power. In retrospect, it seems as if religion was created to enable the moral to tolerate the immorality of the world.

As I engaged with people, Muslims or those of other faiths, it appears that religion is now another barrier, as if it is not enough that humanity is divided by ethnicity, rank, gender, colour, etc. We belong to humanity, yet we relate to different worlds. People forgo a language of peace and compassion; they forgo kindness and gravitate toward a language of violence and transgression that further divides humanity.

The events of 9/11 pushed our worlds even further apart. At work,

I questioned how in the name of my religion I dared approach any of those violated. How dare I think that perhaps what divides our worlds might be the one thing that could bind us? How dare I think that I too had been violated?

Asleep and awake, I could not escape "terror" as radio, TV and print news followed me. I avoided TV news and commentaries except for those I trusted for a balanced view. Reading about the 9/11 events motivated me to read about other incidents in recent history that, although quite different in nature and magnitude, can be classified as terror events; however, these events have been largely devalued and ignored.

Most appalling of these was that of Bhopal, India on 3 December 1984 when shortly after midnight, 40 tons of poison gas (Methyl Isocyanate-MIC) leaked from a pesticide factory. Subsequently, it was determined that the cause of that night gas leak was the turning off of the refrigeration unit to save the company $40 a day. As they slept, three thousand human beings, Indian nationals, were poisoned and died. Within 72 hours, the estimate rose to between eight and ten thousand dead. The factory was a major hazard with none of its safety systems functioning properly. Was this not an act of terror? As many as ten thousand human beings died, three time the number killed in the 9/11 atrocity, because the business manager wanted to save the Dow Chemical Corporation $40 per day.

Reading of Bhopal and other instances of terror did not necessarily make me better understand humanity or make me feel more optimistic. Nevertheless, I persisted in some perhaps perverse sense of solidarity with those who had suffered. I read of the terror inflicted on people – most of which I knew nothing about – who come from different cultural, racial, religious and/or political backgrounds. As I reflected on global warfare, I asked where humanity is going.

Certainly, I am not being consulted about its direction, as I, along with all the "others", am marginalised by the so-called "democratic" leaders of the patriarchal Western world. I do not think one can claim being democratic when democracy is only practised at home. To be truly democratic is to behave consistently within the boundaries of one's own country, with all of its inhabitants and in a global context. The killing of innocent people is a crime, irrespective of geography.

This does not make 9/11 victims less important, less significant. It makes all other terror victims equally important and significant; it makes the value of human life the same everywhere. Terror did not begin in New York City and it did not end there or in the Pentagon or in that Pennsylvania field.

To break the cycle of terror and violence, a tsunami of non-violence is needed. The cycle of terror had a deafening voice that commanded attention. In that deafening roar, all the languages of peace were obscured. Although desperately needed, the language of moderation that can endure and that endorses peace has not been welcomed.

With the media's infatuation with Islam and Muslims, the world observed in awed silence as terror continued to claim more innocent civilian lives. Bali, Beslan, Saudi Arabia, Morocco, Yemen, Somalia, Madrid, and London survived violent atrocities. Lebanon and Palestine have been exhausted by endless invasions and occupations. The violence engulfing Iraq, Afghanistan and Pakistan in civil and international war continues.

I remember well that July 2005 London morning; I was at home that Thursday when I heard the breaking news of the bombings. I was overwhelmed with the feeling of being violated in my home. Although I did not know any of the victims, I felt victimised. I thought of all the people who waited that day for loved ones to return home, but who never would. How could the killing of innocent people be "sold" as a pathway to heaven? How could even the simplest human being buy into such obscene madness?

How can we bear to watch the suffering and pain we inflict on our fellow citizens, neighbours and colleagues? I watched the atrocity on TV; indeed, this was reality television, not surreal imagination. A sense that I was only a step away from persecution haunted me. In the name of my religion again, innocence died second, third and fourth deaths. I am both a victim and a transgressor, despite having no affiliation and no common ground with the trespasser, including that of the religion we profess.

The following day, London triumphed with the creation of a sense of normality. The UK copes with terrorism with the display of an amazing sense of calmness and normality, behaviours that truly defy atrocity. That sense of calm and normality is contagious. Yet I am

## Terror's Real Victory: The Surrender of Rationality

alarmed by my fear of normalisation even when it is in defiance of violence. Surely we cannot accept such violence as "business as usual"!

The following day, I took the underground to London to offer and to receive condolences for the loss, for the violation. Why is it that our "civilian" lives are worthless? As I walked the streets of London tracing the previous day's events, I pondered this question.

As the atrocities continue across regions and continents, it becomes more difficult to comprehend the thrust for destruction. Why are normally rational human beings so susceptible to coercion and manipulation? In the perverted minds of some, the use of terror is a legitimate, moral act that is just in certain circumstances.

Islam, European Muslims and Muslims in Europe re-emerged to occupy the media's centre stage. I followed the media, watching, listening and reading. There was extensive media coverage focused on the veil and its connection to terrorism. Mentally, I juxtaposed the veil and terrorism alongside rape and the mini-skirt. I considered how both terrorism and rape strike indiscriminately, leaving us vulnerable, violated and out of control. While terrorism and rape are different, at the core they are similarly violent acts. The miniskirt does not provoke rape, why would the veil provoke terrorist acts?

As with the unpredictability of the roll of dice, the years roll out, seemingly without pattern and beyond control. Terrorism grows like weeds, choking all in its path. Everywhere, it bares its fangs indiscriminately, targeting and claiming more innocent lives.

In those days after the 2005 London bombings, I took to the streets to protest against atrocities everywhere; indeed, the terrorists claimed more lives in Iraq, in Southern Lebanon and Palestine. I took to the streets to protest using my only asset, "my voice". As I added my voice to the flood of others in opposing violence and terrorism, I questioned if the protests matter; how does taking to the street change the world?

As I write this, the US and the UK troops remain in Iraq; the Iraqi civil war ignites the Sunni Shia divide; the Israeli invasion and assault on Lebanon causes destruction beyond repair; and the hope for the end of the Israeli occupation of Palestinian territory expires. Nevertheless, I continue taking to the street to protest against the inhumanity of humanity, as the coercive silence engulfs the world. I rely on my feet to carry me and on my voice to say "no" to subservient minds and souls. I continue to say "no" to the dying innocent and to children being sacrificed at the altar of the arms trade.

# 14

# Pilgrimage to Childhood

June 2007, walking barefoot, I test myself against the severely polluted sand of my homeland. Walking barefoot is a sensory, tactile act of homage to my childhood. I do not squander the opportunity to be blessed by the grains of sand. The burning sand, the scattered nails and the wood splinters are all part of being a child in my hometown. We were all equally victim to them. There is something elemental about the act of exposing the bare foot. As such, exposure is currently prohibited, *"haram"* for women, in the name of my religion; we were all equally culpable, all subject to censure for violations.

Looking back to childhood, I see myself as a shoeless little girl running around the block where our house sat at one end. The prohibited love of bareness creates a tingling sensation. It races up my spine making me conscious of how my beautiful mother will look at me and my accomplices in crime, my two sisters. The crimes of my sisters might, or might not, go un-noticed. While they do not completely get away with infractions of the rules, my mother holds them to a different code of behaviour, one more relaxed than her standard for me.

I try to remember how little or how big I thought of my world then; did I ever wonder what would become of me? I am a village girl who walked barefoot and rode the donkey cart. Without my father, I lived a simple, unassuming life with my mother and two sisters. That was my world. I shared everything I had with the other three parts of my heart: my mother Maryam and two sisters, Saffiya and Ayah. Despite the distance of that sandy road stretching from my hometown in Saudi Arabia to the United Kingdom's Kingston-upon-Thames, I continue to do so today.

I endeavour to reconstruct the life that led me to become the woman I am today. I trace back to the village from where my world expanded to include a fifth woman, my illiterate maternal grandmother, Fatema. She was a woman with whom I have a deep spiritual connection. Although I loved her dearly, I had never realised how deeply connected I was to her until she departed my world. Her home was and still is my sanctuary; without it, I wonder if I could have faced my world in the way that I did.

Each time I return home, I re-enter the life that I knew intimately as a child. Since the death of Fatema, I no longer seek to understand how I lost and found my sense of navigation of that ancient history. Visiting my maternal great aunt Naima is in itself a pilgrimage to childhood, a journey into the past. She is the only living sister of my beloved Fatema, the last reminder of that loving face with its gentle smile.

Of course on that visit, we were bound to embrace. I kissed her while she held my hand in hers; I left my hand clasped between my blind great aunt's hands as I listened and watched. She spat on her index finger and massaged my wrist with her saliva to protect me from the evil eye and from bad omens.

With tears in my heart, I remembered the many times Fatema had borrowed a shirt of mine or traced my steps to spill melted butter and break eggs to expel the evil eye and thus evict the bad spirit. As I choked on my tears, I felt my heart breaking. In Fatema's memory, I was voiceless, as if in a spell.

Maryam, my ever-immaculate mother, observed the ritual, petrified; grunting, she reprimanded me, "How could you let her massage your wrist with her saliva?" I smiled with the knowledge that my mother knows that the ritual is to prevent the evil spirit from touching me. "It is Fatema's gift to me, how could I refuse?" As we walked away, my mother confessed that at times she was reluctant to embrace and kiss Fatema. "I feel sad for you," I said, although deep in my heart I understand my mother's issues with purity and cleanliness. The visit to my great aunt aroused my longing to see Fatema, if only for a brief moment.

The next day, Maryam and I visited the cemetery. I followed on my mother's heels toward Fatema's final resting place. As we walked, my mother named those we would visit while in the cemetery, but she reaffirmed that we would begin with Fatema.

As we entered the cemetery and before we turned toward Fatema's final resting place, we collected the empty bottles; we each filled two water bottles for Fatema. As we walked among the dead, my mother greeted each of them. As we approached Fatema's site, my mother began to greet and talk to her. We sat at the grave on opposite sides with four bottles of water, the Quran and Fatema.

For Fatema, I read Surah Yaseen from the Quran. I wanted her to hear me reading; I believed that she could. While I recited, in my mind I watched as she traced the holy Quran like in the old days, like always. My mother talked to Fatema while levelling the earth on her grave before pouring water over it. I listened to my mother as she talked to Fatema, "Your grave is moist. Yes, my beloved brother was here earlier; may Allah protect him; he is never late for you." My mother addressed me, "Your uncle does not forego visiting our mother; he is more diligent than I am."

With eyes filled with tears, I smiled at my mother. Mischievously, I reminded her, "I will be diligent. I will always visit you." My good-natured mother with her great wit and sense of humour smiled playfully, "God forbid, we are in the cemetery and you wish me dead." I replied, "No. Not now. Later. Much later." We muffled our laughter. I reminded her of one of her old favourite poems by Iliya Abu Madi.

> Why complain of being wretched
> When in your position earth, sky and stars
> And to you belong the fields, the flowers and the aroma
> Its breeze and its nightingale

As I concluded, my mother reminded me that we are in the cemetery; she moved forward to visit other family members' graves.

Gently, I asked Maryam to show me to Batool's gravesite. Silently, I stood before it. In my heart, I apologised for not respecting her dying wish; I apologised for not calling her before she died, as she had requested through my mother. I asked her forgiveness; deep down I know that I have been granted that forgiveness. In my heart tears flowed, some for Batool and some for her son Suhail, my first love. I opened my soul to inhale the spirit of the dead from the ground beneath me. "One day I will be laid here; I hope near Fatema."

My mother looked at me and commanded, "Let us go." She

continued, "I am really scared of the cemetery and do not like coming here; I do so only out of my love for those who have passed away."

I looked into her face and declared, "I do not mind visiting the graves in the cemetery. I am not afraid of dying." She dismissed my comment, as she does not feel comfortable in serious talk with me about death.

I anticipated that our next stop at Mula Ali's grave was going to be emotionally difficult. My paternal grandfather died on 13 October 2005. When I last saw him at the end of 2004, he looked frail in all respects. His breathing had deteriorated to the extent that he had started using the ventilator. On that final visit, he appeared to have aged overnight. Between us, trust had broken after he stood silently indifferent toward the 2000 family scandal and to the questionable conduct of uncle Najeeb and the letters uncle Najeeb wrote. Mula Ali and I no longer shared a language to openly discuss abuse and emotional manipulation; there was a constant silence, a reminder of the social code surrounding domestic violence, one that I realised I had broken long ago.

As I sat by Mula Ali's grave facing my mother, I sought to contain the space between us and to hold him within it. My mother handed me the Quran to read. I paused, allowing my tears to flow, empowering my sense of abandonment to grow. Memories of past happier times streamed through my consciousness. In his small library, I had spent hours reading and studying; in his company I had recited poetry trying to match his unique recitative skill. As we matured, Mula Ali had reserved a place for each of us to realise our potential and to flourish. As we matured, Mula Ali became more of a companion guiding us with his wisdom, rationality and great sense of fairness. His approach to life had become more relaxed and adaptable to generational differences.

Had he simply grown old and lost the courage, the ability and the will to fight and stand his ground? Since the 2000 rupture, most of our meetings and conversations were filled with an empty space between us; we never really talked, only pretended that we had something to share. We both knew that we were avoiding the difficult conversation. Sitting next to his grave, I realised that I had let go of the struggle to understand. I placed my hand on the sand under which he lies in peace. I watered it and followed my mother's instructions to read from the Quran. While I will never understand why Mula Ali chose the path of indifference, I will always honour who he was. I am reconciled to this contradiction. I vowed then that I would stop trying to understand why Mula Ali never fulfilled his promise to my father in reprimanding uncle Najeeb. I realised that I have to live with that sore spot in my heart while never forgetting the man my paternal grandfather had once been.

As I walked in silence among the graves greeting those resting in peace, I was humbled, comforted in the knowledge that all our journeying ends at this station. The distance and the difference between the living and the dead are in the journey.

Leaving the cemetery behind, I walked beside my mother thinking silently about death. Death and life; what a beautiful harmonious journey! I thought of how I want my passing to be commemorated. I continued in silence. I knew that I would make Maryam uncomfortable if I spoke about it.

On 5 June 2007 – precisely twenty-five years after being imprisoned – I lay in bed in my mother's home contemplating life. The house was erected on the site of the west-facing entrance to Fatema's old house; that was the entrance with the old carved wood gate. It was the gate that Fatema secured in a way that enabled her grandchildren to always have access to her home.

In Fatema's former house, childhood memories of this place, of my maternal grandparents and my uncle Hameed surged as both my uncle and grandfather Hajj Ibrahim arrived in the early morning to see me before they left to attend to their daily chores. Uncle Hameed still summons me to his narratives in the same way he did when I was a child. Astonished, I am filled with gratitude as I continue to live in the comfort of his unconditional love and acceptance, gifts that I took for granted. Eternally, memories of both men occupy a prominent place in my mind and heart. Uncle Hameed, like my mother, used to sing for us and tolerated us as we three nieces trailed after him as he did his chores: changing a light bulb, hammering a nail into the wall or as he helped Hajj Ibrahim with his chores at home or on the farm. From memory, I dredge an image of my maternal grandfather excavating sewage for his granddaughters. I treasure the everlasting image of the old man dressed in his rubber work boots, opening up the sewer to rescue a kitten in response to the desperate plea of three little girls. I remember the flood of voices between those discouraging him from diving into the sewage and ours urging him on.

The gift of love of my maternal grandfather and maternal uncle was a privilege. In Fatema's old house, I think of the traditional, religious nature of my maternal uncle and grandparents; yet, they never criticised or even commented on our dress code, our unveiled faces or our work in integrated working environments. Despite our departures from what is customary and traditionally acceptable in our small community, we, as children and adults, were accepted and loved by them.

I recall those childhood days; I recall each of those memorable voices. It seems now that no one has a voice and no one has a choice. Life is simply a succession of one death after another. Pointlessly, I search for life within the cycle of death.

The following day, I walk the streets and encounter faces, shadows of faces that barely sustain life. Why am I knocking at doors in search of love in a town where love is denied? Love becomes synonym to coercion, a list of ideas and feeling dictated by others. I walk the streets of my hometown recalling my childhood paths and tracing those memories. I look at my feet and the hem of my black abbaya, both adorned in dust. I survey the blend of old houses shamelessly contrasted with newly patched walls.

I become mentally aware with ultra heightened senses of that of sight, smell and sound. I become aware of where I live and where I had lived. I notice how the new houses intrude, forcing their newly erected walls into a line of old homes. I smell sautéed onions in preparation for someone's lunch. I recall the child I was and all the times I came home to that particular smell enticing my hunger for my mother's cooking. I am aware of the many glances from local people and immigrant workers. They might wonder if I am an alien or a crazy woman walking through the heat and dust baring my face. I am aware of how alien I feel and how much I struggle with a mindset from which I became the woman I am today. I go tracing my steps around one more time passing alleyways where I played as a child, tracing roads I walked as a teenager bearing the heavy burden of my concealed love.

As I walk, I think of love not only between humans, but that exhibited by humans towards their homes, their lands, their plants, their streets and realms beyond. I continue walking, passing by our old home and that of my maternal grandparents. I stroll the streets once populated by great aunts and uncles and pass the homes of cousins. Then in sorrow, I pass by an empty tract, a land where my paternal grandparents' home once stood. Now, the land is empty and deserted, empty of all life, all the tears and all the joy once celebrated there; only the memories that were once created within its walls remain, scattered among those now alive.

As I walk, I am overcome with the urge to touch old doors; a few remain of carved wood, although most are of iron. In them, old spirits reside. Not too many people walk at that hour before the noon prayer. A few men leave their homes for a nearby mosque. Similarly, a handful of women leave the Hussainiah where they have attended a condolences service or listened to a commemoration of the martyrdom of Imam Hussain.

It had been a long time since I had attended a Hussainiah, a spiritual homage. Those memories brought with them Hussainiah's winter aroma, that of ginger, cinnamon and dried lime tea. In the bustling of women and girls, I observe devotion and love in their commitment to Ahl el Bait, the family of the Prophet [pbuh]. Women, healthy or ill, would make their way in the afternoons to be part of the commemoration which, during such time, is held twice or three times a day depending on the Hussainiah.

Once again, I walk the deserted streets; I am accompanied by memories formed when I roamed as a child. Even between humans and things, love is elusive in a country where its expression is taboo. There is an alarming absence of passion. Women and men deny love's presence much as they avoid the topic of death. It is the unspoken reality of everyday life; we love without the want or need to declare it.

On the following day, I am savouring the morning in bed with my bedroom door ajar; I overhear my mother's relatives and friends as they enter and leave her home early in the morning. As a child, I had learned to trace love in the conversation as their voices softened and hardened accordingly.

Typically, the caller begins with an urgent enquiry or request for a needed cooking ingredient or help. I listen as the urgency moderates or is replaced by more urgent matters that emerge. I hear the pain and the joy as my mother's women friends come and go. Their love is concealed like their pain; both are embodied in the stories they tell, in the issues they discuss.

I rush downstairs upon hearing aunt Anisah's voice. Her presence brings back memories of childhood, adolescence and the pain of growing up. Aunt Anisah, actually my mother's cousin, is the only one Maryam considers a real sister and is thus the only real aunt my sisters and I have. Aunt Anisah's laugh is uninhibited and free spirited like that of a child. Aunt Anisah is robust, and is a skilled pragmatic, negotiator of life. My mother is a delicate and naive idealist.

Sharing time with these two women is one of the best things I can do to nurture my soul. I sit with them as my mother ticks off the list of sick or bereaved people I should visit. Aunt Anisah objects and addresses me without paying attention to what my mother has just said. Her advice: "Do not go, too much trouble. This is hard work and you are only here for a short time." My mother and my aunt continue the discussion; Aunt Anisah continues listing the reasons for why I should not go.

Ignoring me, they carry on talking about what I should or should not do. Between them, I become a little girl; they forget that I am an adult. Passionately, they discuss how each observes social obligations and what I should do. I am not invited to take part in their discussion.

I have an affinity with both of them. I have an affinity with older women and with older people generally. I believe that my mother and my aunt possess the secrets of love and wisdom that bring our worlds together. While their personalities differ dramatically, they are bound for life by love and by blood. They had married on the same day; they had their children at approximately the same time; and they lived together or were neighbours for many long years.

Both are loving, caring, generous and extremely hospitable. They are conservative and clear about their commitments and obligations to loved ones and their community. They are both resilient and witty. Both are highly moral and had always demanded that we daughters do the right thing. Fortunately for us, they had never learned to spoil us.

"What are you smiling at?" my aunt asks. I am unaware of doing so;

however, I tell her that my sisters and I inherited her pragmatism and that her daughter Wafyah is sensitive like my mother.

My aunt laughs again and then asks, "What do you want me to cook for you? *Saiadiyah?*" I accept happily, eager for her to cook her special fish and rice dish. As she leaves, my aunt repeats, "Do not go around visiting; do not follow your mother." They launch into another conversation before she departs with a giggle.

*In my memories, I return to childhood, to her house. My mother and aunt stand talking in low voices at the gate. As if yesterday, we daughters wait in school uniform for the conclusion of the conversation. Their presence, those gates, this place is beautiful.*

On this fifth day of June 2007, I recognise the mystery that is memory. I am fascinated by our recollection of and talk of various life incidents that have left indelible impressions on our minds. Given the paths before and behind us, how do we select what to remember and how to remember it? Quietly, I endeavour to listen, particularly to older people, in order to learn how memories have been selected.

In my experience, it is rare that two people agree on the same version of events. Although they have lived their entire lives in that small Arabian coastal town, this is true of my mother and her sister. Their narrations of their memories differ as greatly as those of their daughters who have lived and journeyed the world far beyond those shores.

From those musings, I wandered to reflect on my fears: the fear of abandonment and the fear of being trapped. Feeling abandoned once by my father, and once by Seif, do I fear another abandonment? Given my experience with love, will I surrender to love again only to be betrayed? Does my fear of entrapment repel intimacy? Do I spurn love for fear of betrayal? Perhaps I will remain forever trapped between my fear of abandonment and fear of being trapped. While conscious of both fears, I preserve my options.

Back to the reality of my mother's home, I am keenly aware of her determination to monitor my social duties and obligations. My life abroad does not change her views of how I should fulfil my obligations towards our community. I am more keenly aware of her need for control than in the past.

Now, I am also more aware of how annoyed I am with my mother's quest for my perfection; endlessly, she interrupts my conversations on the telephone and in person to edit or correct my sentences. She adds the dot, the commas, the exclamation and question marks. She revises and corrects with either a mocking smile or a frown depending on the size of my errors. As I challenge her, I question which voice is speaking and which voice is being heard?

Knowing that it will annoy her, I ask if she wants to write a transcript that I can follow. I acknowledge that I annoy my mother; it gets to her and makes her feel awkward. I apologise but not without mentioning how we women lose our voices.

In the days ahead, I observe how my mother, my aunt and many other women suffer in silence. My countrywomen use their voices to speak exclusively of their children and their husbands' needs, worries, ambitions and disappointments. Their voices fail to speak of their own unfulfilled personal dreams and desires. While simple, they are unable to talk about them; rather, women choose to avoid speaking of their dreams and desires.

In their conversations, I trace how these women unknowingly neglect themselves and other women; they establish the same limited expectations, the same strict demands that had forced them to abandon their dreams and desires. I listen to the language they use; I trace how love is illustrated in the coded, harsh symbols with which they reproach themselves for any sign of self-indulgence.

Yet I want only to embrace this community of women celebrating both my bond with them and my alienation from them. Those women, whom I love, adore and respect, are powerful reminders of the transformation of my life. I remind myself that for these women, my life away from their boundaries is an illusion.

When I return home I am the young girl, the little woman in need of their loving guidance. In the rules of engagement there, my voice must echo their voices, their language and their world, a world where I remain at its periphery. For the fleeting moments in their territory, I am no longer limited by the fear of being excluded; I am no longer limited by the fear of echoing their voices. I am more keenly aware of the necessity to censor my words, my heart and my mind. Away from that milieu, my voice will always freely rebound.

My mother and I resume our reconciliation routine to determine in whose voice I am to speak. It is the highlight of my annual holiday with her; as my holiday nears its end, we both acknowledge that we repeat this reconciliation every day that we are together.

At night my mother concludes the day questioning, "Why do we argue so much when we have such a limited time together." Dear Maryam reckons, *"We must be insane."* I make no response before we go off to bed assured of a similar argument the following day and assured of our mutual devotion and love.

In her house, I am content; my heart and I savour blissful peace. Here, I am in my mother's house, in Fatema's old house, and in the presence of Fatema's spirit. I count my blessings; I review my gratitude for Fatema, for my mother, for my aunt, for my mother's friends, for my sisters and the spirits of all my women friends who embrace and nurture me.

I close my eyes while keeping my heart wide open. I encourage the voices of all my friends to echo freely. Tenaciously, wholeheartedly, I hold on to all my accumulated friendships. I hold on to friendships that evolved from childhood; to those bound by time, place and purpose; and to those forged in the service of a cause. Drifting, I reflect on home-grown friendships that are the products of my mother's relationships. Reviewing my circle of friends, I can separate the lifelong friends from the transient acquaintances. Before I slip into sleep, I embrace all their voices as I relish the bonds these friendships have nurtured and continue to nurture.

## *Friendship: A Soliloquy*

*I recall the beginnings, the voices of childhood friends running around the block of houses in a game of tag and chase. I see the sun-kissed skins and the slim, dust-covered legs and tiny feet. I recall the gathering at the bus stop in the early morning and the line up at the sweets stall. There, we exchanged our quarter-riyal coins for chewing gum and lollipops to share on the school bus or during school recess. I recall the summer seasons when a lucky few would travel; most of us would stay behind with the heat and the humidity. I recall the afternoon gatherings and the evening visits, as they were the highlights of our summer holidays.*

*Time raced ahead; one day we went to sleep as innocent*

*children and woke up at the threshold of puberty. While tripping into our teenage bodies, we clung to our innocence. We did our homework and studied together; we recited Quran verses and poetry, as friends checked the accuracy of our recitations. We took our final exams together; at times, we even failed them together. We shared hairbrushes and lice; we brushed each other's hair, braided it or rolled it in into a bun. We borrowed each other's books and clothes. We learned to dance together; we laughed at how lousy, potentially good or hopeless each was in acquiring decent dancing skills.*

*Magically, our bodies developed undeniable adult characteristics; as was the custom, we avoided talk of our bodies or menstrual cycles. We sought our friends as refuges from sibling and family quarrels and to irritate siblings and family. At times, we chose our friends over our siblings as we fell in and out of love. On such occasions, our friends became bridges between the lovers' hearts. Our friends were our alibis, our messengers, our mediators, our love counsellors and* consolers.

*Our friends were our best allies, our most gruelling critics and our most dreaded competitors in love. Within the same small circle of friends, we were bound to fall for the same person. Often we chose to remain silent about matters of the heart; sometimes, we chose to fight for those we loved; at other times, we chose to fight for our friend's right to love. We recovered from our broken hearts, aided by the love and friendships that sustained us. We fell out of love and laughed about how silly we had behaved.*

*We learned to smoke together; we got into mischief and were reprimanded together. We became involved in politics together; in time, we were enthralled by politics together.*

*We woke again and found ourselves at the threshold of adulthood; we graduated from high school and said our farewells. In pursuit of higher education, we were sent off in different directions, often to different countries.*

*Through our numerous separations, I became fonder of those childhood friends. The memories of their friendships have lightened my load as I have journeyed. On the long, lonely journey, the playful voices of my friends come alive. In their absence, I recall my friends as they discreetly drew my attention to blood* stains created when my menstrual cycle betrayed me; I recall them as they straightened my dress or skirt that had become stuck in the folds of my buttocks; I recall them as they reminded me that I had forgotten to close my pants zipper. There have been many times that I longed to have them command my attention, to lend me a sanitary towel and to accompany me to the ladies' room.

Only among such intimates would a friend dare question if I had just passed gas; only they would point out my bad breath and the lice in my hair. Only my intimate friends would frown and scold me and yet remain there for me. In my friends, I sought refuge for my broken heart; I knew that I was secure and protected in their love and commitment. I returned again and again to the friendships that had protected me in my pain and that celebrated my triumphs. When I knocked at their doors, those friends embraced me in sorrow as well as in joy.

Then, we were uprooted and scattered into different lands. As I go about my life choosing new books to read, I wonder if my friends are reading the same authors. I recall the many books that danced between our hands; I hear our voices as we resisted exchanging certain treasures or lending to one another. After pointing out the lousy quality of the writing or the irresponsibility of the borrower toward our books, we ended up sharing them, along with our clothing, shoes, jewellery and our lives. Eventually, we misplaced or lost them. We promised never again to share, borrow or lend; of course, we did so the next day.

I recall that, with much fondness, my friends would point out how frail and weak I look when I lose weight. Of course the next time I see them, they point out, with great alacrity, that I am getting fat. Given my frequent bodily changes, I pray that my friends lose and gain weight as often as I do; in that event, I could always count on borrowing their clothing when in Saudi Arabia. That would ease my predicament when invited unexpectedly to an occasion for which I have no appropriate attire.

My heart rejoices in recalling my younger sister's comment about my body's disproportion between small breasts and big buttocks. Fondly, I recollect the exact enquiry of both sisters, "Are you going out dressed like this?" Both urged me to change into clothing of my choice from their wardrobes. As sisters, as friends, *we bond in our longing for approval, secure within the comfort of friendship; as we get older and possibly wiser, we become undeniably more juvenile. We note how young we feel as our spirits defy time and age. Nevertheless, we are aware of our age as we observe our children graduating from high schools, matriculating into university, starting careers and getting married.*

As the light dims in my bedroom, I imagine the world map; following my heart, I trace my friendships from Saudi Arabia throughout the Arabian Gulf, the Middle East and Africa to North and South America. From there, I vault to Asia, Australia, New Zealand and then in a polar leap to the UK and Europe. From there, I retrace my steps to Saudi Arabia where I learned the basic principles of friendship: love, respect, unconditional acceptance, truthfulness, dignity and integrity. Along the way, I learned that true friends would never let you compromise any of these.

Now in my friendships, there is more laughter, more openness and more cooking. Politics is of far less importance. Within my friendships, I am now more conscious of *being*, rather than *doing*. We recall how lovingly envious, harsh, funny or silly we were as kids and teenagers. I think we are now even more lovingly honest and able to express positive envy. At times, we are transparent, direct, honest, even verbally cruel or harsh; we are also funnier and sillier as we grow in our trust that our friendships expand with age and life experiences. As I listen to the voices of my women friends, their laughter and tears enrich me. I am delighted when I enter my friends' homes and find they are reading different books, or have read the same books I know. I rejoice when I enter their homes to hear music, singers, and songs that I love and new ones that they have learned to love. I take great satisfaction in the blossoming of my friends, as they discover their potential, their talents and new friendships.

In my friends' presence, I surrender to their strength and to their stories, even when from a distance. Yet, when I return home, time and space contract, as if we had never parted. Our friendships resume from where we stopped the last time.

We are tempted by politics, which flow into our ordinary lives bringing disappointments and frustrations. Briefly, we become more passionate and emotional; however, the conversation ends with an exchange of recipes, further dinner plans, requests for favourite foods and more complaints about the limited time we have together. In the end, we abandon the living room to conclude, usually, at the kitchen table.

I lay in bed content in the knowledge that within those friendships, I am anchored in love, respect and acceptance. I lay in bed content and smiling, despite being irritated by my mother's relentless search for me the previous evening. Again, I allowed her to make me feel like a sixteen-year-old Cinderella who must return home before the clock strikes midnight when the magic will expire. Maryam fears imposition by the less than perfect me on my friends. She is keenly sensitive to the need not to impose oneself even when in the company of friends.

With the directory in one hand and receiver in the other, she would have dialled every friend until she located me. Only when she had reminded me of the late hour and requested that I return home before she turned off the lights could she retire to bed. Nevertheless, I inspect myself to verify to myself and prove to her that my age is forty-seven not sixteen.

While I smile at that image of Maryam, I curse the telephone and mobile inventions that enable my mother to track me and to remind me that it is late and to command me to come home. Part of me wants to get upset, to have a row with Maryam; in the end, I remind myself that I am only here for a few weeks and that giving her some control will create no lasting damage. I reason that I might as well be sixteen, as she will sulk in the morning. I do not fight; I wait until the evening when I pretend to sulk before laughter breaks out between us. We both know that friendship will lure me into staying up late. I remind her that we have the same fight every year.

I contemplate, *Only your mother, her friends who also mother you, your sisters, and your friends would give you orders and directions totally oblivious to the fact that you are hitting middle age*. Will I always be a sixteen-year-old, naive and fragile girl to them? I embrace their abundant love and their wit as much as time permits and as long as I can tolerate before I become smothered.

On returning to my roots, I rediscover my sisters, the core of my friendships, my lifelong accomplices who like me have been blessed by Fatema and Maryam. They too inherited a natural protective charm crafted of free-spirited love. While it binds us, that love has freed us to be independent in our togetherness.

Constant unconditional love and commitment with all the usual sibling rivalries, challenges, disagreements and frictions define my friendships with my sisters. In rediscovering sisterhood friendships, I encounter a surprise: I realise that if they were not my sisters I would have chosen them to be my best intimate friends.

My older sister's intricate schemes with their ulterior motives entrap me without fail. Facilely, Saffiya cons me no matter how alert I am and no matter how many questions I ask about the purpose of her invitations. Defeated by her charm, I conceal my laughter as I rush to join her. The joy of these "two-hour" escapades with my sister ends with me panting, as the two hours become an entire day of activities and chores that unfold. Nevertheless, I rarely say "no" to her schemes or invitations.

Ayah, my younger sister, is less subtle: she does not leave her wishes for the interpretation of others, including her sisters. She clearly lists on post-it notes her precise wishes and requirements. Her post-it notes embody her sense of humour and wit that are bound to lighten the heart and soul. As the youngest among the three of us, she is always saved by that wit and humour, by the post-it notes she leaves behind.

In different ways, we sisters share our lives, our worries and joys. I marvel at the love and friendship that bound us; my sisters still fear to burden me, despite their trust and my reassurances. I smile as I decide to reach out to Ayah, as she will instinctively ask if she was the first to hear my news: *"Did you tell your sister?"* Before I can respond, she ascertains *"You told her first, didn't you?"*

Unfailingly she reminds me of my childhood and adolescent anxiety about sharing; I dreaded doom if I shared and similarly felt doomed if I did not share. With their wit and bubbly natures, my sisters bring into my life exotic spices, flavours, scents, flowers and seasons. They unknowingly carry within them the spirits of Fatema and Maryam, the spirit of childhood and of friendships. These two strong-willed and stubborn women never fail to remind me of my position as a middle child; I am lodged, even joyfully trapped between them. As I age alongside my sisters, I observe our resemblance to our mother's spirit.

While others view us as similar, I think of how different we three are. Our views, philosophies and approaches to life vary starkly. Within our cores, we internalised the values of love and compassion that Maryam instilled in us. We differ and we agree; we share an openness that absorbs differences and disagreements. To others we may seem alike and we may seem to influence each other; in fact, we are independent of each other. Among ourselves, we recognise our stubborn, well-grounded unique personalities. We share opinions and give suggestions; at the end of the day, we end up doing what works for us as individuals. God forbid if we should have to please one another. Such behaviour would not go unnoticed, as a voice will announce, "You suggested this and I did as you recommended." We fight over whose side the third sister takes and we fight over the lack of support for an idea or a decision. Whether we choose silence or declare our position, we know with whom the other sister is siding. As children, we insisted that the third party had to take sides; as adults we demand the same. We fight, laugh and go to dinner only to carry on with the discussion.

Without friendship, our relationship and sisterhood would be flaccid, bland. Like friends, we enjoy complaining to each other about one another. We never stray far from child-like behaviours. I struggle between competing desires: to love them in the way that I choose as opposed to loving them in the manner they prefer. I am equally grateful for the friendships and the quarrels.

I enjoy and love being around them as they go about their daily chores with husbands and children. I attempt to be inconspicuous and do my best not to intrude, but often I fail myself and I fail them. We share an unspoken pledge to be there for one another, to love and respect the other, their decisions, and their choices without necessarily agreeing with them. There is space between us to grow and to be. I observed my sisters as they grew into other friendships and as they shared their joy and love; I know that our friendship is like a nest and we birds will fly away and return; however, we will never forsake our best friends or our friendships.

As I journey through my friendship memories, I think of the gender divide that defines it. Social and cultural codes erected the wall that marginalises cross-gender friendships. As children, our male friends played with us in the streets, they went with us to the palm field and they studied with us; then, one day we woke up in a segregated world. We were told that it was improper to have male friends. It became illicit and that wall was constructed between us.

No one asked or wondered how we were to deal with the bond that we had nurtured with our male friends. One day they were part of our life; the next day we were excluded from their lives, and they were banned from our world.

Most of my male friendships were sentenced to extinction; the few that remained were largely overshadowed by female friendships. However, a handful survived childhood and puberty to evolve in defiance of social and cultural codes; they did so only because they are members of an extended all-inclusive circle of family and friends.

As I discover and re-discover, I am fascinated by my male friends' language of friendship. They allude to their hopes, pains, sorrows, desires, fears and disappointments. Amiably, their voices project over the telephone in a manner similar to that of my female friends; they are checking on me, just wondering how I am, requesting help, seeking a suggestion or simply verifying some gossip they have heard about me from other friends.

I wove friendships into my life and into my memories; some are with my sisters, others with friends; some have been by chance and some have been cultivated purposely. Friendships are like the making of a quilt that I do not intend to finish; there is always room for one more patch to stitch into it.

Friendship is a magnificent human device that functions like a sieve; it sifts and sorts people in our lives into categories of best friends, transient friends and old address book friends retained in order to refresh memory.

With our friends, we live their love stories, from beginning to end. We endorse some and disapprove of others; always, we pray that they will be happy and that the person to whom they are attracted is worthy of their love. We burden our friends' lovers and partners with our expectations; we impose upon them our perceptions of how best to treat our friends; and then we criticise them for not living up to our expectations.

As our friends become parents, we accompany them on the journey. Invited or not, we join the management team to parent their children. Their partners and their children inherit aunts and uncles who multiply through life. We experience annoyance, exasperation with children and partners; conveniently, we forget that our friends chose the lives they pursue. In the end, we hope that they are happy and content with the outcome, despite the frustrations of life's normal rhythms.

We watch as our friends drift away from the relationships, the essence of what brought them together with their husbands and partners. We watch as they shift their focus away from themselves to their partners; subsequently, we watch as they shift their focus to centre it on children, obligations, responsibilities and duties. We observe our friends as they convert their love relationships into duties, responsibilities and obligations. As the partnership matures, they dance to different tunes; they no longer revisit the essence of their relationship and what brought them together.

As friends, we fail to remind them of that. We watch them move away from *being* in the relationship to *doing* the relationship. We notice – but make no comment – as our friends avoid discussing abusive relationships, avoid the disclosure of their disappointments, of their struggles. Instead, they busy themselves with their children's needs, with social obligations, with shopping and cooking.

We fail our friends as we shy away from pointing out to them what we observe and what needs to be said. We fail our friends, as we do not have the courage to let them know that we recognise their struggle and that we are there when they need our support. We notice as our friends become less secure in their relationships and less secure in themselves; helplessly, we watch as their once high self-esteem slides into the depths, often accompanied by depression.

We fail our friends, as we are too frightened of making them even more insecure. We do not acknowledge them adequately; we do not point out their accomplishments and congratulate them on their brilliant coping skills. We forget to remind them of their special gifts, of the unique and beautiful individuals they are. We fail to reassure them that they can count on our unwavering love no matter their decisions.

We create protection charms around our friends that blind us from recognising the transformation in their lives with marriage and children. As we have remained constant, we assume that we are as important in our friends' lives as before; in fact, they may be at a stage where all that they need from us is to be there for them. Their needs are for our trust and unconditional love, their freedom and their humanity. To set them free is to let them know that we love them and that they are free to remain close, to drift away and to drift back, secure that they will always have our friendship.

At times, I am alarmed as I observe how we hold on to friendships, confining our friends with our own perceptions and expectations. We feel abandoned by our friends when they do not sense our changing needs; in fact, it is we who failed to express our wants, needs, desires and expectations of them as we age. With age we change and are transformed by experience. We assume that our friends are aware of our change and our need to reform our friendship. Half-heartedly and selectively we listen to our friends as we search for our own echo in their voices.

We fail our friends and ourselves when we stop asking for clarification of their statements and responses. We do not challenge for fear of losing their friendship. In the end, we lose them out of fear.

Consciously or unconsciously, we hold back from opening our hearts and souls. We abandon our memories of friendships, failing to remember that they have provided us with some of our most rewarding life experiences. Some of them may also be among the most challenging and disappointing life experiences. At times we feel trapped in our friendships; we fail our friends and ourselves when we do not confront such challenges openly. Rather, we drift away as friendships evolve into other friendships eternally transforming us.

In our memories, we are bound to the voices of friends, voices that recall childhood mischief. We find comfort in recalling the past. Our reconstructed and recreated memories may not resemble the actual experience; they are the essence of what we want to remember. When together, we friends recollect and reconstruct our memories often beyond the recognition of the other participants in the experiences.

From the past, I recall the voices that intimately echo as we friends congregated on the beach, around desert campfires, a swimming pool or a kitchen table. I recall my friendships, free of any prohibitions. I am fascinated by our different perceptions of the world and of our struggles with and without friendships. I am captivated by memories of past voices and faces that besiege me but that remain in the here and now.

Friends who have the desire and the potential to flourish alone and in social groupings nurture friendships. I have grown into and out of friendships; in each I have learned and flourished within those I have mastered, those in which I have failed and those that have failed me. The voices of the many friends I have had and have now remain intimate, sensual, stimulating, priceless and profoundly humane. Having found my own language, my own voice, I no longer feel trapped in my friendships.

## Back to reality

On waking the following morning, I know deep in my heart that although I am rooted here my wings have expanded beyond this confinement. Supplications drift upward from Al Manar television in the downstairs living room as my mother prepares her breakfast. Listening to the supplications filling the morning air, I am reminded of Fatema's recitations, which I sorely miss.

I realise that even more I miss hearing my mother's voice. In my childhood, her singing had filled the air; those were the days before singing and music became viewed as undesirable, verging on illicit activities. Despite yearning for my mother's singing and recitations of poetry, I love being in her presence, in her house, in my town, in my homeland.

On joining her, I am surprised by her enquiry about the case of the annulment of a Saudi woman's marriage while she was pregnant with her second child. I am surprised because questioning the verdicts of Islamic courts is illicit.

Fatima and Mansour's case attracted national and international media attention. Fatima's half brothers secured a court ruling to annul her marriage of three years to Mansour. The half brothers based their case on tribal lineage, claiming that Mansour's is not of the same noble status as Fatima's tribe. In Islam, marriage and divorce are based on consent. Even with consent, divorce cannot be granted until a pregnant wife delivers the child.

Yet a Saudi judge had defied the Islamic ruling stated clearly in the Quran. Her family – "the noble tribe" – decided that her husband was not of noble lineage; therefore, they had the right to annul her marriage despite the fact that Fatima had married Mansour with her father's blessing. Both Fatima and Mansour ended up in prison. Whose Islam is this? The Prophet's (pbuh) message is to establish a community of believers who are valued based on individual virtue and conduct, not that of the tribe. The judge's verdict was an annulment of the Prophet's (pbuh) message and tradition.

Fatima is one of the very few women whose stories and voices made it to the Saudi court system; when they appear, it is typically the tribe that wins. With my mother, I share stories of other women whose marriages were annulled by their uncles or brothers based on tribal and family demands. I tell her of young women who are held captive in their family homes because the chosen partner was not of a noble tribe.

It is illegitimate to question a Sharia court's judgment for annulment based on tribal lineage. In annulling the marriage of Fatima and Mansour for which her father had given permission, the Sharia court violated the Islamic Sharia law and created a grave injustice; it not only forced upon Fatima a divorce against her consent, but it disputed the Islamic Sharia's justice discourse. Have these judges forgotten that divorce is the most loathed prohibition?

"How can such a situation be possible in a country that claims to be the guardian of the two holiest places of Islam?" I muse aloud. My mother's tone of voice changes. "Do not talk like that! You will get yourself arrested," she says, recalling my past imprisonment.

What would happen if women held vigil in front of the court to protest this inhumane and un-Islamic verdict? How many women do you know who are NOT subjugated by the rules of the tribes, of the families of the patriarch? Why are men allowed to reinterpret religion to twist the law in favour of the tribe? Why are Saudi judges not held accountable for such improper revisions of religion?

My mother abandons the conversation; I am disheartened as I consider the gross injustice. Bearing in mind all the newborn girls and young women I know and all of those I do not know who will face similar challenges, I despair. I wonder how women here cope, how they make sense of living in a homeland that denies them the right to choose a marriage partner. How were my countrywomen made so incompetent, so insignificant that even religion cannot protect them from the tribal code? Like refugees, women are exiled within the boundaries of their homeland.

I had learned what it means to be exiled in my homeland and I had learned to live in exile. *"My homeland, even if unjust, is cherished, and my kinfolk, even if frugal, are noble,"* my mother recites to remind me that a homeland is to be valued despite its hypocrisies, complexity and harshness.

A homeland is where the humanity of its citizens and residents is held at the highest level of respect; it is a place where justice is served not in favour of tribes, but in the service of humanity. I am at ease in recognising my exile; I do not have to tolerate or accept my homeland's hypocrisy, complexity and harshness. I had learned that living in it is not a requirement for loving a homeland. I know that nothing, including the wonderful people and friendships that I have here, can offset its reality. I love and admire my family and friends; I admire their survival and coping skills, the strength they have to live and love life here.

Listening to the supplications that replaced the music and songs of my childhood, I roused myself to re-confront the reasons for which I had departed. I had chosen self-exile not because I could no longer live at home; rather I had realised that I wanted to pursue a life consistent with my aspirations. I felt that I owed it to myself to create a fuller, richer life than would be possible if I remained at home.

It was not because women here, like their sisters around the world, are reduced to sexual beings, exclusively objects of sexual desires. It was not because of the religious police, or not being allowed to drive, or not having access to engineering and many other fields. It was not because of my imprisonment or for being denied the research job at King Saud University because I am a Shia. It was not because my existence is measured according to what the patriarchal system confers or that birth in this land does not warrant the right of citizenship. It was not because of the insignificance of human life. It was not because the government and the people in my country transgress and trespass on other people just because they can, knowing that they are protected from international humanitarian laws by the tribal law of the land.

Rather, I departed in search of a home, a place where I can pursue life to my utmost potential as a human being, as a woman and as a citizen. I left in search of a place where I count as a person, where my life counts.

I had learned that there is no perfect place where government is created and functions to serve humanity; however, there are a number of lands where an ordinary woman like me counts. There is a land where I can live where I am not viewed as a natural hazard because I am a woman. There is a land where I can take for granted the simple act of going out of my home without the fear of being violated because of allegations of immodesty. There is a land where I can walk in public without feeling that I am transgressing or trespassing on male-only territories. There is a land where the law does not require me to have a male guardian. There is a land where as a middle age, single woman, I am not suspected of wrongdoing or of a shameful past. There is a land where I can board an aeroplane and will not be asked to change seats because the gentleman next to me is offended because I am not dressed modestly despite my enveloping black abbaya. There is a land where daily I can pursue simple human activities without every act being judged on the licit/illicit scale.

Because humanity is imperfect, there is no perfect land, perfect country, perfect society or perfect government; however, there are lands where the human, the citizen counts, where government institutions are not perfect but they are established to serve society. I am not so naive as to assume that there is a perfect world. There is no place on earth that is absolutely just and fair, absolutely humane; yet there are these lands where rights and obligations are defined and are served irrespective of gender. There are lands where I am accountable for my own deeds; when I am treated unfairly, I have the right to challenge the system and demand justice. There are lands where I am respected simply because I am human. Thus, I packed my luggage leaving with the recognition that although I could stay in Fatema's home and in my native land for ever, I would be eternally restless if I did so.

# 15

# Resumption of the Journey

Upon my return home to the UK, the Islamic headscarf debate had been reignited to take the media's centre stage. I followed the news, collecting newspaper articles and listening to the discussions. I journeyed in search of women's true voices, irrespective of their origin or whether they are in veils or in mini-skirts. Cautiously, I observed how the voice of the European Muslim woman manifested itself in a debate that should have been driven by them. As a woman, I have been denied access to religious and political discourse; in such arenas, I had experienced manipulation and coercion. Thus, I am intrigued by this headscarf debate as it intersects gender, religion and politics.

As the debate unfolds, I observed European Muslim women in an effort to understand how they project their voices in this discourse. I am reminded of how Muslim women have been denied the right to access the Quran and Islamic teaching. Similarly within the secular domain their voices were rarely heard. In the UK, the religious and the secular male-dominant institutions claim the right to dictate the proper dress code for women.

I was not surprised by the debate. It is not the first time that the secular has utilised its institutions to control religion and to curb the European Muslim woman's quest for freedom to choose. As I had lived much of my life where religious institutions had curbed my freedom of choice, I found relevance in our shared experience as women. Therefore, I detected the implicit religious code within the secular. In the European drive to ban the headscarf, I traced a sense of defeat. European Muslim women who choose to wear the headscarf threaten the secular; they are viewed as voices of defiance.

As I passed through airports, hotels, offices, shopping malls and food venues throughout Europe, the headscarf became more visible, as if the debate had triggered consciousness of it. I observed Muslim women at work, with their families and enjoying courtship rituals with prospective males. I observed European Muslims as they create new meaning of their unique identity, at once European and Muslim. As I observed, I became conscious of my irritation with the secular disposition of the headscarf. This imposed dichotomy into secular and religious realms is irrelevant.

State prosecution of offences related to women's headwear contrasts starkly between those for Muslim women and those for European Muslim women; the former are officially prosecuted in their Muslim cultures when unveiled. The latter are officially prosecuted when veiled in their secular cultures.

Two items of women's apparel – the headscarf and the mini-skirt – are the symbolic ammunition of choice on the cultural battleground. Just as the headscarf/veil war is waged to maintain patriarchal political and social control, the mini-skirt battles undergird patriarchal political and social control. In both, the opponents – the tolerant and the intolerant – manipulate the dress code to employ these two items to sexualise the female.

Universally, the mini-skirt has been adopted as the *legitimate* public symbol of freely informed choice; on the contrary, it is a consciously manipulated drive toward the sexualisation of the female. The mini-skirt symbolises societal pressure for conformance of the woman's measurements to those pleasing to men. Similarly, the headscarf is seen as the *illegitimate* public symbol of incompetent choice, i.e., women are incompetent to choose and thus the state must legislate for her. Such state control stigmatises women; it reduces them to sexual beings in its assumption of the incompetence of women to choose intelligently.

Veiled, unveiled and/or in a mini-skirt, women have been alienated from the process of choice. I am challenged by my own convictions. It seems that Muslim women never have the right to choose to veil or unveil. Similarly, non-Muslim women never have a legitimate right to reject the mini-skirt, except with advanced age. Both confront similar pressures; women's free choices are severely limited as they are curtailed by the dominant – religious and secular – patriarchy.

I presume that secular Europe is exercising the same impulse that fundamental Muslims do when forcing women to veil. Secular Europe drives to unveil European Muslim women to liberate them from the headscarf; the assumption is that Muslim women are incapable of making their own decisions. Both the secular and the religious forces deny women the right to choose. Veiled and unveiled, the European Muslim women's voice, with its unique religious and secular experiences, is marginalised within the headscarf debate. Explicitly and implicitly, Europe determined the Muslim women's legitimate dress code within its domain.

Within Europe, Islam is criticised for justifying dominance over the female; meanwhile, secular Europe claims to guarantee individual liberties through the denial to Muslim women of the freedom of choice in dress. Am I alone in identifying this contradiction? As the debate ebbed, I continued searching for woman's voice, for all women's voices.

Not atypically, women suppressed their voices and the headscarf debate faded; it disappeared from the front page and from the list of leading articles. I wonder if my voice counts in the headscarf debate. Do I count as a European Muslim woman who has lived in the UK for the last ten years? Are my views discounted as my experiences are not relevant to the native-born European Muslim woman? While the distinction is never clear, I know that my experience of being a Muslim woman in Europe is inherently different from that of a European Muslim woman. Nevertheless, any such distinction should not exclude me from the headscarf debate.

I continued to examine the headscarf issues in view of the Quran's instructions regarding modesty. I revisited various Quran verses that state clearly a preference of modesty for both women and men. Each person seemed to have her or his own interpretation of what constitutes modesty, how to define the headscarf and the veiling of women. The measurements, interpretations or variations about modesty and veiling seemed endless. I observed the colourful, diverse ways in which women express their modesty; the headscarf is different from one Muslim woman to the next.

Through discussions, I learned that Muslim women in Europe and beyond each had a different reason for adopting the headscarf. To some, it is an identity, to others defiance or simply belief and faith in

Allah's preference. For many other women, parents, guardians, communities and government enforce the wearing of it.

Neither the headscarf nor the mini-skirt should define or limit women. Certainly, our perceptions of ourselves influence our dress and our perceptions of the dress of others. We express the identity that we create in our dress. As an unveiled Muslim woman, I confront perceptions of the stereotypical Muslim woman; the enquirer's perception is shattered by my non-conformance to that stereotype. Unveiled or veiled, women remain on the defensive; as always, women have to justify everything from existence to the right to choose.

I remind myself of the blessing of friendship as it was through my strong-willed friends – veiled and unveiled – that I had learned to appreciate the right of women to choose. They also taught me to suspend negative perceptions, as dress codes as such do not define women.

With the fading of the headscarf debate, I turn my attention to the topic of Muslim women interculturalists in preparation for a conference in Grenada, Spain. One of the topics I am to address is how Islam influenced my identity. Searching for a starting point, I recollect the enlightened view on veiling of my paternal grandfather Mula Ali. Once, the town's dignitaries – all men, of course – summoned him to answer why his daughters and granddaughters were not veiling their faces. His firm position was that Islam does not require women to conceal their faces. Suddenly, I realised that he never urged the headscarf/the hijab for any of the women of his kin.

Amidst the current atrocities, violence, prejudice and extremism, I write about the Islam that I had lived as a child; then, Islam was simply about believers having faith in Allah. Had I been a naive child who never paid attention to how Islam was negotiated and practised? I closed my eyes and followed my grandmothers in their white prayer cloaks; between prayers, they left their prayer mats to tend to their cooking, the children and the elderly. I contemplate the licit/illicit balance sheet; over time, the licit has been reduced and the illicit increased exponentially. Thus, the principles and ethics of Islam and the conduct of Muslims have been defined negatively in terms of the illicit.

## Resumption of the Journey

As the time for the conference nears, I have a recurrent dream of my paternal grandmother in her white prayer cloak. *In it, she is walking in a fruit garden as if she just had returned from travelling. She instructs me to sit down as she unfolds a piece of cloth; it resembles those she used to wrap gifts that she brought from her pilgrimage to Mecca. She displays beaded necklaces and asks me to choose one before she offered the others to my sisters and aunts. I choose a beautiful emerald green necklace. She says, "It is what I had selected for you, but I wanted you to choose. No one except you should wear it."*

*My dream ends with my maternal grandmother's voice in supplication to Allah. I slept on a straw mat so close that I could reach out and touch the beautiful mole on the right side of her chin.* I wake, not sure if I have been dreaming or have lived momentarily in the world of my grandmothers. It seems that their scents and voices linger.

I reflect on my spiritual journey as I have evolved from devout religious practice to the defiance and eventually to reconciliation with religion; now I am in tune with my spirituality, with the way I want to live my faith without mediatory intervention.

Fatema's voice echoes in supplication: *"May Allah protect you."* As I set forth, her voice recites *Al-Kursi*'s verse, *"Allah? There is no God but He – the Living, the self-subsisting, Eternal. No slumber can seize Him nor sleep. His are all things in the heavens and on earth. Who is there can intercede in His presence except as He permitteth? He knoweth what (appeareth to His creatures as) before or after or behind them. Nor shall they compass aught of His knowledge except as He willeth. His Throne doth extend over the heavens and the earth, and He feeleth no fatigue in guarding and preserving them for He is the Most High, the Supreme (in glory)"* (Surah, Al-Baqara, 2:255).

# 16

# Two Thousand and Eight

It has been nineteen years since I left my homeland in search of a home. As I examined how being born a Muslim Shia has influenced my identity, I am aware that it was a natural influence but one that has always been a secondary factor. In this journey stage, I live between religious [KSA] and secular [UK] countries; this duality impacts upon my interactions with others. At once, I am a woman, an Arab and a Muslim Shia. I am at once a citizen of the KSA and of the UK; I struggle with such labels, as none accurately defines me.

My ever-evolving identity is deeply entrenched in my Arabic heritage and the Arabic language, one that I defy through my writing. This act of defiance obliges me to reflect on my choice of English for my writing. As I reflect on my poetic Arabic language, my identity and the various currents that I allow into my heart, mind and soul, I recognise the unique me with multiple identities and yet grounded in my humanity. My identity is simply that of a human being who is always conscious of the journey and that my life is but a passing moment. Being a woman, an Arab, a Muslim Shia, a daughter, a sister, an aunt, a cousin and a friend are dichotomous descriptors, the final touches of the portrait.

While I am the sum of these various identities, I struggle to project my strong, distinctive, clear voice that mirrors my soul precisely. Daily, I question why people expect me to fit into a mould. Daily, I realise that someone somewhere would rather like to suffocate me in a one-size-fits-all-women box. I realise that I despise ornate frames as they restrain the beauty of an authentic portrait. I struggle and tire of battle which diminishes my interest in the world around me. For some time now I have been able to hear the actual voice speaking to me; now, I recognise the voice of men in the words of women.

    I battle with my own conceptions of voice, of identity and of freedom; I long for the simplicity of colourful humanity without the distractions and prejudices. I struggle against the prejudices of others as they gently or forcibly question the confidence I demonstrate in myself, in my voice. I know that I am like a palm tree that requires hard work to reap its fruit. I am eternally rooted in the earth of my homeland with branches extending into the larger world. When necessary, I have bent with the winds of life without necessarily having to break. When I die, I will be like the palm tree as it reaches out to the sky. Have people the curiosity to know me beyond my rough edges? Will they invest the time to linger, to unearth what is beneath or will they simply walk away? Typically, people quickly form their ideas about me; with equally deft assurance, they also develop precise ideas about how I should or should not behave.

    I know that to rise above the imperfections of humanity requires hard work and rigorous discipline. I also know that the beauty of our humanity is found within its imperfections. *Why does being a woman have to be so difficult and sometimes seemingly impossible?* I continue to probe as other women surrender to self-doubt; others develop insecurities with themselves, their body images, their relationships; and others sustain the unending battle of trying to fit the mould. I resist and question as I am prompted to look a little more subservient, a little more attractive, a little more desirable and to remain silent, unobtrusive. I ask as I listen to women wondering what became of the person they once were, their relationships, their husbands, their children and their careers. I ask as I listen to women repeatedly saying "I do not have a choice." I ask as I listen to women who fail to see their radiant beauty that does not fit the marketplace beauty standards and specifications. I continue asking as women comment on how lucky I am that I have never married and never had to cope with husband and children. Those women are right in assuming that I am happy with the choices I have made in life; however, they fail to realise that I have paid and continue to pay a substantial price for my happiness.

I continue to question as women assume that I have an easy life; indeed, some would not mind trading places with me. Women and men alike fail to recognise that I have spent a lifetime in battle just because I am a woman. Nineteen years ago, I left my home in search of another only to confront more battles. I have spent a lifetime in pursuit of respect and acceptance of who I am. At best I have been accorded tolerance. As I have continued to live across cultures and borders, I have learned that tolerance is easy. I shuttle between gender segregated and gender integrated zones without complication. Respect and acceptance require the hard work of self-criticism, self-sacrifice and self-discipline; they require that we remember what it means to be human.

As I read the Human Rights Watch report of April, 2008, *Perpetual Minors: Human Rights Abuses Stemming from Male Guardianship and Sex Segregation in Saudi Arabia*, I was reminded of how hard it is to be human. I restrain my tears as I reflect on the recent processing of my identification card in Saudi Arabia, my homeland. I reflect on how a simple process of updating an identity card becomes a harsh reminder, a painful process in the life of the perpetual minor. Every simple legal and bureaucratic process becomes a tool of humiliation with respect to women. Women employees in those bureaucracies are equally adept at humiliating and victimising women, in expressing the contempt for women that they have learned from the Saudi society's attitude toward women. I reflect on arguments contrary to basic human common sense, to rational and critical thinking that perpetuate the male myth that women are minors in every sense of the word.

Islam is being undermined in favour of the tribal patriarch. In my native land, men are even more subservient than women. Daily, men fail to confront their own lack of control; therefore, they compensate by clipping the wings of women in order to ensure their dominance and to assuage their egos. I am neither sad for nor envious of my countrymen as they are more delusional, more heavily censored and more manipulated than women. Everything in Saudi Arabia seemed to have been designed to serve the perpetual-minor mindset. The whole society embraces a new code of non-Islamic pseudo Islam in order to maintain the status of women as perpetual minors.

The perpetual minors will mature and the system will change only when men who disagree with and oppose the guardianship rule overturn it. To do that, they must surrender their control and endorse the right of women to live as capable adults. Unless change occurs, women will have to find new ways of living as minors. We will remain minors, without respect or protection; we will continue to be devalued and abused.

As I read the report, I celebrated my status, i.e., I only have to be a minor for the few weeks each year that I visit my mother. I did not know whether to rejoice or to grieve as I crossed the border into Bahrain after the border official addressed me, *"Next year, you will not need your guardian's permission to travel unaccompanied."* Surprised by my enquiry, he replied, *"You will be fifty years old and you will no longer require a clearance to travel unaccompanied."*

I find that rule even more irrational and more insulting. Is that it? Was I that threatening? Now, at age fifty, I am no longer viewed as a viable good; I am past my use-by date. The whole system is created around the underlying assumption of unbridled sexuality. From the patriarchal view of my homeland, I had an expiration date. At the age of fifty, I no longer need to be protected from my own desires, as I am no longer desirable by the other.

I reflected on the officer's words; they conveyed the official declaration of my expiration at the age of fifty. At that moment I wished that I could sit down over a cup of tea with this young officer and tell him how I had longed for being in love and being loved. I wanted to tell him that as I grew older my chances narrowed and my options became limited to divorced, widowed or married men. I wanted to confess that twice I fell in love with married men only to discover that I was the interruption, the gift in their journey to rediscover how much they loved and longed for their wives. I had been vulnerable, open to the possibility of being truly loved. I had struggled to retain balance and to exit such relationships wounded yet whole.

I had wrestled with the morality of love. The question was not about the morality of concealing love; the question of morality in love is in the sacrifice. Therefore, I had learned to act immorally by not allowing my heart to fall in love again. I had learned successfully how to escape both love and desire in favour of being virtuous and moral. I no longer have issues nor do I think anyone else has an issue with the immorality I exercise on myself. In denial, in being immoral toward myself, I return home desolate and alone to bury my heart beneath my pillow and wash my sorrow with my tears.

I have no issues with immorality when I lie about wanting to be in love or being in love; I know that love at my age is viewed as immoral. I do not question myself about the morality of burying my love alive! Thus, as I turn the page, I advance a year and forget about love and desire as middle age, single women like me do not have the right to love or desire as declared by the expiration date. As I leave the Saudi border behind, I think in admiration of all the women who remain there and choose or perhaps do not choose their daily battle every day to remain human. For them, I mourn.

On the ninth of August 2008, I was distracted from mourning Saudi women to mourn the unexpected loss of a vital influence on Arab consciousness. Al Jazeera television programming was interrupted with the news of the death of Mahmoud Darwish, the gifted poet whose poetry narrated in simple accounts the history of the Palestinian suffering and struggle for independence; he died following heart surgery. My tears flowed as one of the leading, most revered voices of the ongoing Palestinian struggle was silenced, never to be eclipsed. I mourned knowing that his words will resonate beyond the Israeli occupation and beyond the Israeli government's effort to ban his poetry from the classrooms of young Israeli people.

With tears flooding from my eyes, I turned to my nephew to exclaim, "You do not know what Darwish's dying means!" I continued despite my nephew's astonished gaze, "Darwish died, you do not understand the Palestinian history, the Arabic language, the poetry." Although I had never had the honour to attend his readings, Darwish's poetry of the simple pleasures of love, life, freedom and suffering hummed in my soul. I mourn Darwish; I mourn the Palestinians who weep and suffer.

Shortly after Darwish's death, Israel invaded Gaza to inflict further suffering. From the end of 2008 through the beginning of 2009, Israel waged war on Gaza with artillery land and air attacks on that narrow prison. One and one-half million Palestinians were ghettoised by the state of Israel, by the democratic military state's determination to crush Hamas. I recalled Darwish's poetry:

> Record I am an Arab
> With Identification card number 50000
> I have eight children and the ninth will be born after a summer

At the same time I recalled the words of two Israeli Prime Ministers:

> [The Palestinians] would be crushed like grasshoppers ... heads smashed against the boulders and walls.
> (Yitzhak Shamir in a speech to Jewish settlers. New York Times, 1 April 1988)

> Israel may have the right to put others on trials, but certainly no one has the right to put the Jewish people and the state of Israel on trial.
> (Ariel Sharon, 25 March 2001, quoted in BBC News Online)

The Israeli sentiment of 2008/2009 has not changed from that of 1956; it remains the underlying assumption of the Israeli state. I think of all my Jewish friends and colleagues and the Jewish Israeli intellectuals whose voices are censored. I think of the vicious cycle of violence. I think of the contempt that drives humans to such degrees of inhumanity. I consider those Israeli soldiers who learn how to and are encouraged to rape Palestinian women. From those lessons, they learn how to rape other women, Israeli women. I think of the nameless Israeli women who will be raped because the army generals approved the rape of other women and who will remain silent in the protection of a violent State. A country that has been created on violence and atrocity cannot create peace and is bound to perpetuate a state of violence.

I drop my pen as I lose my ability to continue writing; I watch as silence and muteness engulf the world while hundreds of civilians die as Israel again cries wolf. Israel adopts the same argument the Nazi generals used to kill many Jews in Europe. I become violently ill as I watch the Arab world paralysed by its fear of losing US protection. I become violently ill with the realisation that those Israeli fighter planes bombarding Gaza's innocent civilians are being refuelled from the Arab world's oil. Indeed those planes may have been launched from any of the numerous US military bases in the Arab world. I am repelled by my own repulsiveness, tainted by the morally repugnant behaviour of my Arab people; my own resentment and anger toward the silence in the Arab world are palpable. The Arab nations have become herds of lambs led by lambs.

Again, I take to the streets of London to demonstrate, to protest against the atrocities. I have only my feet and my voice to walk and chant for the innocent Palestinians, to oppose the ongoing brutal, unjustified atrocity of the Israeli state. What would those nations of lambs lose if all the Arabs stopped working and took to the streets? How many thousands would each Arab government kill or imprison? What would it take for the Israeli civilians to realise that for every act of outward violence there will be an act of inward violence? Peace can never be achieved through violence. Israel needs to disarm before it has the legitimacy to call for disarming its neighbours. It needs to respect the voice of peace to secure its borders; Israel needs to realise that the Israelis are not the only humans of value. Peace can only be achieved through peace.

Mahmoud Darwish, in his last published poem wrote:

> I am like you ... I was named by coincidence
> and belonged to a family by coincidence

He concluded it:

> I could have been someone else
> I could have been somewhere else.

I marched the streets of London while the stunned Arab nations largely remained silent. I protested the killing of civilians in Gaza as I had protested the earlier slaughter in Lebanon. I marvelled at the absence of Arab voices. Just as in 1982, the Arab nations observed silence and practised self-censorship while the last of the Palestinian fighters were deported from Beirut. Then they witnessed the slaughter of women, children and the elderly in the Sabra and Shatila refugee camps. Silence is how we protested then and compulsory silence is how we protest now.

The Arab leadership seems to have learned nothing between 1982 and 2009. Over those years, they have silently watched the slaughter at their doorsteps. Without exception, the Arab leadership and the majority of the Arab nations have been pre-conditioned to accept the inevitability of the mass slaughter that lies ahead.

I am one of the millions of Arab nationals who have been stunned by that indiscriminate slaughter. Momentarily, I can raise my voice in protest. Because I live under the protection of a Western government, my voice can be heard. Protected by UK and European law, I dare to act. I struggle to free myself of the fear of persecution that would result from protest behaviour in my native land. From painful experience, I know that my fear is real. In the UK, I take my chances.

My protest, I realised, is not for and about Palestine alone. It is about the dream of a different future for humanity; it is about the possibility of creating an alternative language of peace to replace the belligerent language of war that has dominated the history of humanity. My concern is not only about external world conflicts but also for internal civil conflicts.

While there is a pause in the Israeli violence, humanity has not seen the end of atrocities on defenceless Gaza civilians. There has been no global pause in violence and no hope that we will witness the end of atrocities against humanity.

Violence perpetuates violence; violence impacts both aggressors and survivors. In the presence of artillery, the voice of peace is extinguished. If we misguidedly believe that the violence and destruction of humanity that we watch on TV does not touch our daily lives, we need to rethink our position. If we believe that the random gang killings on London's streets are isolated incidents unrelated to what happens in Gaza, let us look deeper. Atrocity and violence are interlinked. They are all symptoms of the alienation of the majority of the world's citizens and the marginalisation of their voices.

As long as we can hear only the sounds of bomb blasts, automatic rifle fire and knife blades, we will fail to create a language for peace. When the only language we have is that of more power, control and money, we will fail to create peace. When the Arab leadership remains silent under US/Israeli pressure in order to protect their governments and to secure their positions, they are saying yes to the slaughter.

When Muslim clergymen condemn peaceful demonstrations

against atrocities as evil and as distractions from worshipping God, they are not doing so in the service of God. They do so to secure their position and in the service of violence.

I dream of a world at peace; I believe that peace is possible. I believe it is the only option. It is an individual and collective responsibility to confront violence and atrocity. There is and should be no place in our world today for passive reactions such as: "It is not my problem. Why should I care? Let them kill each other!" Passivity and isolationism are no longer options for humanity in our interdependent world. Passivity produces more violence and aggression at the home front, in our neighbourhoods.

The continuation of military attacks and aggression is not the worst thing that occurred in Gaza or in any other scene of violence. By far the worst outcomes are the psychological and emotional damages that scar civilian lives between now and the next wave of aggression.

I could say that I am lucky because I was not born a Palestinian. Just imagine how many Europeans silently voiced the same sentiment about European Jews over sixty years ago. Indeed, history repeats itself.

It is possible that you and I will be the targets of the next round of atrocities and violence. Perhaps we will be chosen because we were born on the opposite side of the fence – perhaps we were at the wrong place at the wrong time – perhaps we dared to speak out against violence. For humanity, there is only one way out – it is to create a language of peace, to be committed to peace. The only possible pre-condition to negotiating peace is *peace* itself. The slaughter must be stopped.

Among the important lessons I have learned is that one needs permission to dream – to have the right – as a citizen – to choose. As a citizen in my native homeland of Saudi Arabia, I did not have that right. While I had learned that my approach was not necessarily the best one, I also discovered that the alternatives were severely limited, if not non-existent. Since learning those lessons, I have learned a lot about the stunning of the human before the slaughter, a practice similar to that used on livestock before the butchery begins. Stunned silence has become the price of life, the price of survival.

For the conference, I am asked for a biography to justify my voice, my opinion and my positions. My public biography is a list that censors out the true me; rather, it acknowledges the schools from which I graduated, my employment and what the world accepts as my ambition. My biography does not tell you that I am legitimate, a woman, an Arab, a Muslim Shia. I am a citizen of this world and your sister/fellow human. The reader may choose to consider me a victim, survivor or a witness to the millions of human beings waiting their turn for slaughter.

My life is about more than education, work and ambition; it is about the realisation that I must answer with my true, authentic voice. My true biography is about being in touch with who I am; it is a quest to reveal the internal lightness.

I live to rediscover the fluttering of butterflies and the earth as it awakens beneath my feet as I walk the streets in joy or pain. My life has been a revelation; it has unfolded herein as my biography. I began with an image that now I can call myself. Eternally, I have believed that women's lives are of value; they are whole, complete and worthy despite the value assigned to them in their cultures, their homelands.

As I reflect on identity, I reflect on the life I have lived and the life ahead. I recognise that I have pursued a life quite different from that of most women. I have pursued the joy of being in my life. I came of age under the radar and out of the spotlight. Before maturity, I had taken shortcuts to grow; then I was not fully cognisant of the ramifications of my chosen journey. I created my life as I lived it, in an effort to get closer to the real me. Influenced by external events, I moved from one extreme to another. Through it all, I grew with the love that surrounded me: with the birth of each of my nephews, nieces and best friends' children; and with the joy of forging new bonds with my sisters, parents, loved ones and best friends. I have stretched my heart, my soul and my being to encompass all of those who have touched my life.

Along the way, the journey became even more difficult and more intense. I persevered, bringing to the challenge my love, courage, compassion, understanding and respect for the complexity of the human being and of life. I continue to evolve with new wounds, new cracks and new scars. My wounds remain tender.

I am not a survivor. I am alive as I embrace and rejoice in the blessings of love and tenderness. I celebrate my being and the journey to be truly me. Through it all my life has been and continues to be painfully beautiful and fulfilling. Each day is a celebration of the rediscovery that I am living differently, that I am fighting, loving, giving and working differently. I am living my feminine way of doing things.

I dream always of a better world, of humanity that lives up to its name and purpose; inevitably, reality impinges as the dream fades. As I was leaving Riyadh airport on 24 March 2009, the young officer spoiled my brief celebration of my new non-perpetual minor status. When he asked for my unaccompanied travel permit, he noticed my shock. I responded, "I am fifty years old, I no longer need permission." He responded, "It is not my rule, I am new on the job. I was not informed of this rule change." As I took out the permit, I breathed easily; I learned long ago never to trust my homeland's systems, I never travel without my permit.

I waited at Riyadh Airport for the BMI flight to London. While waiting, I confronted my stereotypes, my fears and my pessimism as Pakistani children pretended to shoot at a moving target with plastic guns. I am one of their targets. I look into the faces of innocence while my mind fast-forwards twenty years: will these children be staging world terror or will they be staging world peace? Fervently, I hope for the latter.

Before I boarded the plane, a European gentleman stood before me reminding me instantly of Seif. The gentleman caressed his hair and flicked his head back in precisely the same motion that personified Seif. My heart skipped a thousand beats. This December, it will be six years since Seif died. I reached for my address book wherein I noted the latest contact I had for him when he was in London.

I realized that this opportunity was another gift. I was strongly tempted to approach the gentleman and ask if he knew Seif; if he responded negatively, I would say, *"You remind me of a loved one who is no longer with us but who is laid to rest in this city."* Worried that the gentleman might think me mad, I resisted the impulse.

From my address book, another name caught my eye; *in 1991* while I lived in California, Pablo represented the possibility of love. Still today, I am not sure if it is fortunate or unfortunate that he came during a time when my heart and soul were sealed. I was inaccessible. I was and perhaps I am still afraid of being loved and afraid of loving.

I smiled as an image and a conversation resurfaced. *Upbeat and beaming he proposed as we walked down the streets of Berkeley, "Muna, only for once, I would like to see you dressed in a mini skirt, knee-high, high-heeled boots and a short winter coat. Believe me you will look sexy." I drew a deep breath and marvelled at men's ability to dismiss women's strongest convictions. I ridiculed him and told him that he was lucky that I was not going to kick him for his sexist proposal. I dismissed what he said, which came to him as no surprise. Nevertheless, Pablo continued smiling. I replied, "That is not for me Pablo. I will stick to dressing like the modest gypsies."*

As I waited to board the plane, I reminisced. It had been almost two decades since I received Pablo's proposal daring me to change my look to please him. I thought of how much I have grown, changed and matured and how much I have not changed. I smiled and thought to myself: I still do not own a mini-skirt or knee-high, high-heeled boots. I have no niqab or hijab; I possess the essence of the mini-skirt, the niqab and the hijab; I own both the statement of freedom and its modesty without owning the fashion apparel.

I thought of Pablo and wondered what had become of him. Pablo was an invitation, a possibility of love that I spurned. Perhaps, I have intentionally or unintentionally resisted love; I may have always been petrified of it; indeed, I may have always been afraid of being trapped between my desire to love and my fear of being loved.

I boarded the flight and returned to the UK savouring the images of water below and the places I have visited. I felt blessed by life, content.

Memories that belong to another place and another time captivate me. From that place, an old, beloved face emerges to grace my reverie. I reflect on the absence of my father, a male role model within our family of women. I wonder if that absence explains, in part, my strength and my attraction to the community of women among whom I was raised. Those women lived in despair, in the absence of education and with limited resources. They were the friends and neighbours of my mother. By extension, they were all my mothers.

I chose to write about my journey to womanhood in which the East, the West, Islam and secularism were formative influences. I grew up in a different era, a different world. I experienced Islam in its simpler ways. As I navigated the defiance-of-religion stage of life, I grew to understand what is religious and what is cultural. I learned that it is exclusively men who interpret Islam; this is the case with all other religions as well. For many years, I lived in the belief that only women in the East are powerless, underprivileged. I have learned how we women collectively empower men to maintain their superiority. At the beginning and at the end, I am an Arab Muslim Shia woman; the world may or may not be interested in my voice, in my journey.

*Since the 1960s*, I have shuttled between East and West; I am now exhausted by the overwhelming body of work there is to be done for women and for men. My voice even now betrays me. In the distance of long ago, I see the child that I was, playing at the courtyard of my maternal grandparents' house. I hear the voice calling and I recognise the term of endearment.

*Fatema bint Abdallah's voice calls in supplication; I see her face and I know her smile. Her fingers caress my forehead. I sense her warm breath. Fatema bint Abdallah, my maternal grandmother, is my homeland and my homeland is where she now lies in rest. I walked the cemetery with her. We continue walking in silence; she keeps me warm, connected and whole.* Fatema bint Abdallah: I feel sad for people without a Fatema in their lives.

Waiting on Waterloo Station's Platform Four for my homebound train, I am open to all that is conceivable. Each day, life begins with a new promise of love, friendship, adventure, challenge and much more. I contemplate: *What is next for me?* Hesitantly, I continue my internal debate: Shall I embrace and pursue a new moral challenge? Shall I confine myself within the safe confines of moral behaviours, never to discover new boundaries, never to discover a new me?

I look toward the horizon. I breathe deeply. I close my eyes and embrace all the voices of possibilities for a better world, a better place, for the next challenge, the next agony and the coming joy. I smile as I look forward to ageing gracefully. As the train approaches the platform, I joyfully open my heart to invite the winds to blow all the possibilities of life and learning in my direction.

I board to continue the journey alone but not lonely. Homeward bound, I know that alone I have matured and have nurtured a strong sense of self-confidence within the friendship I forged with my voice.

I board.
I know her, she who walks in my shadow
I know her, the woman with a choice
The woman who holds the truth
The woman without a voice.

# Dedication

Fatema – Where she walked, compassion followed.

You made the wait in darkness a beautiful journey toward the conquest of voice.

Our souls and hearts are like houses of the sheerest glass. In times of crisis, some panes will withstand shocks. Others will shatter fatally. While the house, like the soul and the heart, may recover, each will always retain scars, some visible, some invisible. Some survivors can feel the spidery lines of their scars; with their fingers, they can trace them line-by-line and stitch-by-stitch. Memories are maps of our feelings and of those scars.

I nourish such a scar, an October memento, one engraved deep into my soul. Tears stream down my face and sear my soul with October's approach each year. Now, Fatema is nowhere near to brush away my tears with the hem of her black veil.

Quietly, serenely, she drifted into and out of my life. My maternal grandmother, Fatema, proudly bore the name of the Prophet's daughter, a name revered in Islam. In Saudi Arabia, the Eastern Province is home to most of the Kingdom's minority Muslim Shia and most of its black gold (oil). There I was born and grew up.

Fatema's legacy to me is my distinctive voice and indelible memories. Only Fatema could envelop me in the love that lingered long after she departed this life on the first of October 1994.

Tenderly woven childhood memories adorn my scar. In her house, I slept on a straw mat, resting my head on a hard cushion during the hot summer midday. Often, I sensed the cool *mishmar* (a light, gaily coloured cover of sheerest cotton commonly used by Muslim Shia women in their homes) being spread over my body. In my slumber, I absorbed the fresh fragrant Arabic basil wrapped within the *mishmar*'s hem. Dozing, I heard the *"Bism Ellah al rahman al raheem"* and I recognized Fatema reciting from the Quran: "In the name of God most gracious, most merciful".

On the first of October each year, I lie awake reminiscing. Since Fatema's death in 1994, I sense her warm scent ever more vividly. It is in hand-washed clothing, in sautéed onions and boiled rice and in fresh garden herbs. Eternally, I associate her scent with that of the freshly wiped sweat of her elderly parents whom she bathed and cared for daily.

Fatema's grey eyes could not disguise her sunny disposition. Under her influence, I experienced childhood days of rainbow-crowned, blue skies. In her smile I found a safe harbour. Fatema parted her curly henna-coloured hair from the middle, dividing it into two braids that gently embraced her round face. When she lost her front teeth, she gained a baby's smile.

Fatema had a scar on her forehead, a token reminder of one special warm winter morning long ago. It resulted from a cut she sustained from an empty tin. My little sister Ayah found the tin empty of her favourite sweet and threw a tantrum and the tin.

I remember waking in Fatema's house where the air carried a hint of Arabic jasmine and basil rising from beneath the light dewdrops. On rising, I savoured the freshly baked bread, cheese, watermelon jam, *halwa* (a tapioca sweet), *rahash* (a sesame seed/sugar sweet) and fresh cream. The aroma of boiling cardamom-laced Arabic coffee filled the air. Fatema complemented it with hot milk, spiced with saffron and cardamom.

As children, our seasons revolved around Fatema. On summer nights at her house, we were mesmerised with fairy tails, legends and myths. Nightly, she concluded with an offer of delicious, cold Vimto drinks.

On winter days, we roasted chestnuts and listened enthralled to Fatema's father's exotic tales of his past. In the spring, Fatema dyed our hands with henna and tucked Arabic basil within the folds of our braids.

During autumn, she asked us to count the stacked date baskets and showed us the large date-molasses collecting receptacle. We were allowed to relish the cool sweetness from the baskets of compressed dates that hung over the spring-cooled container. The molasses drips were collected for future household use or for the market. The rich sweet molasses is a necessity for *luqaymat* (the sweet dumplings) at *iftar*, the evening meal for breaking the daily fast in Ramadhan.

From Fatema's house, we went to my grandfather's farm. There we harvested fresh dates, figs and *lauz*. Annually, the sesame seeds were harvested and dried on Fatema's roof. I can still taste the first handful of roasted sesame seeds that she placed in the palm of my hand.

When we first practised fasting in Ramadhan, Fatema kept leftovers for us to ease our hunger during the long days without food. During *Hajj*, Fatema helped us make *ise'na*, offerings of small barley-filled baskets. She would weave small hanging straw baskets or save old coffee tins, making drainage holes in their bases. Then she would give us soil and barley seeds to plant. Our offerings were then placed on her courtyard brick wall. Faithfully, we watered them every day. On the first day of *Eid el Hajj* (the three-day festival that concludes the pilgrimage to Mecca), she taught us a song for the pilgrims. Then she watched as we drowned our fully grown barley baskets in the flowing water channel. That was our offering to Allah for safeguarding the pilgrims.

Next to Fatema's house our *Eid* swing swayed between the tallest palm trees. It was the most beautiful in the neighbourhood.

On Thursday nights, I read *"Halal al-Mashakel"* to Fatema and her friends. It is a story of Ali Ibn Abi Talib, the Muslim Shia's first Imam, and the cousin and son-in-law of the Prophet Mohammed (pbuh) that symbolises the sharing of the wealth of Allah's blessings. The Thursday observance was Fatema's weekly offering and thanks for Allah's blessing. I went home blessed with reading and lots of sweets and roasted peanuts.

At an early age, I learned the directions to Fatema's house, my sanctuary. My sisters and I knew that her house was always open. Although she locked her room, she did it in a way that we children could always open it to find a safe haven.

I never heard Fatema complain. It was against her nature. Silently, she attended to her daily chores. Each summer day, she would quietly sweep the house, wash the clothes, cook the meals, bathe her parents, weave the coloured straw baskets to store the winter dates, and make plain straw mats. In the winter, she rose early to boil the washing water for her husband. Then she would bring wood for her father's fire and light the kerosene heater in her room.

Three little girls (my sisters and I) waited impatiently for the completion of her endless chores, longing for the nights. With our souls attuned, we listened to Fatema's magical fairy tales. Forever, we were enchanted.

While Fatema was narrating, her hands massaged the three little heads resting on her lap, played with our hair and searched for lice. Her voice floated towards the sky accompanied by the ticking sound of lice crushed between her thumbnails.

Once, Fatema interrupted her tales to explain the reason behind the lice. For her, it was the attraction of our sweet blood. We objected strenuously but continued to listen. Fatema laughed and continued her battle with lice, trying DDT, kerosene and mercury. In the end, the lice won the battle.

Throughout those evenings, we played with the charm that hung around her neck. Fatema's healing charm was a mystery that intrigued three little girls. No one knew when Fatema parted with it. Also, it was not known how the curious little girls tore open the leather pouch and read the enclosed scribbled words. No questions were asked of us. Fatema waited, terrified that the evil eye would strike again before a new charm could be procured to safeguard her soul.

One day my mother, tired of our incessant questions about the charm, agreed to tell us the story after extracting our promise that we would never mention it to Fatema or another soul. She revealed that years earlier Fatema, on losing her voice, became irrational and had to be physically detained in a room within the extended family home. Perhaps it was the loss of three children or the unexplained alienation of her husband that precipitated her collapse and her retreat into muteness. Subsequently, relatives looked after Fatema's two remaining children.

Under detention, Fatema was deemed cursed. Those who passed the house heard her pacing her room and her weeping echo night and day. The only people who dared to visit were her husband and her sisters. They were greeted with silence. A year passed before Fatema regained her balance and her voice was restored.

My mother conveyed to us that in her dream Fatema saw a revelation. She rose the following morning as if she had slept momentarily. Subsequently, she approached her cousin's wife and asked for one of his personal items: a newly tailored *thobe*. Then, she went to bathe and to pray. On exiting that room, Fatema wore a healing charm composed and designed especially for her by a religious man and blessed by the will of Allah.

For the remainder of her life, Fatema wore the charm that silenced that threatening voice. Inside the faded brown leather pouch nestled a yellow paper with illegible words. With her tormented soul, Fatema guarded the charmed words praying day and night not to lose herself to the evil eye again. No one including Fatema could explain what had happened. She never spoke of it, but behaved as if it were a living force within her, suppressed only by her healing charm.

Now, there are no fairy tales, no legends to charm my ears. The magic of Fatema's storytelling ended. But long before that, I had drifted away from Fatema and from my home on the shores of that distant gulf. Over the years, her powerful silence nurtured a distinctive voice that became my own.

On return from my self-imposed exile, she said little. Her eyes stared into mine, questioning my extended absence. In that time, she had come to love me a little more. From her eyes, I traced the radiant pain to her soul. Smothering her tears, she uttered words I could understand. "You came back," were Fatema's last words to me. In the middle of nowhere, I stopped trying to make sense of life and used her sorrow and pain as a locus to reconceive my own.

Often in my reveries, I find myself at Fatema's doorstep. I push open the door to her room where I am embraced by silence, by emptiness. Fatema's scent lingers in the air. Her face is placid while her voice echoes within me. I see her small, grey eyes smiling with ancient and current tears that flood her face. I see my fingers tracing her scarred forehead.

I smile as I stroke Fatema's bracelet now adorning my wrist. I wear it like she wore her charm. I think of death and am not terrified. If I die now I know that I have Fatema, her soul and her voice within me. Consoled with this thought, I stand at the crossroads of my life, when all is conceivable.

After Fatema's death I hoped to find her healing charm. Subsequently, I learned that it was removed when she became critically ill. Divested by the loss of her lifesaving charm, she must have been terrified of being locked out of life once more. Perhaps she thought of giving up life before the evil eye struck again.

Instead of the charm, I received the gold bracelets that she rarely wore. On that occasion, I boldly spoke my thought out loud: "Fatema's gold bracelets are divine." Mother responded immediately: "Ask Allah for forgiveness." Today, I smile as I remember her reaction convinced of how divine Fatema is.

Clearly, I remember the day Mother called to ask if I was still interested in a memento of Fatema. She said, "Your grandfather has her two gold bracelets and wants to sell them and donate the money to the poor." My pulse quickened and I was a child again, gently stroked by Fatema's fingers. "I want Fatema's bracelets, please." Happily, my mother intervened.

Wearing Fatema's bracelets, I arrived at my younger sister's doorstep. Filled with joyful tears, her eyes lit up: "Are these Fatema's bracelets? How did you get them? I would die for one," she pleaded. With joy, I smiled at my sister. "Well, one of them is for Fatema's great-granddaughter, her coming of age gift." I removed the bracelet and locked it around my sister's wrist. "You can keep it for her until she comes of age."

Fifteen years have passed since Fatema's departure. *How could I lose so many days, Ya Immy [Mother]*? Now I return to sleep at her house. I feel the cool cotton *mishmar* being spread over my body. I hear Fatema's supplication of *Bism Ellah*. I smell Arabic basil and jasmine. I am walking through my grandfather's farm, toward the sea in the mist of a summer morning. Behind me is the farmhouse where Fatema watches; her face is before me, beckoning me. I walk through palm and fig trees hearing her chanting into my soul.

I tell Fatema, "I had a weird dream." She smiles *"Inshalla khair"* (Good omen, God willing). As she smiles, I continue to stretch my hand toward her forehead. I try to stroke the scar, but I cannot. I drift into slumber.